FRANK MILLER'S
DAREDEVIL
AND
THE ENDS OF
HEROISM

EDITED BY COREY K. CREEKMUR, CRAIG FISCHER,
CHARLES HATFIELD, JEET HEER, AND ANA MERINO

Volumes in the *Comics Culture* series explore the artistic, historical, social, and cultural significance of newspaper comic strips, comic books, and graphic novels, with individual titles devoted to focused studies of key titles, characters, writers, and artists throughout the history of comics; additional books in the series address major themes or topics in comics studies, including prominent genres, national traditions, and significant historical and theoretical issues. The series recognizes comics of all varieties, from mainstream comic books to graphic nonfiction, produced between the late 19th century and the present. The books in the series are intended to contribute significantly to the rapidly expanding field of comics studies but are also designed to appeal to comics fans and casual readers who seek smart critical engagement with the best examples of the form.

FRANK MILLER'S *DAREDEVIL*

AND THE ENDS OF HEROISM

Paul Young

RUTGERS UNIVERSITY PRESS
NEW BRUNSWICK, NEW JERSEY, AND LONDON

A BRITISH CATALOGING-IN-PUBLICATION RECORD FOR THIS BOOK IS AVAILABLE
FROM THE BRITISH LIBRARY.
LIBRARY OF CONGRESS CATALOGING-IN-PUBLICATION DATA
Young, Paul, 1968–
Frank Miller's *Daredevil* and the ends of heroism / Paul Young.
pages cm. — (Comics culture)
Includes bibliographical references and index.
ISBN 978-0-8135-6382-4 (hardcover : alk. paper)
ISBN 978-0-8135-6381-7 (pbk. : alk. paper)
ISBN 978-0-8135-6383-1 (e-book (web pdf))
ISBN 978-0-8135-7303-8 (e-book (epub))
1. Miller, Frank, 1957– Criticism and interpretation. 2. Daredevil (Fictitious character)—
History. 3. Comic books, strips, etc.—United States—History and criticism. 4. Popular
culture—United States. 5. American literature—History and criticism. 6. Myth in literature. 7.
Comic books, strips, etc.—United States—History and criticism. I. Title.
PN6727.M55Z96 2016
741.5'0973—dc23
2015032501

Visit our website: http://rutgerspress.rutgers.edu
Manufactured in the United States of America

I wanted to use a style where the reader had to do a great deal of the work, where a pair of squiggles and a black shadow became an expressive face in the reader's mind.

—Frank Miller, 1991

CONTENTS

ACKNOWLEDGMENTS

I would like to thank Vanderbilt University and Dartmouth College for the resources they so generously gave me to work on this book. I am also infinitely grateful to my wife, Carolyn Dever, for recognizing and abetting my passion for funnybooks and funnybook scholarship, and my son, Noah, who refuels my old fascination with comics and superheroes with his own passions and reminds me every day what it was like, *is* like, to feel what one thinks. Leslie Mitchner, my editor at Rutgers, has been encouraging, inspiring, and frank, all of which helped immeasurably. Corey Creekmur, the series editor of Comics Culture, believed in what I was doing before I sent him a single page and has seen me through this with the enthusiasm and faith one could only hope to receive from a fellow traveler in the comics studies field; as a rookie in that bullpen, I can only imagine how much more difficult this project would have been without his support.

A very long time ago, Brooks Landon at the University of Iowa let me lecture to his postmodernist fiction course a couple of times about comic-book history, as a run-up to his teaching of Moore and Gibbons's *Watchmen*, and thus gave me my first crack at teaching. He didn't have to, but he did, and I will always be grateful for that experience. He also mentored my BA honors thesis on postmodernist aesthetics in graphic novels, which he encouraged me to write in the first place; if only I hadn't dropped comics as an object of study for fear of not being taken seriously in graduate school, I might have done better justice to Brooks's influence, and sooner. The students in my winter 2015 section of Film Studies 41: The Graphic Novel and Film at Dartmouth College inspired me to return to earlier assumptions and claims with fresh eyes. Their passion for the material surprised and thrilled me every week, and despite their understandable trepidation, they accepted my challenge to analyze comics form and style by drawing comics of their own and did so fearlessly. Both their dedication and the fruits of their labor taught me much about what I wanted this book to be.

If it weren't for Westfield Comics, Mile High Comics, and Lone Star Comics, I would have had more spending money growing up, but I would have blown it all on records anyway—so no harm done. Thanks for helping my brother and me build the collection that was the engine behind this book. And to Ted Vanliew, the proprietor of Superworld Comics in Massachusetts and one hell of a nice guy, thank you for helping me bridge my past as a young collector to my present as an old one. I purchased one of my most prized books from him and display it proudly in this volume. Ted knows which one.

But I reserve my deepest gratitude for my favorite honorary members of the Mighty Marvel Marching Society: Kyle (Bruce) Phillips, who hooked me up with Marvel's Silver Age via his older brother's collection and did so against the essential backdrop of pool playing, football card trading, movie devouring, hilarity, and goodwill; and my brother, Tim Young, my partner in crime as we "published" comic book after comic book in the seventies and early eighties, with breaks for making action figures fight, listening to the same twelve rock songs every night when KAAY-AM in Little Rock cranked up its power, and going ape over LPs by ELO and Foreigner. Every time we record one of Tim's *Deconstructing Comics* or *To the Batpoles!* podcasts together, I feel oddly like I'm still knocking around our family's home in southern Iowa, hunting old ham nets to use for Spider-Man's webbing or random pieces of plastic sheeting to "preserve" our precious *X-Men* and *Spider-Man* comics, or racing home from the Comic Shoppe / Pinball Place on our bikes to dump the newest issues of our favorites out onto the carpet and dig in. To paraphrase Ben Urich, this one's for you, Tim.

A NOTE ON THE TEXTS AND IMAGES

I have chosen not to footnote individual issues of comic books for a simple reason: source failure. By "failure," I mean that referencing the original comics discussed herein means offering sources that few readers besides collectors of the *Daredevil* series could refer to, while referencing collections published later means giving unclear page numbers to editions that have, in most cases, gone out of print at the time of this writing (the *Daredevil Visionaries: Frank Miller* three-volume paperback series included). Some collections are continuously paginated, while others rely on the original paginations of the comics for navigation; some have tables of contents, others lack them. At the time of this writing, the reader's best bet would be to have the three-volume *Daredevil by Frank Miller and Klaus Janson* series (2008–2009) on hand, for following along.

Ideally, impractical though it is, the reader would have all the issues mentioned here and have leisure to flip through them while reading my commentary, finding the correct pages via the images and picking up their context along the way. What makes that situation preferable to reading along in a reprint volume is that I firmly believe in experiencing comics originally published on newsprint, *on newsprint*. Miller and Janson composed and finessed these pages in full knowledge of how poor the printing process was, how limited their color palette, and how grayish-tan their "whites" would be thanks to the intrinsically off-white-to-tan quality of the paper stock—and they planned accordingly. They also knew that full-page advertisements would be inserted every few pages in their stories once they were published in the traditional "pamphlet" form and worked around them to achieve effects like two-page spreads and well-timed reveals of a character or an event, doubtless with the help of editor Denny O'Neil. This was before DC's mideighties experiments with whiter, sturdier paper, with and without glossy coating, for such miniseries as *Ronin*, *Camelot 3000*, *Watchmen*, and *Batman: The Dark Knight Returns*, and Marvel's "Special Edition" reprint series, which "upgraded" classic arcs from *Strange Tales* (Doctor Strange), *Warlock*, *The Avengers*, and other series—including an odd pastiche called *The Elektra Saga*, a miniseries that used Miller's original artwork from *Daredevil* and new, third-person text boxes to create a chronological account of Elektra's life and death. Then as now, stories reprinted from newsprint comics look sharp and vibrant on Baxter stock and its successors, but they don't look like the comics did. The closest equivalent I can describe to paging through *Daredevil* #158–191 on glossy paper is the experience of seeing a historically crucial film like *The Wizard of Oz* "upgraded" to digital 3D: I recognize what I see as a reference to the original, but it is neither a bastardization of the original nor the same thing only better; it is, simply, not the same thing.

At the risk of being accused of lo-fi hipsterism, I have taken the figures in this book from my personal copies of individual issues whenever possible, for the following reason: to offer even a hint of their original impact, one has to have a sense of what could and could not be done with newsprint, the limits it presented to fine line work and color choice, and the pulpy texture that Miller and Janson worked with, not against, when rendering *Daredevil*. Seeing Miller's original *Daredevil* issues on glossy paper turns the murky blacks and watery, dank pastels that Janson and Glynis Wein used to set the mood into a fireworks display of primary colors, as though every page were a cover trying to nab our attention rather than a page engineered to move us through a plot at a particular pace. The material, sensory history of the comic book as an object—the individual copy with its bent corners and its bleachy scent of aging newsprint—is lost, and with it goes much of the impact of the child's first encounter with a particular comic book, the experience of stumbling across a specific, eye-catching issue with nothing to guide one's engagement with it except the object itself.

FRANK MILLER'S
DAREDEVIL
AND
THE ENDS OF
HEROISM

DEALING WITH THE DEVIL

If you were reading superhero comics thirty-odd years ago, hearing the words "Frank Miller's *Daredevil*" will give you visions. Long-forgotten panels will hijack your brain as though it's 1982 all over again. No doubt the specific images you recall will differ from mine, but then there were so many that stood out: a finger poking out of the darkness of a pool hall to stop a cue ball in midshot; a series of seven panels turning the act of setting fire to a notebook into a monument to a news reporter's selflessness; a borderless long-shot panel in which a laughing assassin runs a rival through with her own weapon, her leotard tenting against the *sai* as she sags like a marionette. Some of the images simultaneously repel me and beg my admiration. Once they took hold of me, hate them or love them, I couldn't chase them out of my head. And I never did.

As I dig through my comic-book collection in search of the frames that sparked these mental pictures, two realizations strike me. First, I remember Miller's panels accurately, nearly down to the smallest detail (this from a person who can't recall street names in his own neighborhood). Second, they're all taken from sequences with a common purpose: to slow time by stretching split seconds across multiple panels in an arrangement Scott McCloud calls moment-to-moment closure.[1] A superhero comic has to deliver big, climactic plot turns to earn its market share, and such turns often get concentrated into single panels or full-page splashes. But Miller's dynamic panels are tiny by comparison, and individually they mean little or nothing if removed from their context. As Miller has frequently acknowledged, he based such time-lapse sequences on the work of Bernard Krigstein, a cartoonist who never drew a superhero in his entire career. Krigstein drew crime, horror, and science-fiction stories during the heyday of EC Comics, publisher of *Mad* and primary target of the 1954 Senate Subcommittee Hearings into Juvenile Delinquency, but his peculiar combination of dynamism and grotesquerie has kept him obscure compared to such celebrated EC creators as Wally Wood, Jack Davis, and Harvey Kurtzman. I had never seen Krigstein's work when I first encountered Miller's moment-to-moment sequences. All I knew was that I had never seen time move so excruciatingly slowly in a comic book before, and yet my experience of the panels was not annoyance at the slowed pace but fascination at the dramatic impact they created. Static though the panels themselves may be, like individual frames from a strip of film, these scenes *move*. Though they developed actions incrementally instead of emblematizing them, that choice on Miller's part somehow caused me to store these images in my head not as snapshots of actions but as complete actions in themselves. He embedded entire sequences in my mind's eye like a magician forcing an unwitting volunteer to pick a predetermined card. The scenes, and many others like them during Miller's four-year run on *Daredevil*, all riff on the work of Krigstein in that they transform plot events into climactic expressions of surprise, monumentality, or horror that make the storytelling as prominent as the events themselves (see figure 1).[2]

If a distinction may be drawn between how Miller and Krigstein delineate climactic moments like these, it's in the different levels of

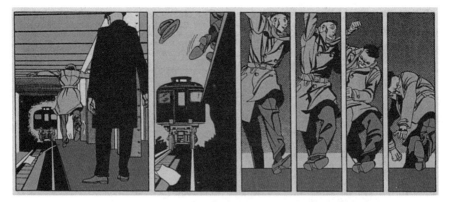

FIGURE 1. Bernard Krigstein art from "Master Race," *Impact* #1 (EC, April 1954).

editorial control their incremental panels express. Krigstein multiplies panels to make dull scripts more dramatic. Miller uses them to do what Krigstein probably wished he had more freedom to do: to produce dramatic effects at preordained moments in the narrative, moments he chose himself. For unlike Krigstein and many of his contemporaries, Miller vied for, and got, the opportunity to write *Daredevil* as well as draw it. Artist-writers were few and far between during the Bronze Age of US comics. The big stars at Marvel Comics in the 1970s were writer-editors like Marv Wolfman and Steve Englehart. However, after Miller got his hands on Ol' Horn-Head, as cocreator Stan Lee nicknamed the character, suddenly it seemed that every artist in the industry was chomping at the bit to write the comics they drew.

Why did Miller's Daredevil blow my twelve-year-old mind? Was it the dynamics of angle and contrast? Was it the urgency of the line work, made even more breathless by Klaus Janson's scratchy inking style? Was it the muted palette that Glynis Wein and later Janson himself employed when coloring the series? Or was it the chilling content of panels like the ones that stick in my head so tenaciously—violent, abrupt, sometimes sickening, sometimes absurdly crude freeze-frames of high comic-book melodrama? If actions speak louder than words in most mainstream comics, Miller made every act of *Daredevil*'s characters into the loudest explosions comics had made since the Thing routinely stomped Yancy Street into rubble in Jack Kirby's *The Fantastic Four* more than a decade earlier.

What follows is an attempt to assess the peculiar staying power of these images and of the stories they injected with so much energy. In describing and appreciating Miller's multi-issue *Daredevil* run, I also want to limn *Daredevil*'s moment in the history of superhero comics, a moment that changed what they meant and how they expressed it, for better or for worse depending on whom you ask. This moment bleeds into the present in several forms: in Miller's work on and off the Daredevil character in the years following the celebrated run; in how Daredevil would be handled by subsequent creators; and in the mainstreaming of superhero comic books beyond their traditional market of children and lifelong fans in the form of graphic novels containing grim, violent, and/or erotic "adult" content and successful Hollywood franchises. In redefining the Daredevil character, Miller defined himself as a creator whose grim but reflexive approach to superheroes profoundly affected the history of each character he tackled thereafter. His phenomenal success in the 1980s dramatically altered standard creative practices at Marvel and DC. In the process, he and other creators who felt cheated by the comics industry's work-made-for-hire business model redefined superhero comics as an industry in which successful creators shared in the profits generated by their creations and in some cases even gained the independence to publish characters and stories owned by them alone.

That said, Miller's influence on superhero comics has been as frustrating, and potentially damaging to comics as we know them, as it was initially exhilarating. The industry charged through the nineties, fueled by a fundamental misreading of Miller's success as a matter of telling "gritty" stories of heroes who bled buckets and were no longer averse to killing their enemies, breaking with the superheroic convention of revering life for its own sake that dated back to the developmental phases of Superman, Batman, and Wonder Woman in the early forties.[3] Marvel in particular tried to exploit the fans' unquenchable thirst for Wolverine, the Punisher, and other merciless "Milleresque" heroes by glutting the market with new series and "special" issues, often bearing covers that were sparkly, holographic, and expensive to produce and collect. The hope was that the vigorous collector's market for longer, pricier issues of such series as *Daredevil* (the death of Elektra in #181) and *Uncanny X-Men* (the death of Phoenix / Jean Grey in #137) would tempt collectors to invest in multiple copies of every double-sized or shiny comic that rolled off the presses. To reinvigorate sales after the crash that resulted from this flood of not-so-special specials, the publishers Marvel and DC have tried everything from digital distribution to turning every series they publish into subplots of monstrous crossover events. Now, with the outlandish success of Marvel's film-production division, superhero comics seem more and more like supplements to their own filmed adaptations, complete with character depictions and story arcs that increasingly treat the films, not the comics, as canonical.

Obviously, Miller is not to blame for self-destructive industry practices. And on the positive side, his success helped attract more attention to comics from the cultural mainstream. Along with other popular creators—such strange bedfellows as the cerebral *Watchmen* writer Alan Moore and Todd McFarlane, the *Spider-Man* artist who infamously devalued stories and storytelling in favor of splashy styl-ization—who abhorred being treated as interchangeable day labor-ers by an industry that could not have prospered so without them, Miller helped pave the way for broader acceptance of comic books and graphic novels as worthy of critical scrutiny outside the realm of fandom. This book, then, tracks a cartoonist through his first major series run with one eye fixed on the present of what has tradition-ally been the American mass media's least respected enterprise. This is a present in which blockbuster superhero movies have made even Marvel's Thor, for decades a character virtually unknown beyond fan culture, into a household name. But it's also a time in which Alison Bechdel's *Fun Home*, a graphic memoir of her childhood and her clos-eted father's suicide that resembles Miller's work about as much as Art Spiegelman's *Maus* resembles a 1970s Spire Christian Comic, can find a major publisher, become a bestseller and a critical favorite, spawn an award-winning Broadway musical, and earn its creator a MacArthur "genius" fellowship. This is not to say that Miller sparked the assimila-tion of autobiographical or feminist comics into the mainstream.[4] Still, without his rise to fame as a superhero cartoonist in the 1980s, along-side the critical success of such other high-profile creators as Lynda Barry, Spiegelman, Neil Gaiman, Harvey Pekar, and Chris Ware, fewer publishers today would take a chance on publishing a funnybook, no matter what its length or who its intended audience.

It's even more difficult to imagine the creators' rights movement of the mid-1980s making the rapid gains it did without Miller. *Dare-devil* was an early volley in the industry's shift from an oligopoly that assigned work-for-hire staff and freelance creators to write, draw, let-ter, color, and edit the adventures of corporate trademark characters to a more complex market in which retention of rights to characters and stories has become a common work incentive for creators. Along with Moore, Jim Starlin, Steve Gerber, Chris Claremont, and John Byrne, Miller spawned (pun intended) a second wave of richer and more powerful creators like Todd McFarlane, a work-for-hire artist for Marvel who rapidly gained the capital to found a successful comics publishing company of his own. Miller and his cadre began this trend by selling thousands of copies of individual comics every month in the midst of what had been a creative and financial lull, proving to creators and suits alike that there was a genuinely growing market for comics, if you were willing to give readers superhero stories that exceeded their expectations of innovation and stylistic singularity, recognizing and tweaking genre conventions all the while. And Miller's bitter fight against censorship within and without the comics business helped erode one of the most persistent obstacles to the raising of expectations for comics. The "adult" audience he pitched to may have been the audience of R-rated action movies rather than readers of George Eliot, but by courting an older audience with more diverse tastes in fiction, he helped dispel the notion that the only world comics could offer was one crammed with bulbously endowed men and women wearing costumes that looked alternately like military uniforms, B&D gear, and porno-inspired lingerie.

Frank Miller's initial run as penciler, then as writer/penciler, and finally as writer/layout artist on *Daredevil* began with issue #158 (cover date May 1979) and ended with #191 (February 1983).[5] Prior to Miller's arrival, Marvel Comics published *Daredevil* every other month, an indication of the series's lackluster sales compared to hit monthly series like *The Amazing Spider-Man* and *The Fantastic Four*. The print-run statistics published in #158 (necessary for the publisher to claim legal ownership of the character and book) list the paid circulation average as 111,559 copies per issue. When the Statement of Ownership report appeared in *Daredevil* #181 (April 1982), the devastating climax of Elektra's career, it lists the paid circulation average as 276,812, more than twice the number of copies listed just three years earlier. In 1983, Miller left the series as the most coveted talent in the industry—an industry that until then had rarely promoted artists or writers as selling points, reserving any such publicity for major coups like Jack Kirby's defection from Marvel to DC Comics in the early 1970s. The fact that, as his run on *Daredevil* drew to a close, Miller himself jumped from Marvel to DC to produce *Ronin* (1983), a six-issue "prestige" format miniseries over which Miller retained full ownership, further demonstrates the transformative effect his *Daredevil* had on what had been the most fiscally conservative of creative industries. Miller didn't begin the comics creators' rights movement—that honor probably goes to, among others, Miller's mentor Neal Adams—but the steam it gained after Miller's *Daredevil* run reminds us how important his early career was to its development. Without *Daredevil*'s popularity, he might not have gained the creative and economic clout that made him such an effective advocate for creators' ownership of the characters, stories, and original artwork that had made mountains of money for their corporate bosses.

All that said, however, I would be remiss to pretend that my interest in this topic is strictly aesthetic or historical. Miller's *Daredevil* has haunted me for some thirty years now. Consider this book part critical study and part exorcism attempt, one I'm pretty certain will fail to purge me of either the images or the rotating feelings of attraction and apprehension they inspire. When I was a nebbishy preteen comics reader, a big fan of Spider-Man because he was a nebbish too, I was frightened by Miller's *Daredevil* even as I sneaked issues into my parents' house under cover of a brown paper bag and a nylon jacket (my father, an open-minded Lutheran minister, would not have taken a superhero in a red devil suit very seriously, but my grandmother would have shamed me down the stairs and back up again had she caught even the remotest glimpse of such an abomination). I was also confused by what looked to me then like Miller and Janson's glaring inconsistency as renderers of Daredevil and his urban world. Sometimes the artwork looked effortless, elemental, as though it couldn't have been drawn any other way; other times it looked flat-out awful, though no less purposeful or decisive. All I knew for certain was that *this guy is young and green and more confident in his own vision than anyone else in the business. Something big is happening here and I don't know what it is, but I do know that if I miss an issue, I'll never figure it out. Daredevil* was the first series that hooked me by way of a creator rather than a character. It began my decades-long struggle with Auteurist's Syndrome, the dog-like adulation of a comics creator that underwrote my discovery that comics were a craft.

Dear reader, I understand your doubt at this point. I know what even some of the most generous among you are thinking: *Frank Miller? Frank Miller?! There's nothing redeemable about his work anymore, if there ever was. His Batman stories justify taking the law into one's own hands as violently as possible.* Sin City *is openly misogynistic, and considering the castrating monster he made of Daredevil's soul mate/archvillain Elektra, there's little cause to wonder whether that misogyny drives even his earliest work.* 300, *his account of the Spartans' heroic defeat at Thermopylae, is as xenophobic regarding their Persian enemies as the Spartans were themselves. What's to be gained from an analysis of his early Daredevil run besides confirmation of what we already know?* To me, however, this last question is anything but rhetorical. Even now, as much as Miller's politics frost me, as wretched as I find his work's gender politics, and as frustrated as I am by the seemingly panel-to-panel plotting of his recent work compared to the intricate arcs he designed for *Daredevil,* I am still haunted by what those images showed me and what they meant to me beyond what they depicted. Today, as I shake my head mournfully while flipping through such recent work as his anti-Al-Qaeda propaganda gore-fest *Holy Terror* (2011), I am more curious than ever how and why those *Daredevil* panels have proven impossible to ditch. By articulating the nature of the hold they exert on my imagination, I hope to shed some light on how Miller brought *Daredevil* back from the brink of cancellation and what that success meant for the discourse of superhero comics past, present, and future.

I also want to dig into the value system Miller constructed in *Daredevil,* one in which the conservative hardliner's concern to make an example of the guilty clashes repeatedly with the liberal reformist's concern to both protect victims of crime and guarantee the just treatment of its perpetrators. Contrary to what one might expect from the xenophobic atmosphere of *Holy Terror,* however, these clashes were not depictions of liberalism as the superhero's straw man but thoughtful examinations of both sides of the debate. Miller's own life as a public figure illustrates a distinctly American tale about how libertarian shades of liberal ideals—including liberalism's critique of vigilante justice, a foundational concept of the superhero genre—could be twisted so easily into justifications for the "War on Terror" after the coordinated, deadly attacks on New York and other US targets of September 11, 2001. Rather than counting Miller himself merely as representative of that turn, however, I take *Daredevil*'s reflexive commentary on the fundamental ideals of superhero comics—liberty, community protection, and sacrifice—as a public airing of thorny questions regarding the American ideal of justice that, for many avowed liberals as well as conservatives, received their unequivocal answer with 9/11: kill the bastards who threaten our way of life, and to hell with taking prisoners. This bramble of ideology, creative expression, and commercialism is not my focus, nor do I pretend my ruminations on it are definitive. But they will, I hope, provoke a new thread in the ongoing discussion about the American passion for superheroes that began nearly eight decades ago, just a year before Hitler rolled into Poland, with Super-man.

My brother and I started collecting Marvel comics in 1977 or '78, spurred by several years of ingesting Silver Age *Spider-Man* and *Fantastic Four* comics that my older brother's best friend inherited from *his* older brother, an avid collector in the sixties and early seventies. The collection represented nearly every non-funny-animal comic a kid growing up in Centerville, Iowa, could find back then, with emphasis on anything and everything drawn by Jack Kirby, Marvel's sine qua non. By the time I began buying *Daredevil* for myself, after giving an issue (#159) away as a party favor in 1979, my brother and I had read the *Marvel Tales* reprints of the deaths of Gwen Stacy and the Green Goblin from *Amazing Spider-Man* #121–122, so we had a more sober sense of the mortality of comics characters than our friend's Silver Age issues had on offer. Back then, Spider-Man's Aunt May nearly died every six months or so, only to return to her usual ox-like frailty two or three issues later; and while the occasional minor criminal got shot to death, there was never any blood, and Spidey's life never changed as a result.

But not even the Green Goblin throwing Spider-Man's beloved Gwen off a bridge to her death and then accidentally impaling himself on the pointy metal ears of his own bat glider could have prepared me for what Miller would do with Daredevil. *Daredevil* was a violent comic in ways that mainstream, Comics Code–approved books had never been before. Beginning tentatively with issues #164–166 and in earnest with #175 a year later, I devoured *Daredevil* in spite of, and doubtless also because of, its simple, sketchy, sometimes gruesome images of heartless crime and the acts of vigilantism Miller prescribed to cure it. In Miller's world, when people were punched or shot, blood was spilled in quantities not seen since the g(l)ory days of EC horror comics. And there was stabbing, a lot of stabbing, something that had practically disappeared with the inception of the Code, likely because it was an easy act of violence to imitate. There was throat slashing galore, too, as Daredevil's nemesis, Bullseye, weaponized everything from a coroner's scalpel to the ace of spades from an ordinary deck of cards and aimed straight for the neck. After swallowing that imagery a few times, I could never play cards with my family or even wear an open-collared dress shirt without feeling strangely vulnerable.

And a lot of people died, from nameless walk-ons to central characters. As Sean Howe discusses in *Marvel Comics: The Untold Story*, superheroes and the environments they inhabit rarely change for good, at least not since Stan Lee demanded that his writers and artists deliver only the illusion of change. They might suffer protracted spirals of destruction, but the spirals were always followed by reversals of fortune that returned the world to its initial state.[6] Such reversals didn't happen under Miller's watch, and so seeing murders in *Daredevil* was a new, visceral experience for me. I hated the cheapness of human life it reflected, having been raised to be nonviolent to the point of docility, but I found it difficult to sort out whether Miller was cheapening life gratuitously or justifying Daredevil's vigilantism. At the same time, these killings attracted me with their novelty, their forbidden nature, and most of all their finality. Good and bad people alike died horribly, suddenly. These stories had real endings, endings in which characters weren't just beaten up and then got better: they died, and they stayed dead. Compared to most comics I read and to what my brother and I called the "Bash-Pow Fights" of the 1966 *Batman* TV series, the stakes here were astronomical.

The more general revelation here was that there were other ways to draw comics and outline stories beyond Stan Lee's mandate that displacement must equal zero. Even though the violence was genre driven and sensationalized rather than naturalistic in the strictest sense, reading Miller's *Daredevil* introduced me to the idea that a spectrum of representational possibilities existed for comics. The anatomically correct musculature drawn by Neal Adams (even the body he drew for Superman looked a little rangy) and the awkward but verisimilar facial expressions of his figures had set the standards for realist superhero comics as early as 1970. By contrast, in *Daredevil* Miller scrapped accurate anatomy whenever he needed a character's body to signify something beyond that body's existence in space. While critics and fans frequently called *Daredevil* gritty and realistic, Miller's loose, delirious approach to rendering his hero's stories makes realism seem like the wrong term. Like modernist and postmodernist art in general, Miller's pictures didn't support illusionism. Rather, they focused our attention on the act of creating comics. By acknowledging and even playing up the medium's rank artificiality, Miller freed himself to his expressionist impulses, impulses that "serious" superhero cartoonists had largely ceded to funny-animal strips and political cartoons.

In the years since I first read *Daredevil* as a gape-mouthed kid sprawled on my NFL bedspread, I have learned to appreciate how much Miller's expressionist sensibility depended on his shrewd understanding of genre. Interviews demonstrate that he understood from the beginning how genre conventions present a creator not simply with limits but also with opportunities to improvise within and discover detours around these same limits. Despite my differences with Miller and his work today, and despite his tendencies toward the same impossible physiologies, exaggerated secondary sexual characteristics, and impossible or unlikely plot twists that still rule mainstream comics, I still experience that run of *Daredevil* as a work of subtlety, restraint, and political complexity. To reread the run alongside Miller's analyses of genre fiction in his interviews is to realize how much that complexity owed to his approach to the conventions that confront any creator of superhero stories. The difference between *Daredevil* and the contemporaneous soap-and-space opera that was *X-Men* as depicted by Chris Claremont, Dave Cockrum, John Byrne, and Terry Austin, or even the trippy Marvel experiments of the mid-'70s like Steve Gerber and Frank Brunner's *Howard the Duck* or Jim Starlin's *Warlock*, might productively be boiled down to Miller's focus on the conventions of the genre in which he worked. Regardless of what I and many others imagined he was doing at the time, Miller was not making superheroes more realistic in the way that, say, Alan Moore and Dave Gibbons confronted costumed vigilantism with real-world physics, politics, media, and sexuality. Rather, he was exploring the internal makeup of the superhero genre, poking around for contradictions and paradoxes, with the similarly stylized "realist" genre of crime fiction as his probe.

Now, thirty years after our first meeting on a spinner rack at the local convenience store, I am in a better position to get my head around what Miller's take on Daredevil did to me. The precise moment at which I met his Daredevil, and my personal experience with comics up to that point in my childhood, has at least as much to do with my take on the phenomenon as does my education as a film and media scholar. Miller took a character type that thousands of introverted little kids like me and tens of thousands of angsty adolescents (also like me, only a little later) employed to process their sense of themselves as outsiders and risked undermining that function by calling our attention to the fact that somebody actually *made* this stuff, that there was more to drawing comics than skintight costumes and dynamic layouts featuring Kirbyesque homunculi who threw punches with their feet planted eight feet apart.

One bit of this "more" I refer to was visual symbolism, the way Miller exploited the sizes, proportions, and relative positions of objects and figures to express meanings in excess of what his dialogue or depictions could supply on their own. Hot on the heels of my introduction to Marvel's parody series *Not Brand Echh!* (1967–69), a *Mad*-magazine-style ribbing of Marvel's own Silver Age heroes (and everyone else's), my early glimpses of Miller's metaphorical expressionism got me wondering about what reflexivity could produce beyond parodic five-page stories with cute titles like "The Amazing Spidey-Man!" or "Charlie America!" My brother and I, ever ready to plagiarize whatever we admired, each came up with parody series of our own at the respective ages of twelve and nine. We drew, lettered, and colored them on sheets of used typing paper from my father's office trash can.

Those attempts at reflexive humor were my first steps toward realizing that undercutting generic types and plots was not only funny; it could also become a means for investigating the nuts and bolts of a medium. We began with shameless swipes from *Echh!*, ranging from the titles we gave our anthologies (my brother's was "Not Brand Yegch!," while mine was "Not Brand Ugg!") to the umpteen tiny gags that Marie Severin, Tom Sutton, and Kirby himself crammed into the panel backgrounds of *Echh!* in imitation of *Mad*'s Bill Elder. By around 1982, when I drew my last cover for what I eventually called "Not Brand Ugh!," I had also been writing and drawing "serious" Spider-Man stories for several years. Perhaps influenced by my desire to become a superhero cartoonist myself, I had begun to use parody less to imitate than to outline my difficulties with Miller's *Daredevil*. For that last cover, I cast the hairy eyeball of irony on Miller's cover for *Daredevil* #170, which featured the Kingpin of Crime, a grotesquely fat Spider-Man villain, looming over New York City skyscrapers like King Kong and gripping a doll-sized Daredevil—Fay Wray with a billy club—in one fist (see figure 2).

For the second segment of what was to be a three-part story about my oh-so-clever character "Staredevil," a hero who overpowered his foes by beating them at stare-down contests, I redrew Miller's cover to poke fun at its dramatic misrepresentation of scale. While grasped

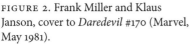

FIGURE 2. Frank Miller and Klaus Janson, cover to *Daredevil* #170 (Marvel, May 1981).

FIGURE 3. Paul Young, "Ugh! #7" (c. 1982–83).

in one of the skinny insect legs of my brother's parody of Marvel's Kingpin, called the Stingpin (a bald, rotund, human-scaled bee with a long pointy stinger-nose), Staredevil, tongue poised on upper lip in the manner of Dennis the Menace aiming a slingshot, thinks to himself, "I sure hope this is just symbolic!" (see figure 3)

That drawing implies that I found the symbolic exaggeration of Miller's cover funny, plain and simple. True enough. Back in 1982, I just wanted my cover to be funny to those who knew Miller's work, that is, my brother (who was very nearly my only reader). Looking at it now, however, I experience it as a coded message from my younger self to my older self, a clue about my attraction to a bloody, scary, pessimistic superhero series that I didn't want to love but did. Like the moment-to-moment panel sequences I described earlier, *Daredevil* #170's cover stared back at me like a Rubik's Cube I had to solve by trial and error alone. The absurdity of it prevented me from enjoying it as a gripping coming attraction and then moving on. Why would

Miller, a professional cartoonist, plop a gargantuan Kingpin into the middle of a "serious" comic cover? How did he decide when and how to do things like that? Was it okay for a cartoonist to exaggerate that openly for immediate effect—after all, Marvel's and DC's covers frequently exaggerated or outright misrepresented the issue's contents to sell more copies—or did taking liberties with basic rules of proportion violate the unwritten pact between superhero cartoonists and their readers that nothing must distract from our absorption in the plot? My "Not Brand Ugh" cover now seems a crude attempt to put those questions on paper and a sign of my recognition that Miller was asking them. It alludes to a subversive enjoyment in laying bare the conventions of comics art that Miller instilled in me without my realizing it. Thinking of it now still makes me feel in my gut the raw need to draw comics, even though my hands more or less gave up drawing twenty years ago.

In the world of comics and sequential art studies, Miller's 1980s *Batman* stories, *Batman: The Dark Knight Returns* (1986) and *Batman: Year One* (1987), and the projects he hatched after them have all but eclipsed his *Daredevil* stint as an object of scholarly research.[7] It's not difficult to find articles and chapters about *The Dark Knight Returns*, but after nearly four years of searching, I have yet to find any sustained analysis of Miller's *Daredevil* run outside of such mass-market specialty magazines as *Comics Feature, Amazing Heroes,* and the *Comics Journal* and such obscure one-offs as an incisive review, written by Miller's fellow comics creator Alan Moore, published in a Marvel UK anthology comic not long after Miller began writing *Daredevil* as well as drawing it.[8] Considering the series's importance in its time and Miller's mainstream appeal since *The Dark Knight*, this lack of attention seems bizarre. Miller's *Daredevil* runs neck and neck with Claremont and Byrne's thirty-five-issue collaboration on *Uncanny X-Men* (1977–81) as one of the most influential superhero runs since the key Lee-Ditko and Lee-Kirby arcs of the Silver Age. Certainly a great many creative teams since Miller have vied for critical attention as well: the Ann Nocenti–John Romita Jr. run that began after Miller's second go at the character in 1986 (the seven-issue "Born Again" arc); D. G. Chichester's consecutive runs with the artists Lee Weeks and Scott McDaniel, in which Chichester resurrected Elektra, a Miller creation that Miller himself had wanted to stay dead; and revered runs by Brian Michael Bendis and Alex Maleev, Ed Brubaker and Michael Lark, and (since the series's acclaimed reboots in 2011) Mark Waid, Paolo Rivera, Marcos Martin, and Chris Samnee. Whichever *Daredevil* creative team one prefers, however, the simple fact is that comics critics have yet to take seriously the question of why Miller's *Daredevil* caught fire in its time or even to come to terms with its relationship to Miller's work after *Daredevil* and the legacy it handed on to other creators who worked on the series. I suspect that Miller's recent notoriety, drawn by his hawkish public pronouncements and the increasingly Manichean quality of his works since 9/11, undercuts the value of these questions for some people. As I will demonstrate, however, the politics of his comics has never been as simple as it appears, and *Daredevil* provides the code to crack its historical complexities, particularly regarding the uneasy satirical links he has continually drawn between vigilantism and fascism.

Chapter 1 discusses the state of Daredevil when Miller came to the series, while chapter 2 delves into how Miller's approach as artist and writer redefined the character and his world. These chapters also attempt to come to terms with Miller's sensibility of genre conventions—in this case, the conventions of the superhero comic and the hard-boiled crime novel—both as templates for familiar, entertaining graphic storytelling and as creatively productive limitations. Though I take seriously Miller's belief, repeated in several interviews, that his *Daredevil* was a crime book first and a superhero book second, I challenge it a bit by exploring the debts Miller's *Daredevil* owes to the mythos of the Marvel superhero as a two-dimensional type defined by two traits above all: superhuman "powers" and a sense of responsibility driven by equal parts beneficence, guilt, and revenge. Chapter 2 also discusses Miller's approach to secondary characters—one of few nods he made to the character's history—as complements to Matt Murdock's characterization more than individual characters with backstories. Chapter 3 spotlights the main adversaries of Miller's Daredevil: the Kingpin, Elektra, and Bullseye. Though Elektra was Miller's creation, he used her to explore a gap in Daredevil's past, the heretofore untold story of Matt's transformation from vision-impaired teenager to costumed crusader. Miller used both the Kingpin (an old Spider-Man villain) and Bullseye (a member of Daredevil's lackluster rogues gallery) to perform similar functions by pressuring Matt/Daredevil into exposing exactly what makes him tick, sometimes to his disadvantage as a heroic character in the average-guy-as-role-model sense that defined Marvel's Silver Age.

Chapter 4 focuses on the visual and formal qualities of *Daredevil*. Difficult as it is to nail down, I attempt to describe the peculiarity of the artwork produced by Miller and inker Klaus Janson, its dependence on a minimalism-cum-grotesquery reminiscent of such singular Atomic Age and Silver Age cartoonists as Krigstein, Steve Ditko (responsible for Charlton horror stories, Atlas science fiction/fantasy, *Amazing Spider-Man*, Hulk in *Tales to Astonish*, and *Doctor Strange*), and Gil Kane (*Green Lantern*, *Spider-Man*, scores of Marvel covers in the 1970s). The influence Miller invokes most frequently is Will Eisner, the Golden Age writer-artist whose crime-busting character the Spirit became a channel for experiments in storytelling that made Eisner legendary among cartoonists. I also try to fill a hole in Miller criticism by analyzing his *Daredevil* page layouts, which match Eisner's and Krigstein's for pure graphic ingenuity without exactly imitating either of them. In combination with the muted coloring and Joe Rosen's hard-boiled lettering, Miller and Janson's line art exuded both grimness and a sheer joy in manipulating physical reality that revolted against the aesthetic pomposity of many Marvel series at the end of the 1970s.

Then there is an interlude in which I discuss the most notorious issue of Miller's run, *Daredevil* #181, with Paul Young, age thirteen. Writing it made it possible for me to finish this book, a task that has simultaneously brought me great pleasure and inexplicable dread, to the consternation of my kind and patient editors. This dialogue is my attempt to figure out why this has been such a masochistic project for me, using as its medium an analysis of the single issue that cemented Miller's residence in my head: "Last Hand," in *Daredevil* #181 (April 1982). You are in a better position than I to judge the success of this attempt.

The conclusion brings the *Daredevil* years to bear on Miller's work since the mid-1980s. Miller's best comics strain against the limitations imposed by genres, and as such, I reference some of his later and most celebrated works (as well as a succès de scandale or two) to position the 1979–83 *Daredevil* run in the history of Miller's work as well as the history of superhero comics' entrance into a more mainstream market—cynically speaking, the market for R-rated thrillers; more idealistically speaking, the market for ambitious exploitations of late-twentieth-century multimedia literacy—that made sophisticated demands of superhero comics in some ways and reghettoized them as entertaining but disposable mass culture in others. These other Miller works (and I reiterate that they are referenced but not explored in depth) include *Ronin* (DC, 1983); *Batman: The Dark Knight Returns* (DC, 1986); *Batman: Year One* (as writer with artist David Mazzucchelli, *Batman* #404–407, DC, 1987); *Sin City* (Dark Horse, 1991–present); *Batman: The Dark Knight Strikes Again* (DC, 2001–2002); *300* (Dark Horse, 1998); and *All-Star Batman and Robin* (as writer with artist Jim Lee, DC, 2005–2008). Miller positioned Daredevil less as Mickey Spillaine's Mike Hammer in long johns than as a souped-up policeman, but since then, his vigilante heroes have leaned increasingly toward the Spillaine approach, enacting Hammer's conviction that the ruthless pursuit of justice trumps any law that would restrain it. Miller's increasingly vitriolic, anti-Muslim response to the terrorist attacks on September 11, 2001, has pushed him even further into Spillane territory. His graphic novel *Holy Terror* (Legendary, 2011), a wish-fulfillment fantasy of a superhero literally knocking the teeth out of jihadists, has dramatically polarized Miller's fans, as has his November 2011 blog screed against the Occupy Wall Street movement that, among other things, chides protestors for criticizing American capitalism when they could better use their energy battling anti-American terrorists. The most difficult question I pose in the conclusion is also the simplest to state: Is cartoonist Miller the hate-monger that Miller the public figure seems to be? If so, has this tendency always fueled his work? Moot as this question may seem to Miller's detractors, it gets more complicated when we take into account the subtlety with which he represents the relationship between justice and the law in *Daredevil* and then track that sensibility through to his present work.

Miller's second run as writer of *Daredevil* (again with Mazzucchelli as artist, #227–233, 1986, collectively titled *Born Again*) helps focus the conclusion. It provides occasion to meditate on the success of Miller's use of Daredevil to deconstruct a crucial paradox of the superhero genre: the hero's determination to serve justice, on the one hand, and his messier quotidian experiences with specific lawbreakers and the justice system, on the other. *Born Again*, sometimes hailed by critics as the definitive take on Daredevil the character, strips Matt Murdock of his house, his possessions, his reputation, and his license to practice law—the last and strongest tie *Daredevil* had to an argument against vigilantism. Now that Miller regularly and apparently unironically favors jingoistic and vengeful heroes, do his first and second runs on *Daredevil* stand as the intellectual high point in his examination of superheroic ideals? Or might we understand them now as merely tamer versions of his present glorification of kicking ass without even taking names? Or must it be either? To what degree does the fact that the majority of his best-known works are superhero stories—a genre that still teeters on the lower rungs of the mass-culture ladder in spite of many breakthroughs—inflect how readers come to such decisions about the work or its creator? In 1982, I wanted to know why *Daredevil* read and looked like a grown-up's series compared to my perennial favorite, *The Amazing Spider-Man*. The middle-aged me still wants to know why I thought so then, but more important, I also want to know why I still think so now, in spite of everything Miller has produced since. Let the exorcism begin.

OUR STORY SO FAR

Daredevil, like his more famous predecessors the Fantastic Four and Spider-Man (introduced in 1961 and 1962, respectively), became a costumed crime fighter for the most principled of reasons: to defend the innocent and vulnerable from violence. A brilliant, philanthropic attorney by day, by night Matt Murdock wears a bright-red devil costume, complete with horns and a big "DD" emblazoned on his chest, and confronts injustices that the police cannot or will not put right. In other words, this upstanding citizen-hero—a licensed defender of the rule of law on behalf of the those in need of defending, whether alleged perpetrators or victims—harbors an equal and opposite drive to take the law into his own hands, a drive so close to the surface of his identity that to unleash it is as simple as a change of clothes.

Nothing about this formula differs fundamentally from the superhero blueprint as Peter Coogan describes it, beginning with Superman: he has a mission to protect the innocent, powers beyond those of normal people, and a secret identity that he vigorously protects. Yet from the beginning, Daredevil stood apart. He lacks the augmented strength of his peers (though he still possesses abilities premised on science fiction, as I'll discuss); like Batman, he had to train his body to be stronger, faster, and more agile than those of his enemies. He is older, more mature, and more settled when he commits to wearing the mask than is Spider-Man, who begins his wall-crawling career while still in high school. And his professional association with the justice system turns Spidey's persecution by the police on its head. Matt Murdock is, if not the first attorney-superhero, then surely the first attorney in a Silver Age Marvel comic to wear tights. Marvel got its reputation for realism in the Silver Age in part by paying more than lip service to how superheroes keep body and soul together in their off hours. This is not to say that the secret identities of DC's heroes were not integral to their stories. Clark Kent's job as a newspaper reporter was a convenient way to keep Superman informed about threats to the city of Metropolis.[1] However, the civilian professions of Marvel heroes were, at their most suggestive, linked logically and expressively to their identities as costumed adventurers. Peter Parker is a freelance news photographer who sells selfies of his alter ego battling costumed criminals, but he never gets market value for them and is always broke, a situation befitting his not-so-secret identity as Midtown High's resident nebbish. Tony Stark, a multimillionaire inventor and arms manufacturer, keeps his own heart beating after a land-mine explosion in Vietnam by constructing Iron Man's armor, a cross between a life-support system and a single-passenger tank that prevents him from stripping to the waist to go swimming or (presumably) go to bed with one of his many glamorous paramours, lest his chest plate give his secret away. Being a millionaire playboy-inventor-superhero doesn't get much more tragic than that.

Matt Murdock goes Spider-Man and Iron Man one better. He is blind—as blind as justice itself—and yet he risks his life daily as Daredevil to keep his beloved Hell's Kitchen as safe as he can. The pun on "blind justice" inherent in this situation is hardly subtle, but if the character's history is any indication, developing the pun into a substantial theme of the series was harder than it looked.

One barrier to its development seems to have been the need to make *Daredevil* sell, and the path of least resistance to that goal was for Marvel to imitate its past successes. In one of Miller's earliest extensive interviews, he agrees with the interviewer, Dwight Decker, that "Daredevil always seemed like Spider-Man's weak sister" but then asserts Daredevil's potential to be something quite different from the very beginning. "The first few issues [of the series], particularly the run of issues that Wally Wood drew and Stan Lee wrote [issues #5–11], had an approach to the character that Stan later lost. He played up the blindness and the fact that Matt is a lawyer, and made him something special."[2] Miller isn't wrong to claim that the early issues exploit the blind-justice theme with more focus than the series would for years afterward, but for the most part, lawyering is just Matt Murdock's day job. The law firm he shares with his friend Franklin "Foggy" Nelson functions as a plot device, with every case providing supervillains for Daredevil to fight. Even in issue #7, renowned for DD's mismatched battle with the superhuman Sub-Mariner, Lee and Wood get the bad guy on the good guy's radar by making the suddenly litigious Sub-Mariner pick a law firm at random and end up, of course, at the door of Nelson and Murdock, green swim trunks and all. This sounds like a clever use of coincidence until one notes that Lee had already used a similar conceit three times in the first six issues.

The duality of Murdock's professional and secret lives offers a gift to any writer willing to lean on the oppositions between the two. But no other single issue from those first years matches the intensity with which *Daredevil* #1 contrasts Daredevil's vigilantism with Murdock's sworn duty to the law. The debut issue, dated April 1964, was written by Stan Lee, Marvel's Silver Age editor in chief and head manager of its expanding universe of characters, and drawn by Bill Everett, an industry veteran who created the Sub-Mariner in 1939, back when Martin Goodman's Marvel was known as Timely Comics.[3] The issue begins with the titular hero, clad in the yellow-and-reddish-black acrobat's leotard he wore for his first six issues, beating the heck out of a roomful of thugs. As they sag, defeated, against the walls of their hideout, Daredevil demands they produce their boss, Roscoe Sweeney, a boxing "manager" also known as the Fixer (for reasons easy enough to guess).

Then a lengthy flashback sequence unfolds the origin of our hero. Matt Murdock is the son of a washed-up boxer, Jack "Battlin'" Murdock, a widower who raises his son alone in a working-class New York neighborhood that the series later identified as Hell's Kitchen. Known as Midtown West or Clinton today, Hell's Kitchen was a nineteenth-century Irish slum known for its gang violence but also for its bohemian aura; geographically it overlapped with both Times Square and Broadway and was the first home of the Actors Studio. In 1963, its reputation was still mixed enough that New Yorkers would probably have recognized Hell's Kitchen in *Daredevil* #1 from Battlin' Jack's working-class Irish vibe and the hardscrabble look of Everett's location drawings. In comics, at least, one can hardly beat Marvel origin stories of the early sixties for their narrative and thematic economy.

The flashback begins with Matt as a boy standing, his shoulder to the picture plane, before his enormous father as they converse in a living room containing some beaten-up furniture. Jack, a self-proclaimed "uneducated pug," sits in an easy chair with his hands on Matt's shoulders and makes him promise to earn his living with brains, not brawn. But Lee quickly establishes the inherent conflict of this promise: the elder Murdock lacks the resources to send his son to college when the time comes. To raise the cash for Matt's education, he signs a contract with the Fixer, portrayed by Everett as a scowling old bookie from Central Casting, though he looks uncannily like Leonid Brezhnev with one of Fidel Castro's cigars stuffed in his mouth. (Brezhnev did not replace Nikita Khrushchev as leader of the USSR until October 1964, but considering the virulent anticommunism of contemporary Iron Man, Thor, and Ant-Man/Giant-Man stories, the resemblance is difficult to ignore.) Such a bald-faced proclamation of seaminess as the Fixer's nickname surely would have raised a red flag for most people who aren't characters in comic books, but in Marvel's Silver Age, secondary characters like Jack Murdock fulfilled their pre-destined functions no matter how unlikely they were. What matters for the origin is that Jack has regular gigs in the ring but only because the Fixer plans to clear Jack's path to a championship match, thus fixing the odds against his opponent, and then force Jack to take a dive so the Fixer can make a fortune on illegal bets placed on his boxer to win.

Once this setup is in place, Lee starts piling on the irony. Matt saves an elderly blind man from being hit by a truck at a crosswalk, only to be blinded himself by radioactive material the truck was carrying; though his eyes no longer see, the radiation permanently heightens Matt's senses and grants him a sixth "radar" sense that allows him to navigate the world like an especially deft bat; Jack wins the biggest match of his career, but the Fixer's henchman promptly kills him for refusing to throw the fight; the blind-as-justice Matt Murdock fulfills one promise to his father by studying his way into a top law school but breaks the other promise—to shun physical conflict—by training himself to fight, dressing as a devil, and pursuing the Fixer into a subway station with the intent of placing him before a jury of his peers. Daredevil catches up to the Fixer just as the old shark has a heart attack and dies. He then extracts a confession from the Fixer's hit man just as police officers arrive at the scene. Case closed.

Daredevil #1 traffics in poetic justice, Marvel origin-story style. For all the ironic reversals dogging the hero, nothing shakes our faith in his goodness. Bad things happen to good people like Matt Murdock's father and Peter Parker's doomed Uncle Ben for a higher purpose, to make heroes of young men, and bad things happen to bad people like Ben's killer and the Fixer because they're simultaneously the worst and best kinds of bad for adolescent male readers: daddy killers. They allow Matt and Peter to distance themselves from their father figures while paying their vengeful respects to the patriarchy that now promises them a spot at the top.

Yet Daredevil's path to glory has a darker dimension than Spider-Man's because in this case, the killer pays with his life. If Spider-Man's origin emphasizes Peter Parker's moral motivation for becoming a costumed crime fighter via its twist ending, Peter's realization that a thief he did not even attempt to stop went on to murder his uncle, *Daredevil* #1 begs a different question of superheroic ethics: What punishment does the criminal deserve for killing the hero's father figure, and who decides? Lee and Everett's answer is obviously the righteous wrath of Matt Murdock, the spunky blind kid in the red-and-yellow suit, but it is a wrath that falls short of murder. It's not DD's fault that the Fixer suffers cardiac arrest when he gets caught. But this answer is not as unambiguously positive as one might expect. Though the death of the Fixer is coincidental, his sudden heart attack plays like a preadolescent revenge fantasy turned adult nightmare, particularly when we consider the legal career on which Matt has already embarked when he suits up for the first time. On this pivotal day, only a few days after his graduation from law school, Matt enforces the law extralegally and winds up handing down a death sentence all on his own. As if to emphasize the shaky moral ground on which he stands, he falsely claims to have tape-recorded the Fixer's confession to trick the Fixer's hit man into confessing. Of course, we're rooting for Battlin' Jack's boy all the way, but something smells faintly rotten in Hell's Kitchen.

The story moves so fast that we have no chance to dwell on Matt's losses any more than Matt himself does. After Jack's death, Matt mourns him for exactly one panel before he's back in a law school classroom plotting to catch his father's killer and looking forward to a bright future as partner in a new firm. But even the relentless forward momentum of the origin story cannot disperse the ethical ambiguity of the Fixer's death and the questions it raises about Matt's motives for chasing him down. Matt has, after all, rigged himself a second identity that tables civil determinations about guilt, innocence, or punishment until after he's interrogated suspects himself.

Lee never recognized, or at least never revisited, the complicated snapshot of vigilante justice that he and Everett put to paper in *Daredevil* #1. He probably couldn't have even if he had wanted to. There was plenty of space in the Marvel lineup for a misunderstood hero like Spider-Man or a bickering family like the Fantastic Four but no place for a cold-blooded vigilante, not if the series that Martin Goodman published was to bear the seal of the Comics Code Authority, the comics industry's collectively supported office of censorship. But I still find it a bit chilling to read the last panels of *Daredevil* #1, in which the uncostumed Matt casts a tall shadow of Daredevil, horns and all, on the wall of his new office at Nelson and Murdock as his thought balloon reads, "Dad, wherever you are . . . I kinda hope you're resting easier now!" Here Matt seems proud of his victory over injustice in the subway station, but as its onlookers, we have witnessed how justice can be twisted by ruthlessness. Now we have proof of how oblivious Matt is to the contradiction. He talks like an angel, but the shadow knows he's a devil even when he isn't wearing the ugly suit. Now that he has a law degree and his own firm at his disposal, one might reasonably ask, what sort of extralegal havoc will Matt Murdock wreak next?

By 1979, some fifteen years later, the use of Matt's profession for thematic purposes had all but evaporated long ago. The irony of a blind attorney who assaults alleged perpetrators without trying them first had long dissipated. It was now convention, pure and simple. Apparently it took a creator with nothing whatsoever at stake in the character to turn that neglected theme into Daredevil's vital engine, a paradox that every subsequent creator would have to acknowledge from that point forward.

A DEVIL WITHOUT ADVOCATES

By 1978, the history of *Daredevil* was littered with failed attempts to generate greater interest in the character. Murdock had joked his way through street fights like Spider-Man, dabbled in the spy business like Nick Fury, played at Errol Flynn–style adventuring, and fought cosmic and supernatural threats like those usually faced by the Fantastic Four and Captain Marvel. More daring was the decision to make the ex-Soviet spy Natasha Romanoff, a.k.a. the Black Widow, Matt's crime-fighting partner (beginning when she fishes him out of New York Harbor in *Daredevil* #81) and also his lover. But even the Widow's complaints about Matt's insensitivity to gender politics read like a dull echo of how Janet van Dyne, a.k.a. the Wasp, resented the condescension of her partner/boyfriend Ant-Man in the *Tales to Astonish* anthology series and later in *The Avengers*. The Widow's bitterness was only deepened and made more specific than the Wasp's, in keeping with second-wave feminism circa 1971, though most of her complaints sound like snide attempts by the writers to paint feminism as a victim mentality. Even less conventional decisions involved electing the nebbishy defense attorney Foggy Nelson as New York's district attorney (*Daredevil* #48–130) and having Col. Nick Fury invite him to become an agent of S.H.I.E.L.D., Marvel's answer to Ian Fleming's SIS (#123; much to the nation's relief, Foggy turned Fury down). Scriptwriters even turned to science fiction and fantasy for inspiration. At one point, DD battled the Mandrill, a half-ape mutant who could have been lifted from an H. G. Wells novel ghostwritten by H. P. Lovecraft. The Mandrill emits a pheromone that makes women unable to resist his commands—surely the oddest Marvel villain I've ever encountered and surely one of the maverick writer Steve Gerber's less successful experiments in superhero psychedelia.[4] As this story grinds on, the Widow and a bunch of other women get brainwashed into following the Mandrill's every command. Reading it is excruciating, like watching *The Stepford Wives* reedited to tell the story from the perspective of the Stepford husbands. As far as antifeminist apocalyptic nightmares go, the "Fembot" story arc from the contemporary prime-time TV series *The Bionic Woman* was at least more honest about its own misogyny, and it was a hell of a lot scarier, if for no other reason than that the Fembots were led by John Houseman. The Mandrill was no John Houseman.

The crowning glory of editorial desperation, however, may have been displacing Daredevil from Hell's Kitchen. At the time, the most popular Marvel heroes were all based in New York City; only second-string characters like Ghost Rider or Shang-Chi, Master of Kung Fu, paid the rent elsewhere, leading me to think DD's various relocations were motivated by low sales and a felt need for novelty. Among other touristic turns, he travels to a fictitious South American country to put down an antigovernment rebellion for some reason or other, courtesy of a misfire of a story "ripped from today's screaming headlines" by writer Gerry Conway for *Daredevil* #75–76. Less than a year later, in issue #87, Matt Murdock is "permanently" relocated to San Francisco, where he partners at a high-profile law firm and (daringly) cohabits with the Black Widow. Imagine Spider-Man leaving New York to set up shop in Oklahoma City and live in non-Code-approved sin with Mary Jane Watson, and you'll get a sense of how odd it must have seemed for a superhero to leave the city that had been Marvel's near-proprietary dreamscape since the early sixties, let alone share a home (read: bed) with a lover without putting a ring on it.

After Conway left, Steve Gerber and then Tony Isabella took their mostly unmemorable turns at *Daredevil*. Marv Wolfman injected a bit of new life into the series when he took over as writer-editor (a peculiar Marvel job description that did not survive the 1970s) with #125 (July 1975). Getting back to basics, Wolfman moved Daredevil back to New York and had him split up with the Black Widow, though they attempt to reconcile a couple of times in future issues. In issue #131, Wolfman introduced Bullseye, a professional assassin whose claim to fame is his ability to kill anybody with anything he can throw: "He Never Misses!" Bullseye added some heft to the Daredevil's thin lineup of hyphenated bad guys (the Ani-Men, Leap-Frog, Stilt-Man, Death-Stalker, et al.) and plain-old weirdoes that I primarily associate with the giant heads and tiny faces given them by Joe Orlando, the series's second artist and a fine cartoonist who nevertheless seemed out of his element (the Owl, the Purple Man . . . wait, the *Purple Man*? What's so villainous and scary about *purple*?). A villain who can shoot the hero with a gun is a predictable threat in a Marvel comic; a villain who can kill the hero by flinging everyday objects at high speeds—a paperclip, a playing card, a condiment rack (presumably), et cetera—is genuinely frightening. But Wolfman was writing a passel of other books for Marvel, including its flagship *Amazing Spider-Man*, and after twenty issues, he was dissatisfied enough with his own work that he asked off the series. By his own admission, he didn't have the time or energy to isolate something unique to Daredevil on which he could capitalize.[5] Wolfman's turn as writer was followed by a brief, no-nonsense stint by Jim Shooter, the former DC wunderkind who was to become Marvel's editor in chief in 1978, but the book still couldn't attract the kind of fan following that made Spider-Man popular enough to star in four separate series by 1976.

But even generally solid and inventive writers like Gerber (who did script some lively issues of the series), Englehart, Chris Claremont, and Wolfman couldn't maintain momentum when the art team seemed to change every other issue. Fill-in jobs by the veteran *Daredevil* artist Gene Colan kept popping up among stories by pencilers ranging from the inspired (Gil Kane, whom Miller has called "the perfect fight artist in comics")[6] to the work horsey (*Iron Man* cocreator Don Heck, phoning it in except when pouring the Black Widow into her leotard). The underappreciated Bob Brown, a veteran of the Golden Age, drew twenty-six issues of *Daredevil* between 1974 and his death in 1977, many of them written by Gerber. Their near-regular collaboration made them the most consistent writer-artist team since Stan Lee and Gene Colan in the preceding decade. But such inkers as Heck, Vince Colletta, and Jim Mooney did indifferent, sometimes downright ugly work over Brown's pencils, thus subverting the dynamics of his storytelling and making it impossible for the series to attain the visual consistency that John Romita Sr. gave *Amazing Spider-Man* from the midsixties through the early seventies.

In spite of all the changes, both calculated and accidental, *Daredevil* had a way of gravitating back to an unremarkable status quo. We could attribute this to Lee's general edict that Marvel Comics must offer readers only the illusion of change, but that's only part of the story. There was no momentum behind any of the revisions to the Daredevil mythos because there was no creative continuity, no team that stuck with the book long enough to establish the consistent direction and deep mythology that Jack Kirby and Stan Lee gave *The Fantastic Four* during their decade-long collaboration on the series. By 1978, Colan was still filling in from time to time, almost to the point where he could still be mistaken for the series's regular penciler. All told, Colan had drawn more than eighty issues of the series before leaving it behind. He made his mark on *Daredevil* in many ways, from his unusual page layouts and irregular panel shapes to his tendency to draw the limbs of Daredevil and his adversaries splayed out like the arms of a starfish, heads dipped and shoulders high, as they perform excruciating feats of strength and will. Colan's fluid representations of bodies took advantage of the dynamic possibilities of angled "shots" and forced

FIGURE 4. Gene Colan art (inked by Syd Shores) from *Daredevil* #60 (Marvel, January 1970).

perspective, their ability to make even Matt walking in street clothes look like a fight scene, in ways that few cartoonists have matched (see figure 4). But the fact that Colan's style was synonymous with the character's past made him an unlikely catalyst for a renaissance.

Daredevil had become one of those characters one couldn't imagine the Marvel universe without, but whether he could or should retain his own series was another question. After years of good but not great circulation numbers, with issue #148, *Daredevil* was knocked down to a bimonthly publication schedule, often a step in the direction of canceling a title altogether. The esteemed syndicated cartoonist and *Batman* writer Frank Robbins was then assigned to the series, but his pencils for the single issue he actually drew, #155, are so anatomically stylized and frankly ugly that the issue comes off as a parody of superhero cartooning.[7] The only consistent aspect of the book at this point was Klaus Janson's inking, which began with issue #124 and continued intermittently until the Miller era, when he became a permanent fixture of the series. During that period, Janson's inking was the only thing that made the line art in *Daredevil* any fun to look at. His lines were loose but unapologetically so, dominated by shading lines and crosshatching, heavy on big areas of black. His style was well suited to Colan's expressionist pencil work, on those few occasions when he got a crack at it, but his presence was unmistakable no matter which penciler he took on. Not even Janson could make Carmine Infantino's drawings look like Gil Kane's, but he did make the work of both artists look like his own—no mean feat when inking the pencil drawings of such singular cartoonists.

So what does a comics publisher do with a keystone character that doesn't live up to its sales potential? I suspect that ditching him altogether was never considered an option. Superheroes were almost never killed off in the seventies. Marvel just canceled their series and preserved their trademarks by farming them out to rotating guest-star series like *Marvel Team-Up*, where they could bask in the reflected glory of Spider-Man in any given month, or giving them two-issue arcs in anthology series like *Marvel Spotlight* and *Marvel Premiere*. Daredevil might also have been pushed into a team book. Could *Daredevil* live on in a superteam like the Avengers or the Defenders? Ant-Man, a.k.a. Giant Man, a.k.a. Dr. Hank Pym, never had his own ongoing series outside sharing *Tales to Astonish* with the Hulk in the 1960s, but he remained an Avenger for a couple of decades, staying relatively fresh by continually exchanging old costumes and old super-powers for new ones. But Daredevil was, like Spider-Man before him, a solo act almost by definition. His relationship with Natasha, a partnership considered permanent enough that the series's covers bore the title *Daredevil and the Black Widow* for a while, had been reduced to an awkward friendship by the time Roger McKenzie began writing the series with issue #151 (July 1978). One of McKenzie's resuscitation strategies was to rekindle Murdock's stormy relationship with Heather Glenn, an unpredictable but devoted heiress introduced by Wolfman, Brown, and Janson in #126.

In retrospect, the frustrations that led Wolfman to drop the series after less than two years—a short run for the dedicated Wolfman—reveal a fundamental problem with the character's handling up to that point. Everyone who wrote *Daredevil* had to redefine the nebulous title character, because no one had tried for more than a handful of issues to capitalize on what made Daredevil unique to begin with. The only definitive Daredevil story remained the origin story, while *Amazing Spider-Man* cranked out inspired proof of the character's singularity every couple of years or so, at least during the Silver Age (the monumental Doctor Octopus arc in #31–33, the Green Goblin's discovery of Spider-Man's secret identity in #39–40, and #50's "Spider-Man No More!" immediately come to mind). Rather than being a blind defense attorney who moonlighted as a superhero, Daredevil was a superhero who happened to be an attorney in his spare time. The Matt Murdock identity had become an extension of his life as Ol' Horn Head rather than the other way around, to the point where Matt rarely practiced law, or anything else, except insofar as it served Daredevil's interests.

By the late seventies, even the heightened senses and echolocation powers that set Daredevil apart from Spidey and the rest were exiled to occasional dialogue, thought balloons, and captions. Change the lettering a little, and the drawings could have depicted the exploits of a sighted hero. This wasn't always so, as Miller's remark on the series's first stories suggests. Early issues of *Daredevil* confront directly the aesthetic problems of representing visually Matt's blindness and how his mutated senses manage to overcome it. In the beginning, his radar sense helped constitute the unique look of the series. Over a seven-issue stint beginning with issue #5, the industry legend Wally Wood developed Daredevil's costume from a yellow-and-reddish-black circus-acrobat costume into a sleek red leotard. His more foundational intervention, though, was to grant Daredevil's invisible powers their own iconography. For one panel in issue #5, Wood visualizes DD's radar sense as a series of concentric rings intended to demonstrate how Daredevil's radar sense works. Beginning with issue #8, however, the effect begins to appear regularly simply as a reminder that Matt has this supersense at his constant disposal. Thereafter, the rings appear around the head of Daredevil in the box at the top left corner of each issue's cover, a uniquely Marvel convention that quietly kept readers up on the state of the art of representing their favorite heroes.

Firing on all cylinders creatively (reportedly spurred by Lee's promise of profit sharing, which went unfulfilled),[8] Wood spearheaded another crucial icon in *Daredevil* #8: the waveform that translates Daredevil's enhanced hearing into an electrocardiogram image. From the first issue, Daredevil uses his superhearing as a polygraph; if he picks up irregularities in someone's heartbeat while he or she speaks, he has proof (according to the biological laws of the Marvel universe) that the person is not telling the truth. Lee initially communicated this information via thought balloons and expository boxes. But in #8, when the narration switches from dialogue to Matt's thoughts—"If they talk long enough, I'll use their pulse rates like a lie detector!"— Wood superimposes a spiky, EKG-like wave across three nearly identical frames, increasing the amplitude of the waveform when it passes in front of the two characters in question. Here Wood ingeniously envisions the sonic interference that prevents Matt from determining which one of them is lying. The icon stuck. Sometimes artists arrange it across Matt's face, sometimes behind or above his head, but they always employ it as a projection of Matt's subjective experience of heartbeats.

Wood's trope sets an important precedent for Miller's visualization of story time, as well. The EKG waves in *Daredevil* #8 act simultaneously as reflections of each panel's content—the heightened amplitude indicates an increase in heart rate—and as lit fuses of comic-book temporality, as if sparks were burning across the page from left to right as the suspense rises. Miller was to emulate Wood's strategy at the end of his and Roger McKenzie's retelling of Daredevil's origin in #164. The sharp peaks and valleys of the waveform ramp up the narrative tension right up to the moment that Daredevil's quarry has a fatal heart attack, drawn as a sawtooth curve that changes abruptly into a flat horizontal line.

Passive as Daredevil's powers seem when compared to the Human Torch bursting into flame or the Hulk turning huge and green when he gets angry, Wood's iconography kept Daredevil consistent with these splashier Atomic Age heroes. Taken together, his representations of DD's superhearing and echolocation powers allude to schematic signifiers of electricity, radio waves, radar, and nuclear energy all at once, with the hero's skull acting simultaneously as generator and receiver. By positioning that horned head at the eye of the storm, Wood implies that Matt emits a mental signal, perhaps an audible one, that bounces back to him, allowing him to get a precise bead on distances between himself and spatial targets, obstacles, or foes (prompting the inevitable comparisons to bats' sonar). Unlike Steve Ditko's imaginative but obscure rendering of Spider-Man's spider sense as a gaggle of worm-like squiggles radiating from his brainpan, Wood's icons gave readers a purchase on how a blind superhero might experience physical reality.

By the seventies, these fruits of Wood's ingenuity had long ago sunk to the status of rote conventions that were invisible to any but the newest *Daredevil* reader. DD's radar sense may as well have been a reminder that the reader hadn't grabbed an issue of *Spider-Man* by mistake. By the midseventies, the concentric circles appeared infrequently enough that writers occasionally described it verbally in dubious attempts to keep the character's supersenses relevant to the series. In *Daredevil* #103, Steve Gerber takes a stab at simply narrating the radar sense in boxes that are simultaneously overwritten and weirdly unhinged from the accompanying images, not to mention gratuitously salacious: "For so acute is DD's hearing that he could detect the sound of Natasha's vinyl costume slipping down across Ramrod's sweaty palm—." To quote one of Thomas Pynchon's theatrical patrons in *The Crying of Lot 49* upon seeing a prop representing a torn-out human tongue, "Ick."[9]

Occasionally the concentric rings still waft through *Daredevil*'s 1970s cityscapes, but to little effect. In *Daredevil* #123, Bob Brown makes no attempt to follow Wood's example by illustrating how the quasi-sonar waves are supposed to function. The writer Tony Isabella simply tells us about Murdock's process of accumulating such data over a series of thought balloons, rendering the generic rings redundant. Every thought balloon describing the layout of a room or the location of an enemy portrays Daredevil's radar sense as a multistep process for which the circles provide passive context rather than dynamic representation. If it took as long for him to process the information that his senses gather as it does for us to read the balloons, Daredevil would have his wave-radiating head handed to him in every fight. We cannot forget that our hero is blind, but to my mind, such prolix—and pointless—descriptions of his other, heightened senses ultimately make him seem more disabled, not less.

Daredevil's specificity was thus reduced to halfhearted spins on such Silver Age Marvel staples as secret identity troubles and romantic angst. He reveals his Daredevil identity to his current girlfriend (Heather Glenn) in #150, something Spider-Man often threatened to do during the Silver and Bronze Ages of comics but never followed through, either out of duty to his wall-crawling alter ego's crime-fighting crusade or out of concern that his friends and lovers would become targets of some supervillain's ire. Even this plot just recycled Matt's revelation to his first love, Karen Page, in *Daredevil* #56–57, but at least the run-up to that climactic event didn't involve the invention of a fake twin brother whom Matt made everyone *think* was Daredevil in order to throw his friends off the scent (the notorious "Mike Murdock" subplot of issues #25–41, in which Matt plays Mike as a sighted, flamboyant, hipster jerk). I won't deny that the mid- to late sixties stories are passably enjoyable, largely due to Colan's contribution, or that the early seventies issues have their quirky charm for a historically minded reader today. Yet so far as the character's commercial viability was concerned, Daredevil, having been everything at one time or another, was by the end of the seventies nothing in particular—nothing but a promising concept that the second generation of Mighty Marvel superhero creators failed to realize any more fully than had Stan Lee himself.

By tracking the character's historical straits up to the point where Miller picked up the series in 1979, I do not mean to imply that Miller's take on Daredevil was inevitable, the last possible road to revivification left on the map. Rather, my point is that the time was ripe—overripe even—for an approach founded on the character's internal conflicts and limits, one that would treat his blindness and heightened senses as opportunities for development instead of mere plot devices. By taking up that gauntlet, Miller demonstrated how thoroughly *Daredevil* had lacked these elements up until then and how much their exploitation could enrich the character and the series over time. In the moment, however, Marvel's editorial department was just taking a chance on a rookie freelancer, perhaps hoping to develop a creative chemistry that would spark readers' enthusiasm or perhaps using a bimonthly series with poor sales figures as a safe space for a rookie to prove his worth. Miller had already done some pick-up penciling on other low-risk Marvel stories such as a Doc Samson bit that appeared in the back pages of a *Hulk* annual, and "guest artist" issues of such minor series as *John Carter: Warlord of Mars* and *Marvel Two-in-One*, a team-up book that featured the Thing from *The Fantastic Four*. After filling in as penciler on *Peter Parker, The Spectacular Spider-Man* for a two-issue guest appearance by Daredevil, Miller approached Jim Shooter, now Marvel's editor in chief, about drawing DD regularly.[10]

Issues #27 and #28 of *Spectacular Spider-Man* (February–March 1979) are fascinating for what they reveal about the skills Miller hadn't yet learned and the techniques and preoccupations he had already begun to develop at this early stage. His layout and figure rendering look pretty similar to Brown's, and Frank Springer's inking smacks enough of Vinnie Colletta's scratchy line work to make a contemporary reader wonder if he or she hadn't picked up a copy of *Daredevil* by mistake. It's not impossible to tell this is Miller's work, but it's not easy either, considering both his level of rendering skill and his approach to panel composition at this early stage. Characters' heads take on slightly odd shapes. Frequently Miller unmoors the reader by rendering both Spider-Man and Daredevil from above as they jump and swing over the city. His later work on the *Daredevil* series would move the point of view closer to ground level, stressing Daredevil's harder edge as a detective of the streets and lack of skyward-leaning superpowers; he can't fly, of course, and unlike Spider-Man, he can't stick to the sides of buildings just by touching them but must rely on physical strength and an occasional swing on a nylon cord fired from his multipurpose billy club.

Yet the *Spectacular Spider-Man* issues already evince Miller's interest in panels and layout as opportunities to experiment with the overall design of each page without sacrificing plot momentum. In both issues, he portrays Daredevil's acrobatics in increments within the same panel, following the example of such previous *Daredevil* artists as Gil Kane and, by a more convoluted route, the motion studies of cinema pioneers Eadweard Muybridge or Étienne-Jules Marey. As DD performs a gymnastic pirouette through a barrage of rifle fire on page 3 of *Spectacular Spider-Man* #28 (see figure 5), Miller uses an oversized, horizontally oriented panel to render him at four distinct intervals (his costume colored a pale pink rather than red in those intervals) beginning with his initial position in deep space at the left edge of the panel. The figure then leads our eyes along a reverse-C path to the center, where Daredevil, now five times the height of the image that begins the maneuver (and red rather than pink once again), floats at the panel's left edge, his hand overlapping the panel below to produce a three-dimensional effect of the hero leaping off the page and into the reader's space.

It's a dynamic composition that looks like a beginner's stylistic grandstanding until one comes to grips with its storytelling function within the page as a whole. Though it's the largest panel on a page containing only four panels total—a low number for a Marvel comic of the time—the arc traced by DD's pinkish avatars guides the eye straight to the page's final sound effect ("Fzzzzzz-tt"), a noise motivated by a hail of bullets that shorts out a breaker box and douses the lights. Daredevil dominates the panel not least because Miller stages the four intervals against a mostly white background, but by shoving our eyes downward, Miller ensures that the bottom panel, the cliffhanger that pushes us to turn the page as quickly as possible, gets all the emphasis. Even there Miller takes no chances with the visual

FIGURE 5. Bill Mantlo (script), Frank Miller (pencils), and Frank Springer (inks), "Ashes to Ashes!," *Peter Parker, The Spectacular Spider-Man* #28 (Marvel, March 1979).

plotting, using a black background to make the sparks shooting out of the breaker box the obvious hinge between this page and the battle in the dark—Daredevil's own element—that follows.

At the top of the next page of *Spectacular Spider-Man* #28, Miller provides a more specific harbinger of his layout achievements in *Daredevil* (see figure 6). A four-panel sequence portrays DD punching out a passel of riflemen, the action across these panels broken only by an additional image that pops up between the first two and the last:

a disembodied, frameless close-up of Daredevil's face, his head sur-
rounded by the telltale circles of his radar sense. At the level of design,
the frameless panel creates a pleasing balance between the pairs of
fight panels on either side of it, as do the circles. Miller also alludes to
the function of the radar sense by continuing the circles *into* the fight
panels, illustrating how DD's radar signals permeate the scene. But
the real ingenuity comes across when we notice that Miller completes
the circles not with superposed images of the radar waves but in the
form of semicircular motion lines, signifiers of the punches Daredevil
throws in the four action panels. The punches alternate direction from
panel to panel—up/left, down/left, up/right, down/right—thus making the vectors of the fight scene more dynamic while completing the
radar-sense circles generated by the central image of Daredevil's head.
Miller thus makes the symbol of one invisible phenomenon, motion,
stand for a different invisible phenomenon altogether, the radar sense,
and vice versa. What this sequence demonstrates is the intrinsic tension of the comics page, its capacity for generating narrative sequence
and graphic composition simultaneously. Surely other superhero cartoonists besides Jack Kirby had experimented with gestalt effects like
this before, but in these early DD pages, we get a glimpse of Miller
figuring out how to do it himself in a way specific to this character.
The polysemy of Miller's layout is easy to miss as it ushers the reader
economically through this fight and on to the next plot event. At the
same time, the design is so straightforward that it both demonstrates
how such an effect works and makes an argument for its untried possibilities.

The theme of blindness in this story, written with uncharacteris-
tic inspiration by Bill Mantlo, also uncannily foreshadows Miller's
concern to answer a question that had dogged the character since
the beginning: What makes Daredevil Daredevil and not a bargain-
basement Spider-Man? When the Masked Marauder (the bad guy,
of course) blinds Spidey, Daredevil must train him to use his spider
sense as a kind of radar and to exploit his remaining senses just as DD
always has. With this cunning reversal, Mantlo turns Lee and Everett's
sideways Spider-Man clone into the original to be emulated, the experienced hero who must transform his comrade in arms into a version
of himself in order to save the day. Mantlo thereby gives Daredevil
an aura of authority he has lacked for nearly two decades, splattered

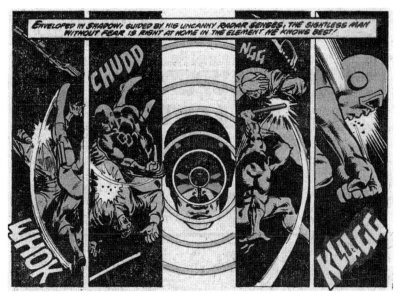

FIGURE 6. Bill Mantlo (script), Frank Miller (pencils), and Frank Springer (inks), "Ashes to Ashes!," *Peter Parker, The Spectacular Spider-Man* #28 (Marvel, March 1979).

as the *Daredevil* series was with self-pitying thought balloons about Matt's tendency to say things he doesn't mean and his uncertainty about whether he most wants to fight for the public good or pursue his own happiness. This is Daredevil's historical turning point, a bring-'em-back-alive war story in which the hero proves willing to sacrifice himself to save a fellow infantryman in the war against violent criminals in tights. A few years (and even a few issues of *Daredevil*) earlier, Matt's thoughts emulated Spidey's self-pitying monologues about his tortured love life. Now his thoughts reflect nothing but his immediate mission. He is all conviction, living entirely in the moment, determined to make the situation right and equally determined to protect the good and the innocent in the process. Daredevil has taken his first major step out of the Webhead's shadow.

COMING ATTRACTIONS

Miller took over as *Daredevil*'s penciler at the end of a four-part story written by Roger McKenzie that featured the supernatural villain

Death-Stalker. Miller's cover for his first issue, *Daredevil* #158, was designed by the "New X-Men" cocreator and Marvel cover editor Dave Cockrum, but regardless of its provenance, it reads now like a harbinger of the grimness of Miller's run.[11] Daredevil, seeking Death-Stalker under bare trees and a humongous full moon, stands crouched in a graveyard ready to fight. He plants his feet in front of a newly dug grave, complete with a headstone that reads, "Rest in Peace Daredevil," while his foe floats menacingly above him, black cape billowing and red eyes glowing through the black void of his face (see figure 7).

Though Daredevil doesn't die in this or any other issue of the run, and the graveyard theme capitalizes on McKenzie's reputation as a horror writer as much as anything else, Cockrum and Miller's cover image provides a neat allegory for the creative crisis the book had suffered for some time and even alludes to the strategy Miller would use to save it. Consider the cover a prediction, a pictorial announcement made by the new creative team: "Moribund though Daredevil is, his stories waterlogged with secondhand ideas, we, the creators whose work lies beneath this cover, will reinvent *Daredevil* as a much darker series, tonally as well as visually. Death stalks Daredevil now." Of course, death theoretically stalks all superheroes whenever they risk their own safety to protect others, but death has rarely looked so menacing in a Marvel comic as it does in this graveyard, where an end is an end that (theoretically) leaves no further story to tell. But like the Death card in the tarot deck, this image does not simply forecast casualties. It signals transformation—the termination of one phase of a life, followed by self-examination in light of the preceding phase. Suspending the hero in this pose of high alert, Cockrum and Miller pluck Daredevil from a comic-book world where violence rarely has permanent effects and drop him into one more like the reader's reality, where the limit of physical violence is defined not by losing consciousness or hauling a villain to jail but by mortality.

The cover of #158 introduces another new theme with a bang: violence. In 1981, Miller argued that "violence is actually the theme of the book" in that his *Daredevil* stories force readers to confront the fact that their favorite peace-keeping heroes require ugly physical violence—others' and their own—to be superheroes at all: "When I do a fight in a story, I would rather show people bleed than not, just to remind readers what they're looking at, and not make it so comfortable

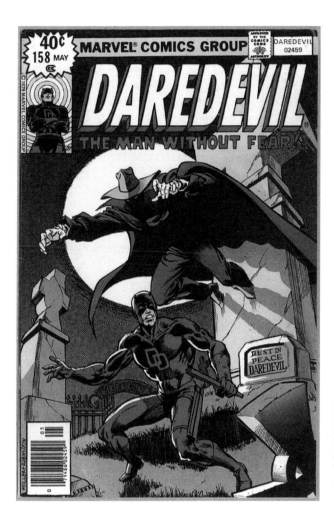

FIGURE 7. Dave Cockrum (design), Frank Miller (pencils), and Josef Rubenstein (inks), cover to *Daredevil* #158 (Marvel, May 1979).

for them that they're really enjoying the fights."[12] The graveyard cover signals the end of inconsequential cartoon violence in *Daredevil* and the beginning of a new focus on violence and the pleasure that comics readers take from it, as well as what violence means to a blind man who pushes himself relentlessly to become a better, faster, more courageous fighter than the sighted criminals he pursues. Daredevil intrigued Miller because he "was always attracted to the superheroes who didn't have any powers." Says Miller, "I particularly liked Daredevil because his chief feature is an impairment."[13] This remark is not as crass as it might seem. What interests Miller about Matt Murdock is not his blindness per se but Matt's self-consciousness about it, the psychological apparatus he has developed to process his blindness, and the possibility that Matt is "overcompensating" for his disability by putting on the suit.[14] The miniplot that this cover constructs thematizes both the perils of Daredevil's literal blindness and the hubris of his blind confidence. His sightless eye line points past the reader's right shoulder, while the ephemeral Death-Stalker makes like an Olympic pole-vaulter from behind his back. Despite Daredevil's being ready to spring on his adversary, despite his ability to pinpoint assailants with his heightened senses, here and now he cannot locate his ruthless enemy. *This* Daredevil believes in himself so completely that even when faced with a supernatural enemy like Death-Stalker, who can render himself immaterial at will, he trusts his radar to make up for the one sense without which both crime fighting and comics would be difficult to imagine. The only problem here is that radar is useless when your adversary is a ghost.

In a single image, the concept of Daredevil is sent straight back to the character's reason for being, back to the murder of Jack Murdock and Matt's unceasing quest for justice, back to Murdock's vulnerability as a blind man fighting a sighted person's battles and his brave but dangerous refusal to recognize the consequences of that vulnerability. And in a very few issues, Miller, first with McKenzie and then on his own, made a project of that return to roots, gradually eschewing the usual supervillain-of-the-month format (or every other month, rather) in favor of a character study that capitalized on the paradox of the blind superhero and the equally stormy paradox of the objectivity of law when faced with the disturbingly subjective nature of justice.

SPIDER-MAN IS A WHINER

For about ten years, from roughly age twelve until I turned twenty-two and started graduate school in English and cinema studies, I read many interviews with creators in the *Comics Journal, Comics Feature,* and anywhere else I could find them to learn how superhero cartoonists approached their craft. When I was about thirteen, I read a joint interview with Miller and Klaus Janson in a magazine called the *Daredevil Chronicles,* part of a series published by an independent company called FantaCo and dedicated to interviews, historical essays, and amateur appreciations of Marvel series. The interview both enthralled and mystified me. Miller and Janson spoke to Peter Sanderson in intricate terms about character development in *Daredevil*. They aired the initial assumptions about Matt Murdock's personality that they had made as creators, their inferences about his past and their ideas about how it shaped his decisions and actions in the present. "What could they possibly be talking about?" I wondered. In spite of Miller's and Janson's assertions, I stubbornly held that character in ongoing comics series was an unambiguous quantity, something superheroes and their supporting casts broadcast to us via dialogue and thought balloons in order to reinforce what we all knew to be the essence of the character. Character was certainly not something beneath the surface, a secret for the plot and artwork to reveal gradually. To me, this kind of scrutiny and subtlety regarding funnybook heroes was something new. What I didn't know then was that it was relatively new to the comic-book industry, as well.

Where characterization was concerned, the so-called Marvel method, Lee's ingenious workflow plan for producing a full-blown line of comics with only a tiny stable of writers, was a mixed blessing. As Charles Hatfield describes it, the Marvel method put the artist in control of storytelling in an unprecedented way: "During the formative period of *The Fantastic Four*, Lee and Kirby seem to have conferred initially about characters and plots, after which Lee prepared treatments or outlines . . . that piloted or prompted Kirby, or gave him narrative targets to shoot for as he broke the story down into pages. Afterwards Lee applied the finishing touch of dialogue and captions."[15] This routine made the artist rather than the writer responsible for solving many, if not all, of the problems involved in leading the characters from one pivotal plot point to another—their actions and bits of stage business and their moods, expressions, and relationships with others. The artist produced the full version of the story—and I do mean produced. Jack Kirby eventually got credit in *The Fantastic Four*, where he was listed as co-"producer" with Lee, for his role in not simply telling "Lee's" stories but turning them from a few scribbled half sentences into full-blown plots.[16] According to the Marvel artist Don Heck, for him the Marvel method meant that Lee would give him ideas about only the beginnings and endings of individual stories and ask him to "fill it in," the narrative equivalent of inbetweening at an animation studio.[17] The writer then pitched cleanup, composing expository narration and appropriate dialogue (something like "adding a laughtrack or music" to a finished film, as Miller puts it) and filling plot holes that had gone unresolved in the images.[18]

I am of two minds about the effect of the Marvel method on characterization. One the one hand, giving diverse artists (Kirby, Ditko, Heck, Everett, Colan, et al.) a free hand over visual portrayal and character interactions probably forced Lee to write dialogue and captions that would gloss what the characters were doing on the page in ways that didn't correspond to his original intent; in effect, he had to interpret the drawn characters in a convincing and consistent way, which likely led to some fresh, unexpected decisions that could be capitalized on in later issues by both artist and writer.[19] On the other hand, in practice, the characters that Lee and Kirby or Lee and Ditko jointly (but not exactly collaboratively) developed could become muddled by disagreements between writer and artist or get stuck with two easily communicable dimensions, such as the Thing's rotation between loyalty and anger or the Human Torch's teenage impulsiveness and his penchant for teasing the Thing. (This was still an advance over DC's characterizations during the same period, in which meticulous, fully executed scripts defined characters by their powers and/or basic agendas, like "good" and "evil" and "victimhood.") Some characters, like Reed Richards or Spider-Man, were conceived thickly enough that the right dialogue could adequately allude to preestablished traits, but both artist and writer were expected to place the greatest emphasis on action, not personality.

The Marvel method, with its odd division of labor between writing and storytelling, probably inhibited some writers from setting up major events several issues in advance and generating anticipation by gradually building the conditions that would produce them. It didn't stop some writers from trying some elaborate preplotting anyway, but on a series like *Daredevil* in the seventies, with its revolving-door creative team, complex foreshadowing probably seemed a futile pursuit. Some members of the Bronze Age generation of writers, represented by such fans-turned-professionals as Steve Englehart and Steve Gerber, returned to DC's practice of writing full scripts before the artist took over, but even for them, characters often functioned like action figures made to suffer ever weirder plot twists.[20]

Daredevil's creative teams had to deal with the extra complication of working in Spidey's shadow, an influence established on *Daredevil's* very first cover. Jack Kirby and Bill Everett's drawing of Daredevil leaping over crooks is dynamic, certainly, but it also borrows a stock fistfight maneuver from Ditko's *Amazing Spider-Man*. If that allusion isn't obvious enough to generate associations for readers, the rookie Daredevil is nearly crowded off the cover by images of Marvel veterans. The words "Remember when we introduced . . . SPIDER-MAN" appear inside a large purple arrow pointed at a nonstandard-looking drawing of Spidey (possibly by Kirby, who never grasped the character's Ditko-generated essence), from which another arrow leads us straight to small head shots of the First Family of Marvel heroes: "Now we continue the mighty Marvel tradition with . . . Daredevil!! . . . A worthy companion magazine to such all-time greats as *The Fantastic Four!*" The vertical column displaying these images takes up more than three-quarters of the comic's height and more than one-third of its width (see figure 8).

FIGURE 8. Jack Kirby and Bill Everett, cover to *Daredevil* #1 (Marvel, April 1964).

Miller made it his project to fulfill the promise of Mantlo's *Spectacular Spider-Man* story by leaving behind the long shadows of Marvel's previous hit characters. Of course, Miller didn't shun opportunities to work with these other characters. He once told the interviewers Richard Howell and Carol Kalish that "Spider-Man is a great character to draw," and he drew a number of polished Spider-Man stories after his guest stint on *Spectacular Spider-Man*, most notably a couple of *Amazing Spider-Man* annuals and a *Marvel Team-Up* annual featuring both Spidey and the Fantastic Four. Miller's problem with Spider-Man was all the angst. "All my reservations about the character are in how he talks, 'cause his visual is still very confident, and very strong—it's just that he never stops whining."[21] Spidey's self-pity, his penchant for martyrdom, and his borderline masochistic self-neglect attracted fans' identification but also made his life more or less a continual nightmare. Even worse, it made his success as a superhero hard for Miller to swallow. Spider-Man's trademark habit of heckling villains during fights only made his effectiveness less believable:

> I don't believe that Spider-Man would last two weeks [as a crime fighter] the way he's conceived. In order to have power over the criminals, you would have to be that rotten; [criminals] would have to accept him as almost one of them. . . . Daredevil has to reach the point where when he walks into a room, they're terrified of him, because he has to be accepted as a force they'll respect. That isn't done much in comic books; it's around in other kinds of fiction. I'm more comfortable with that; I don't see him as being happy go lucky when he's up against a bunch of guys with guns.[22]

Following this logic meant making Daredevil less of a wiseacre than Spider-Man, whose snappy patter (to complicate Miller's negative assessment) expressed the liberation that being Spidey meant for the younger, nerdier Peter Parker. Miller turned DD's knowing sense of humor into a sign of his control over difficult situations and darkened his encounters with the criminal element in order to make that wit harder to mine. "What I have tried to do . . . is to take that character that Stan and Gene did as a swashbuckler and put him in situations where it's impossible for him to be that way."[23] To put it a little differently, Miller finished what Mantlo started by squeezing the last drops of Spider-Man out of Daredevil, thereby testing readers' confidence that they knew Matt Murdock very well at all.

DAREDEVIL VERSUS THE COMPETITION

Instead of courting comparison with other superheroes in hopes that their popularity would rub off on Daredevil, Miller used their example to distinguish the character more sharply. In Peter Sanderson's 1982 joint interview, the inker Klaus Janson describes Miller's Daredevil as, psychologically, a healthier character than either Spider-Man or Batman, the corporate-owned character that Miller did not take on until 1986 with *Batman: The Dark Knight Returns*. Daredevil, Janson says, "seems to have accepted himself" by the eighties; "he's no longer anchored to the past by his relationship to his father or by guilt. He's going ahead."[24] Miller agrees, noting that unlike Spider-Man, whose career is an endless act of penance for his uncle's death, Daredevil "doesn't do what he does because he's guilty about something." He is "positively motivated" now; "he isn't an avenger and he isn't a punisher. . . . He's doing good rather than stopping evil. That really is the essence of the character."[25] While Wolfman had made Matt more "petulant" than he had been in the 1960s, as Miller puts it, Shooter rationalized that petulance as a developmental landmark by putting Murdock through what Miller calls an "emotional adolescence, coming to grips with the world and trying to exert the control he hadn't exerted in the earlier years."[26]

Miller would probably have incited comparisons to Batman in the fan press simply by transforming *Daredevil* into a grittier, more deterministic series, but Miller openly stressed the parallel in his *Daredevil*-era interviews. In 1981, Miller draws an explicit contrast between Daredevil and Batman: "Daredevil . . . operates on a basic motive of love for seeking out justice. . . . [Batman] is punishing those who killed his parents. Batman's focus is on the criminal, Daredevil's is on the victim."[27] Critics picked up on Miller's concern with Daredevil's motives, as well as the productive task of measuring them against those of the Batman. Reviewing Miller's work thus far in the *Comics Journal in 1982*, Ed Via wrote that Miller had made Daredevil "first and foremost a moralist, a person with a strong sense of fairness and . . . compassion, someone whose actions were as directly in line with his convictions as humanly possible."[28] Even Daredevil's scuffles with criminals differed from Batman's in that they were performances rather than acts of vengeance: "I see Matt Murdock as being a grown man and Daredevil as almost being a boy. . . . He believes in everything he's doing and he works very hard at it, but part of him just gets off on jumping around buildings."[29] "I'm also trying to develop him as a guy with a terrific sense of humor, who scares criminals and has a great time doing it. Like [Steve Ditko's DC character] the Creeper, he laughs and laughs and laughs, and thinks [to himself], 'Jeez, they're buying it!'"[30] Miller's favorite means of exposing his hero's antic side was to send Daredevil to Josie's Bar, a fictional dive where New York's entire population of petty thieves seems to turn up every night. Digging for clues to various cases, DD inevitably sparks fights that trash the place, hurling thugs through the front window while Josie protests (for the umpteenth time) that she just had it repaired. Sometimes he even orders a drink first, but as Miller points out, it's always a glass of milk. The milk (and the milk moustache it leaves behind) comically telegraphs Matt's wholesomeness compared to the hardened types guzzling whiskey and beer all around him, but it also underscores Miller's description of DD as Matt's boyish side, the inner child that "comes alive" while playing superhero.[31]

Ultimately, however, the contrast Miller once drew between the borderline psychotic Batman and the psychologically healthy Daredevil sounds like an overstatement of the argument, fronted by the *Village Voice* in 1965 (and echoed in *Esquire* the following year), that "Marvel Comics are the first comic books to evoke, even metaphorically, the Real World."[32] By those lights, "real world" referentiality meant that Marvel heroes dealt openly with persecution, neuroses, and family squabbles and turned out to be their own worst enemies nearly as often as protagonists did in postwar literary fiction. By contrast, DC didn't raise any schlemiels, with the possible exception of Clark Kent, whose inferiority complex is all an act to keep people from noticing that, but for the eyeglasses and the hunched shoulders, he looks exactly like Superman. DC stories followed the logic of such classical storytelling modes as the epic or the chronicle, where decision making is an exponent of action instead of a process inflected by character subtleties and every action thus taken is world-historical in importance. Its editors exiled strong emotion, anxiety, mortality, and other everyday complexities to the infamous imaginary stories of the fifties and early sixties. This means of distinguishing Silver Age Marvel heroes from those of DC hits a snag, however, when we stack Batman's origin up against that of Spider-Man or Daredevil. The emotional crux of all three is the Spidey triumvirate of all-too-human gut reactions: guilt, shame, and a desire for revenge. Indeed, the most obvious precedent for Daredevil's origin is the first version of Batman's origin story in DC's *Detective Comics* #33 (December 1939), in which an anonymous street thug robs and shoots Bruce Wayne's parents before young Bruce's eyes. Batman's origin sets underexamined precedents for many origin stories from Marvel's Silver Age: dead parent, angry child, costume chosen to strike fear into what the Batman of 1939 touts as a "superstitious, cowardly lot" of evildoers, an initial state of helplessness igniting the desire to bulk up and do right. Not unlike the death of Jack Murdock in Daredevil's case, Bruce Wayne's extraordinary childhood loss forges Batman's determination to avenge that loss on all criminals everywhere forever after and to transform himself into a steroidal, bat-eared Sherlock Holmes.

Miller brought the Punisher, then Marvel's most homicidal lead character, into the comparison to develop a pet point about Daredevil's singularity: his duty to the legal system, for better or worse. In 1981, when Richard Howell asked Miller point blank, "Is Daredevil Marvel's Batman?" Miller answered that, no, "the Punisher is Marvel's Batman."[33] Miller argued that, unlike the Batman, whose parents' murder catalyzed every major life decision he made from then on, the death of Battlin' Jack did not have as "big an effect on [Matt] as his father's life, and he is his father's son, being a natural born fighter."[34] The Punisher, by contrast, shares not only Batman's desire to avenge murdered loved ones but also his will to stop killers and drug dealers in their tracks. He exceeds Batman's mission only in that he executes the bad guys on the spot. The Punisher, Miller tells Howell, is "Batman without the impurities. The side of Batman that makes him spare the criminals is something that's added on. It's not part of the basic concept of his character. . . . Daredevil's basic concept is very dissimilar. I see Daredevil as someone who operates on a basic motive of love for seeking out justice."[35] This was not to say, however, that the Punisher's use of deadly force made him less heroic to Miller than Daredevil or Batman were. The Punisher *is* a hero, Miller says, but "I don't consider him a role model. The main difference between him and Daredevil is Daredevil's sense of responsibility to the law. The Punisher is an avenger; he's Batman without the lies built in."[36] The "lies" Miller mentions refer in part to Batman's vow never to kill; he wields a gun only two or three times in his entire first forty-five years in print, due in each case to editorial inattention. While the no-kill rule probably helped keep Batman out of trouble with parents worried over comics' influence on young children, it exacerbated the tension between his desire for justice and his sense that the legal system is inadequate to the task of collaring mass murderers and rooting out corruption. If Batman's prime motive is to champion justice in the legal sense, to quash anarchy and restore social order, then why does he have such contempt for the police and the legal system except insofar as they can help him achieve *his* goals?

But Miller's hero comparisons beg the question, what makes Daredevil any different? Miller's remark that Matt Murdock, unlike Bruce Wayne, was more affected by his father's life than by his death doesn't quite ring true.[37] According to Lee and Everett's origin story, Jack Murdock was not just a prizefighter or a role model to Matt. He was Matt's parole officer, policing his son's natural aggressions in what seems a narcissistic attempt to start his own life over again by proxy. And then he died, violently, after using his fighting skills to triumph over his final opponent. However differently Matt Murdock and Bruce Wayne reacted to their parents' deaths, psychologically speaking both lost their opportunities to detach themselves from their parents in the course of normal development because their parents were violently taken from them. If the adult Murdock is still a boy half the time, dressing up to play a grim tough who talks with his fists, even a half-hearted Freudian account could hardly avoid noting that the murder of his father stunted him, left him with unfinished business he can never transact with Jack but can only process on his own. I don't bring up this point to psychoanalyze a fictional character but rather to suggest that Miller's portrayal of Matt achieves a type of sophistication peculiar to genre fiction and to melodrama in particular. Avenging a father's murder is the conventional thing for a male protagonist to do in crime melodrama, to be sure, but the trope doubles as Freudian shorthand for more quotidian Oedipal tension. Miller maps Matt's psychic interior onto a world defined by conflict—strategizing, reconnaissance, pursuit, and physical violence. Far from turning the character himself into a genre trope, however, Miller manipulates such conventions to construct Matt more subtly than could be accomplished through dialogue or thought balloons alone. He expands the function of an idealized premise driving superhero comics—the hero lacks public sanction for his acts yet abides by the law—by using that premise to motivate Daredevil very narrowly, even two-dimensionally, and then placing the hero into circumstances tailored to explore the gray areas of that ideal. Miller makes the pursuit of swashbuckling an uphill struggle all the way.

Examples of this strategy began to appear even before Miller took on the writing chores. In *Daredevil* #161, four issues into his run, Miller renders what could have been a rote fistfight between Daredevil and Bullseye as a one-sided pummeling that contorts the villain's body grotesquely with every punch. Looking on, the Black Widow, Matt's former lover, comments, "I thought *I* was an enigma . . . but I don't think I've ever seen Matt so grim, so cold-blooded. He's changed. He's not the same man I used to know." Miller didn't write that line, but once McKenzie began writing dialogue for Miller's pages, he may well have observed that Daredevil rarely hit anyone quite that hard (only when Gil Kane was behind the pencil, really) and sensed an opportunity to develop a new complication: this highly controlled individual, as vigilant about the legal system as he is about the physical world he must navigate blind, occasionally loses control *but does not recognize the loss*, while the people around him do. Stick, the leader of a band of do-gooding ninjas (code-named the Chaste, though that happened years after Miller's run), puts the complication perfectly in #188 when he tells one of his teammates, "[Matt] could be as good as what we do as *any* of us . . . if only his head wasn't such a snake pit."

However sincerely Miller claimed Daredevil as a man of the law in interviews, McKenzie and Miller's recap of Daredevil's origin reveals just how deep the snake pit runs. In *Daredevil* #164 (cover dated May 1980), in which Daredevil tells his origin story to the reporter Ben Urich, Miller portrays Matt's pursuit of the Fixer as the culmination of an orphan's vendetta fantasy. Skinny, vertically oriented panes render Daredevil stalking the Fixer moment by agonizing moment, while an EKG line that represents the Fixer's heartbeat runs horizontally across the panels (see figure 9). Visually, Miller subordinates space to time in a way that pays one of his many tributes to Bernard Krigstein, particularly his rendering of another "accidental" death in a train station in the classic EC story "Master Race" from *Impact* #1 (1954) (see figure 1).

In a shrewd analysis published shortly after #164's release, R. C. Harvey describes this scene as representative of McKenzie and Miller's skill at combining word and image so that neither reveals its full meaning without the other: "Sweeney's [the Fixer's] faltering words ['You're a . . . devil . . .'] mean little without the accompanying pictures, and although the pictures alone tell a tale of their own, Sweeney's words give significance to the series: from the lips of a dying criminal whom DD has run to the ground, Daredevil is properly christened."[38] And the significance that Miller and McKenzie inject into the images here reaches beyond the aesthetic impact of their formal decisions in themselves to lead us straight back to "Master Race." Written by the EC editor Al Feldstein, "Master Race" relates the last moments in the life of a German American immigrant named Reissman. In EC's typical O. Henry fashion (the same issue also adapts "The Necklace" by Guy de Maupassant), the second-person narration leads us to believe that the sight of a former concentration-camp officer on the subway has sent Reissman's thoughts back to his own suffering at Belsen. But the penultimate page turns the tables by revealing that Reissman commanded Belsen and that the other man, who ultimately chases Reissman to his death onto the subway tracks, was his prisoner.

Krigstein took what Feldstein intended as a five-page story filled with talking heads and transformed it into an eight-page comics tour de force that concludes by dividing the story's climax into multiple panels (eleven in all) constituting the top half of the final page. Before I start comparing Miller's similar breakdown of the Fixer's death to this sequence from "Master Race," I need to clarify what Krigstein's experiments with time mean for the criticism and theory of comics. Art Spiegelman, a longtime champion of Krigstein's work, dismisses the critics who characterize temporal distensions like this one as "cinematic":

> The two tiers of wordless staccato panels that climax the story have become justly famous among the comics literate. They have often been described as "cinematic," a phrase thoroughly inadequate to the achievement: Krigstein condenses and distends time itself. The short chase that ends Reissman's life takes up about the same number of panels given over to the entire Hitler

FIGURE 9. Frank Miller and Klaus Janson, "Exposé," *Daredevil* #164 (Marvel, May 1980).

decade [on the preceding pages]; Reissman's life floats in space like the suspended matter in a lava lamp. The cumulative effect carries an impact—simultaneously visceral and intellectual—that is unique to comics.[39]

Spiegelman made a finer point about this scene in a 1975 article on "Master Race" that he cowrote with John Benson and David Kasakove. There the authors describe how Krigstein alters "the standard comics 'cinematic' device of repeating an identical scene for two panels, with an object or person moving closer in the second panel." Krigstein, they write, breaks down story time into panels that record slightly different stages in the motion of objects—subway trains, primarily—but makes the unusual move of changing the angle on these objects slightly in each panel, the better to demonstrate the direction of the movement (see figure 10).[40]

Then, at the climax, Krigstein appears to revert to the "cinematic" convention of keeping the point of view rigid. When Reissman falls onto the tracks in front of the incoming train, each of Krigstein's four panels depicting the fall "shows exactly the same viewpoint"—but not, Spiegelman et al. insist, in the interest of producing a cinematic effect. Instead, Krigstein represents the event as "a single visual unit, the four successive heads [of Reissman] forming one curve of descent," thereby creating an effect of abstraction that only a series of side-by-side panels can achieve.[41] The moment has been extended to grant it an impact similar to the horrors depicted in distinct spaces and times on the earlier "Hitler decade" pages. The effect of this parallel is not to monumentalize Reissman but to make the punishment fit the crime. Every second leading up to the train's impact—Reissman struggles for life,

FIGURE 10. Al Feldstein (script) and Bernard Krigstein (art), "Master Race," *Impact* #1 (EC, April 1954).

changing tactics every millisecond, trying to regain his balance, grabbing at the platform—is as tortuous as the months and years of torture and murder represented in each panel depicting the death camp.

Superhero artists had exploited this technique before Miller, perhaps none so elegantly as Jim Steranko, particularly in his later Nick Fury stories in Marvel's *Strange Tales* and his brief stint on *Captain America* (#110–111, #113) in 1969. But in *Daredevil* #164, Miller alludes directly to the climax of "Master Race" in order to address the nature of Matt Murdock's inner conflict. He keeps the same perspective on a single event over multiple panels at five points in *Daredevil* #164, four times to monumentalize a major event (Urich holds up a photograph to Daredevil for identification, forcing DD to admit his blindness and thus his Murdock identity; a military truck driver suffers the heart attack that leads to Matt's accident; the Fixer dies; Ben burns his notebook) and once to visualize Matt's frustration at his failure to get information from Jack's old sparring partner, who never stops swinging at his practice bag during the entire conversation. For the rest of the issue, whenever Miller spreads an event over multiple panels, he keeps shifting the point of view, at one point to reveal that Matt, hiding, can hear both the Fixer's demand that his father throw the championship fight and his father's refusal. The death of the Fixer in the subway station, however, stands out from all of these moments. It follows three pages that show Daredevil mercilessly beating the Fixer's gang and is immediately preceded by three panels that present the Fixer's initial descent into the subway station from slightly different positions. The contrast between the pages of conventionally depicted brutality and the moment-to-moment breakdown of the Fixer's heart attack mimics Krigstein's parallel of Reissman's death with the war years in Belsen. The twist here is that, if the Fixer is to Daredevil as Reissman is to the unnamed prisoner of the camp, systematic violence, for which we initially hold an innocent victim accountable in "Master Race," is in fact perpetrated here by both the villain *and the hero*. That violence culminates with the Fixer, terrified and unable to escape, taking Reissman's fall.

So much for the joyful swashbuckler who cares more about protecting the innocent than punishing the guilty Batman-style. Though Daredevil's adversary dies without the hero laying a hand on him, Daredevil identifies himself as the author of the Fixer's death to the point of reveling in it: "This one's for you, Dad . . . ," he thinks as he stands over the body. In case there are lingering doubts about DD's motive as McKenzie and Miller depict it, here are Miller's own words: "In the original [origin] story . . . Daredevil chased the Fixer down while running on top of a barrel and so didn't know [the Fixer] was having a heart attack. In the version that we did, it came across as much more of a cold-blooded murder on Daredevil's part."[42] When it's all over, one killer is dead, but the other is still at large. This retelling of the origin introduces one of Miller's most consistent and influential themes in *Daredevil*: the dark psychological corners of civil society where public responsibility runs aground on personal desire, as discovered by a volunteer hero who lacks the self-knowledge to recognize when the latter is passing itself off as the former.

If (male) superheroes were born of Oedipal tension, Miller's Daredevil performs masculinity as a state of perpetual suffering, where psychological anguish is Matt Murdock's one and only reward for trying to make himself a transcendent patriarch in the wake of his father's abrupt death. From the perspective of disability studies, José Alaniz claims that behind every rippling-muscled superhero body lies a disabled or dead body that the superbody exists to deny. For Alaniz, Matt Murdock's blindness is both an obstacle he heroically overcomes and just one mask among many that Matt schizophrenically dons every day, another sign of the "hollowness" of his identity. The difference is that his "blind man" performance "reaffirm[s] cultural expectations about the defenselessness of blind people."[43] And the (self-) punishment doesn't stop there. Miller's comics in general are littered with battered male bodies, and Daredevil was the first in line; issue after issue, he becomes more visibly torn, broken, bullet-riddled and bloody than any mainstream superhero before him. The devastation of his body gives him the Oedipal motivation to resurrect himself not just as a man but as a superman who simply will not stop getting up no matter how many times he falls. Writing about the bloodied Batman of Miller's *The Dark Knight Returns*, Theo Finigan calls "the visual representation of the body in pain . . . central to [the] recrudescence of overt patriarchal control" that Batman exerts against the "limp and emasculated figures" of Gotham City's impotent "city fathers."[44] In the process, Daredevil emphasizes the myth about masculinity that superheroic bodies have been spinning all along: when one has the phallus in one's toolkit, no amount of punishment can strip him of it for long. But the cycle of punishment never ends, and therein resides the loose thread that unravels this fantasy of eternal male potency. Matt Murdock's blindness, his one incurable Oedipal wound, is a constant reminder that the ideal of perpetual male regeneration is founded on the lie that within every torn male body stands a superbody defined by constant, tumescent vigilance.

The most loaded distinction between Miller's Daredevil and Batman—a difference that also clarifies the political stakes of Miller's *Batman: The Dark Knight Returns*—is that Batman regrets the limitations that the justice system imposes on him and replaces that system with one of his own, while Daredevil embraces the same limitations, employing them as a barometer that he fully expects to alert him when he goes too far. In Miller's words, "A lot of what the Daredevil character is about is controlling and restraining that which is dangerous within us through law and through rules. He does that with himself."[45] What makes these limits interesting for the reader is testing them. "In any form of fiction, when you want to have a good conflict, you put two things the character loves against one another. I've [done] this several times with Daredevil."[46] This is what McKenzie and Miller did in *Daredevil* #164. They gleaned from *Daredevil* #1 a conflict between Matt's love of justice and his love for his father—or, rather, his ambivalence about his father, which, as Sanderson points out, disinters Jack Murdock from Ben Parker's section of the cemetery. Whereas Uncle Ben towers over Spider-Man like an "idealized symbol," an impossibly good father figure, the task of Jack Murdock's ghost is to haunt Matt in the form of "buried resentment" against his father for failing to offer him anything but a negative path to adult masculinity: Don't be like me. "Show me any guy that doesn't have resentments towards his father," Miller quips.[47] In hindsight, it seems that the seed of Miller's transformation of *Daredevil* from a chronicle of an unequivocal hero to a third-person memoir of a man who misunderstands his own motivations awaited Miller from the moment Lee and Everett's Fixer died in that subway tunnel in issue #1.

Miller takes every opportunity to underscore the tension between Murdock's presumption of universal innocence and the fact that he does not, in fact, leave the law and its enforcement to professionals and elected leaders. The crux of Miller's Daredevil is this contradiction between Matt's passion for fairness and Daredevil's subconscious drive to compromise due process. Miller claimed that the question driving his characterization of Matt/Daredevil was not "why does he dress like a devil and fight crime?" but "why did he become a lawyer?" As a writing exercise, Miller tells Sanderson, he once wrote a story in which Matt tells Ben Urich why he became a crime fighter: "The reason he is Daredevil is because he is scared, that what happened to his father represented a horrible violation . . . of everything that was good and the idea that the bad guys could win terrified him . . . and so he stops it. It only sounds paradoxical that a man without fear would be motivated by fear. He's beating it back and defeating it."[48]

Behind that story of primal masculine hysteria lies a more personal event, a specific patriarchal injustice that set Matt on the path to the law. As a kid, Matt tells Urich in this unpublished story, he got into a fight with bullies and came home bragging to his father about how well he had made out. Jack saw Matt's black eye and slapped him savagely for disobeying his father's command to stay out of fights and make something of himself. Surprised and angered, young Matt stays out all night, sitting atop the Brooklyn Bridge and plotting to become a lawyer because "people needed rules, laws" to protect themselves and others from harm.[49] On this account, it was not Matt's emotional reaction to his father's murder that ushered Matt down his future path. His choice to enforce the law, both officially and unofficially, was his response to a father who first dished out brutality and then fell victim to it. Fittingly, Miller waited to go to press with this tale of Matt's childhood until his final issue, #191, in which Daredevil, realizing he has caught himself in a lie, admits to his most fearsome enemy that he became Daredevil not to fulfill the legacy of his father but to correct him—to discipline him and others who threaten harm to Matt, as young Murdock fantasized of doing that night on the bridge. The secret is finally out. He is his father's son, after all.

INTO THE SNAKE PIT

Unlike scriptwriters at the dawn of Stan Lee's Marvel method, Miller plotted *Daredevil* many issues ahead, laying out the consequences of Matt Murdock's private and public activities in a single, epic arc to which the usual villain-to-villain progression of superhero comics takes a backseat. And whereas in the sixties Lee's Peter Parker hashes out every single crisis in his mind the moment it occurs, some of Matt's choices and reactions along the way stem from obscure motivations that never make it into dialogue or even thought balloons. Miller creates psychological suspense much as Raymond Chandler or Dashiell Hammett do in their detective stories. Even their first-person narration (Chandler's Philip Marlowe stories, Hammett's Continental Op and Nick Charles in *The Thin Man*) withholds information or motivation until it is utterly essential to the reader's comprehension of events, and sometimes not even then. Their third-person narration makes such things even more obscure. We never know what Sam Spade is really thinking in Hammett's *The Maltese Falcon*, even when he cites his professional code to justify throwing his lover to the police in the end. "You have to read an entire Marlowe novel," Miller told Gary Groth in 1998, "before you realize Marlowe's a compulsive do-gooder. He deliberately clouds it with cynicism."[1] It's no secret that Daredevil is a do-gooder, of course. What Miller conceals instead, in his own largely third-person narration, is the motivations and obsessions that Daredevil himself doesn't recognize.

The final scene of *Daredevil* #183, which on the surface is part 1 of a story about how the illegal drug trade affects the lives of young children, epitomizes Matt's lack of self-knowledge. Just a couple of issues earlier, in #181, Matt's college sweetheart, Elektra, now returned as a master assassin with a heart of ice, dies at Bullseye's hand. Unable to accept her death, all hope of redeeming her gone, Matt digs up her body in #182 and must touch her face one last time to convince himself that she is gone for good. Yet here he is in #183, standing in the snow in Central Park in a final-page splash panel, proposing marriage to Heather Glenn. The dialogue is straightforward, the plot utility of the scene unmistakable, and yet it can only bewilder a regular reader of the series. Daredevil just lost the love of his life, a woman who also happened to run afoul of his entire worldview. What could this proposal be but a neurotic attempt to escape the reality of that double loss, a rebound proposal in the worst sense? Matt rarely discusses his upcoming nuptials in subsequent issues; even his thought balloons reveal next to nothing about his abrupt decision. Meanwhile, Heather's family business falls prey to corrupt leadership, and Matt alternates between calling her pet names and belittling her managerial incompetence, sadistically forcing her to acknowledge her dependence on him legally until, finally, she turns to alcohol for solace. By obscuring Matt's intentions so painstakingly, Miller changes what could have been reader anticipation into dread, particularly for poor Heather's sake. This is not the Matt Murdock that Daredevil fans know and admire. This is a figure so traumatized by his failure to stop Elektra's downward spiral that he transforms independent Heather into a vulnerable, flighty woman whom he *can* save, regardless of the cost to her self-respect.

Closing off the hero's mind like this puts a new spin on the tried-and-true Silver Age practice of cultivating identification with the hero. As I discussed in chapter 1, the Marvel method helped raise the ceiling of superheroic character development while placing definite limits on the extent of that development. Lee and his collaborators painted their characters in broad strokes, making them a series of varied screens on which readers could choose to project their own fantasies of heroism. Two characters born of the Marvel method, Thor and the Thing, exemplify this trend especially well. Like down-market Homeric heroes, each possesses a couple of basic traits, such as the Thing's impatience and poor grammar or Thor's narcissism and King James Bible syntax, in addition to their specific powers (the Thing is effectively a human bulldozer, while Thor controls the weather, uses a big stone mallet as a weapon, and hits really hard). While those traits determine their basic reactions to crises, the crises themselves are not tailor-made to put those traits to the test, only to showcase them.

Miller, by contrast, wrote *Daredevil* something like the way a method actor generates stage business: draw a perimeter of goals, desires, weaknesses, history, and subconscious tics around the central character, place said character in one situation after another that challenges the integrity of that perimeter, and plot accordingly. Miller tried something that no Daredevil creator had ever attempted: he mapped out a phantom set of basic character traits that underlay the character's beliefs about himself, traits that *the character did not recognize.* Just as Matt repeatedly tells himself he must bring Elektra to justice but skips numerous opportunities to do it, he cannot acknowledge his sadistic treatment of Heather after Elektra's death because he cannot accept that he would ever act sadistically, especially not where a loved one *and* justice are at stake. The most striking aspect of this delineation is that, unlike Lee's soliloquy-heavy scripting, it depends largely on the absence of layered subjective information. It strikes the same sweet spot that made the most stylish hard-boiled detective fiction of the twenties and thirties look and feel like literary modernism, deeply concerned with the reality of the individual psyche and yet equally concerned to render it enigmatic, inexpressible even by the author pulling the strings.

WITH VERY LITTLE HELP FROM MY FRIENDS

One of Miller's first tasks was to streamline the most inconsistent aspects of *Daredevil.* Central to this revision was Miller's approach to Daredevil's fighting style and his weaponry. Having given up reading superhero comics as a teenager, he returned to the genre with a stealth mission to turn the little-read *Daredevil* into something more like the work that had constituted his amateur portfolio: a crime comic. In *Spectacular Spider-Man* #27 he drew DD's baton at least once in its conventional form, a collapsible cane with a curved end that straightens out into a baton. Having done some research into the physics of it, however, Miller decided that swinging from building to building on a nylon rope shot from a spring-loaded baton was so improbable that it might impede the change in tone he had in mind; after two or three swings over city streets, he learned, anyone attempting that mode of transport would start scraping their boots on the asphalt.[2] But Miller didn't eliminate the baton, which was by now an icon of the series and would likely have been missed by die-hard readers. He kept the icon but scooped out its old narrative functions, refitting it with tasks that better served his needs. Miller's version of the baton is not a trapeze bar but a throwing weapon. To make up for the lost mode of transport, Daredevil now relied on the city itself to transport him. He climbed buildings by grabbing window ledges and jumped from roof to roof or windowsill or awning, occasionally repurposing a flagpole as a springboard.

The *Daredevil* editor and martial arts enthusiast Denny O'Neil once noted that Miller shared his enthusiasm for Asian fighting forms, saying, "I think it's all over his work." Miller grasped the physics of hand-to-hand combat better than many cartoonists did: "What Daredevil does looks to me like it's a heightening of what martial artists do, and what I see guys in the prize ring do. So he [Miller] does it better."[3] Martial arts was a plausible choice, considering that Daredevil lacked the augmented physical strength of most of his superhero peers and could thus profit from a combat style that requires leverage, logistics, and knowledge of the body's vulnerabilities rather than sheer force.

Rather than Miller building on the continuity that preceded him, he also manipulated the secondary characters in *Daredevil* to fit his vision for the main character. In the 1960s, Foggy Nelson and Karen Page, Nelson and Murdock's legal secretary, were nearly the only recurrent secondaries. Lee kicked the series off by pushing Matt, Karen, and Foggy into a typical 1960s Marvel love triangle (see, for example, the Iron Man triangle of Tony Stark, Pepper Potts, and Happy Hogan and the triangle he attempted to set up among the teenage heroes Cyclops and Marvel Girl and their mentor, Professor X [!], in *X-Men* #1 but thereafter dropped). In *Amazing Spider-Man*, navigating the geometry of high school romance gave Peter Parker some depth he could not have accumulated had he holed up with Aunt May in Forest Hills between supervillain attacks. In *Daredevil*, however, Lee established the triangle so early—before we knew anything of substance about Foggy or Karen—that it comes off as the prefabricated dynamic it was. Gerry Conway finally wrote the disillusioned Karen Page out of the series with issue #86, sending her off to pursue an acting career and clearing the way for the Black Widow to replace her as Matt's love interest. As his relationship with the Widow waxed and waned, Heather Glenn, self-avowed party girl and heir to her father's company, Glenn Enterprises, darted in and out of Matt's life. Miller made Heather into Matt's primary civilian lover and a veritable anti-Karen: flighty, materialistic, and apparently casual about her relationship with Matt. She was Daredevil's Dark Lady, a brunette with a pageboy haircut, a casual and flirty manner, and a voracious sexual appetite, to Karen's chaste blond princess whose thought balloons were stuffed with doubts, fears, and frustrations about Matt. Miller's Heather combines genre conventions taken from hard-boiled fiction—think of the gambling Sternwood sister from Chandler's *The Big Sleep*, hiding ulterior motives beneath a decadent persona—with seventies-era male anxiety about women's sexual liberation, an issue already on the table since the arrival of the Black Widow on Daredevil's scene.

Heather's renewed importance to the series caused controversy among fans, but Miller seems to have anticipated their ire, even planned it as part of his effort to shake up the series's status quo. Whereas Stan Lee held that most "major" changes in the Marvel universe, from couples breaking up to the "deaths" of central characters, should only ever be temporary, and fans treated continuity (the consistency of a character's history across creative teams) as the scripture that decreed that stability, Miller viewed this focus on continuity as the root of stagnation, the reason why, in his estimation, Spider-Man and Superman had entered a very real "process of decay" by the early 1980s. "Whatever else has happened in the series [before now] is available to me," Miller told Dwight Decker in 1981, "but I'm not going to be explaining what happened to Mike Murdock, or explaining why Daredevil doesn't have a flare gun in his billyclub anymore. . . . There's so much junk back there. I just can't pay attention to it."[4] The downside of ignoring continuity "junk" was that it flew in the face of readers' desire for comforting familiarity, but young as Miller was, aged twenty-three when he began writing *Daredevil*, he was never eager to please just for the sake of pleasing. He felt a responsibility to do the opposite of what the fans begged of him, to throw them curveballs from every angle, to shock them into reading the next issue to find out what this crazy writer would do with their beloved hero next: "In many ways, making your audience overly comfortable is failing to do your job. What I'm hired to do is to give them something that they don't expect, maybe even something they don't want, but mostly to make them buy the next one. If I gave them what they expected, they probably wouldn't buy it. . . . It's more my job to know what makes a workable comic book than it is theirs, and so I shouldn't be taking pointers from them on how to do it."[5]

Miller took the fans' disdain for Heather as a particular challenge. "I could write her out of the book if I want, it's my option, but I've made up my mind not to," he said in 1981. "I've really come to like the version of her I use. It's just been rather tough describing that version to a really antagonistic audience." Some such antagonists would write letters containing a "nice little review" of a particular issue, he said, "and then [write] 'Get rid of Heather' at the bottom. 'Please shoot Heather.' Stuff like that."[6] In this interview, Carol Kalish presses the question of whether Miller was consciously provoking *Daredevil* readers by making Heather an idiot:

> KALISH: She seems to have been such a bubblehead for so long. Is she a bubblehead?
> MILLER: No. . . . There are certain alarms you can set off: the flighty woman who changes her mind at the drop of a hat is such a stereotype, and such a horrible one, that it makes people very angry. However, legitimate characters may be that way.[7]

In Miller's mind, Heather was neither idiot nor stereotype, and I think he is correct, though using generic or stereotypical tropes of femininity in a superhero comic during the 1980s would (it seems to me) guarantee that whatever subtleties one layered with those tropes would be misunderstood. However one feels about the women of Miller's 1990s noir pastiche *Sin City*, where femmes fatales and "good girls" alike are all killers with the impossible bodies of porno goddesses, the Miller of *Daredevil* was ahead of his audience, and the majority of his contemporaries, regarding the gender politics of a superhero's "girlfriends." Comparing Miller's version of Heather with Matt's love interests over the whole series up to that time, it seems an unassailable point that Heather is a more complicated construct than Lois Lane, Mary Jane Watson, or even Chris "I Write Strong Ladies" Claremont's Jean Grey in *X-Men*. She *is* abrasive, impatient, unlike Gwen Stacy, whose main difficulties with Peter Parker involved his disappearing during dates to fight crime or "loving danger" too much. Gwen scarcely has the volition to think about anything *but* Peter, but rather than obsessing over Matt, Heather finds being ditched or ignored a good reason to stay away from him. For all Heather's flaws, at least she has the feel of a rounded character rather than a male hero's mirror or a wish-fulfillment fantasy for adolescent boys.

None of these last points changes the fact that Heather's function in the series resembles what Laura Mulvey describes as the curse of the classical Hollywood female character: she is there to make men do things, for the desires of men, not women, drive classical plots.[8] But Miller is largely gender neutral regarding this function. For him, *all* Daredevil's secondary characters, whatever their gender or race, exist primarily to hone our sense of who Matt really is. He brings them closer to the foreground than some of his forebears had, but at the same time, he paints them in much broader strokes in order to make them operate less as stereotypes or the furniture of verisimilitude than as functions of Matt Murdock's character. They externalize his basic traits in some cases and provide counterpoint to them in others.

In 1964, the boyish, plump Foggy was the rich benefactor of the Nelson and Murdock firm, a chubby legal lightweight who vied with Matt for Karen's affections and envied his partner's good looks. After years of Foggy's development into a more serious figure, and many serious feuds with Matt that dissolved after a time, Miller returned to what was comic about Foggy. This new-old Foggy is the definition of the awkward outsider, always the only person in the room who either doesn't get the joke or misunderstands it altogether. At the same time, Miller made Foggy a smarter lawyer and a better friend to Matt. If Matt is the eloquent courtroom performer, Miller's Foggy is his necessary complement, the partner who chained himself to the books in law school and knows all the precedents he and his partner will ever need. This trait stems from Miller asking the question "What is Foggy doing here?" as one not of expediency but of character. Looking back over the series, he wondered why, if Foggy is such a schlemiel, the dashing and brilliant attorney Matt Murdock would have stuck with him for the duration and then decided that "Foggy is a human encyclopedia of law. . . . [Matt] can make all the abstract points in the world [in court], and he's very intelligent, but it's Foggy who remembers 'the such and such decision.'"[9]

Miller clearly has fun with the character of Foggy, too. He consistently portrays Foggy as less Matt's rival for Karen's affections or the workhorse who envies the glory his partner earns at trial than a sort of urban hayseed: fearful, full of bluff, accident prone, a rube who never barks an epithet stronger than "Golly." Miller's mainstay joke is that Foggy perpetually overestimates his command over his environment. The story "Guts," in #185, brings this characterization to its zenith. As Foggy investigates corruption at Glenn Enterprises, the caption boxes offer his own hilariously garbled hard-boiled narration as he botches one encounter after another with organized crime yet always manages to come out on top, like Philip Marlowe as portrayed by Mr. Magoo. Behind the scenes, however, Daredevil is assisting Foggy, silently taking out his friend's assailants and finally supporting Foggy's picaresque quest by announcing to the Kingpin, New York's preeminent crime lord, "Don't mess with Guts Nelson." As if the humor weren't enough, "Guts" is also a small wonder of plot economy. It simultaneously turns otherwise banal expository information about Heather's crisis into a central plot, squeezes an issue's worth of comic relief out of a series otherwise defined by its grimness, and demonstrates once again Daredevil's role as a champion of the powerless.

The virtue of limiting Heather's and Foggy's functions this way is that they become purer mirrors, reflecting the highlights of the Murdock character and offering hard looks into his flaws. Foggy is like Matt without the fire in his belly, a smart lawyer who lacks the passion for justice that makes Matt effective as both lawyer and costumed hero. But Foggy's unquestioning loyalty to Matt brings into relief how little Matt gives back to their firm or their friendship, caught up as he is in the melodrama of his secret life. Heather is a film noir femme fatale without the motivation; she's as promiscuous as Kathie Moffatt in Jacques Tourneur's film noir *Out of the Past* (1947), though unlike Kathie, she's already rich, spends her money indifferently, and genuinely loves the hero. But whatever her impulsive nature reveals about Matt's Oedipal development, a standard function of the noir femme fatale, she also highlights his reckless disregard for the feelings of the people closest to him. In #176, Daredevil has lost his radar sense and is brooding on the ledge outside Heather's penthouse when Heather sees him, begs him to come in and dress for "the Pavarotti concert," and then watches as he impulsively throws himself off the ledge as if his radar were still functioning and bounces clumsily off a street-light, nearly missing his next perch. When Heather then thinks, "He—almost fell! He almost died . . . ," her usual impulsiveness recedes to make way for her concern for Matt; for once, she sounds like the reasonable one. True, Matt's impulse to get his old martial arts master to help him regain his radar makes everything (sort of) all right in the end, but rarely has an act of determination on Daredevil's part looked so undisciplined, so suicidal, so *fearful*. In everyday life, between the woman who flirts nonstop and the man who dresses like a Halloween devil and gets stabbed, nearly drowned, shot, and dropped thirty-odd stories from a mob boss's window, the flirtatious woman with ambivalent feelings about her superhero boyfriend would win the averageness sweepstakes every time.

It might surprise those who are familiar with Miller's *Daredevil* that I place the two-bit thug Turk, a Miller creation who rarely appears for more than a page or two in any given story, in the upper tier of secondary characters as well. Turk, a dopey African American crook who wanders in and out of the Kingpin's employ, exists to be Daredevil's punching bag. He and his partner, Grotto, hatch scheme after scheme of petty thievery and revenge to the accompaniment of Turk's boasts about his brilliance, only to be hyperbolically undone by Daredevil. Miller insisted that Turk was one of the series's most "popular" characters. However, US mass culture has reduced black men to mindless scapegoats for white people's amusement for nearly two centuries, and Turk doesn't exactly ditch the trend, as he overflows with the blackface minstrel's fatuous self-aggrandizement one page and takes a "comic" pratfall off a helicopter ladder the next. In Dwight Decker's interview, Miller sheepishly discusses a scene in #170 in which Daredevil spontaneously smashes through a car windshield to kick Turk in the chest, acknowledging it as a moment when he "went too far" with the violence, to the point where Miller might be accused of racism.[10] But without letting Miller off the hook for these infractions, I submit that in Turk's functions with regard to Matt's character, he more closely resembles Heather and Foggy than Amos and Andy. He's a one-note wonder, an ersatz Laurel to Foggy's Hardy, but like Heather "the gorgeous girlfriend" and Foggy "the overweight partner," Turk's primary function is to sharpen the definition of Daredevil as "the dumb thug." His braggadocio is so over the top, and his lack of brains and courage so pronounced, that he becomes a doppelgänger to Daredevil right down to having a plus-size sidekick. If he is himself ridiculous, he manages by association to make Daredevil's pained-looking grimness, his Lee Marvin act if you will, look a bit ridiculous, too.

If these characters are really as limited as I make them out to be, the reason may lie in Miller's philosophy of art, in which rules, whether self-imposed or enforced from without, make artists work harder to invent new complications and dynamics without breaking them, whether they're the conventions of a genre or the Comics Code's ban on explicit sex, drug use, and graphic violence. Though in the mideighties he characterized the much-discussed comic-book ratings system as an infringement on cartoonists' First Amendment rights, on other fronts, he still counseled that creators "need walls to push against": "I've seen very little good work that's been created without supervision of some sort . . . [or] without fairly strict rules. Even when I've gotten a great degree of freedom, I've set myself rigid rules to follow."[11] To hear Miller tell it, the most generative of all such limits is genre, and his master genre for this claim is comics:

> Comics are a literary form, and the pictures have to serve almost as words in a sentence. . . . Comics have to tell the reader that a thing is happening or that a particular character is a particular character. In Daredevil's case, it's the horns and the chest emblem that make him immediately identifiable. But it goes deeper than that. It affects the basic style of the drawing. That's why so many [cartoonists] are total mannerists. They use familiar, comfortable images. If you were to render each picture photographically, you would probably lose the reader's interest or bore them. . . . We're only a few steps away from funny-animal drawing. This is in no way disparaging what we do.[12]

These comments, made more than a decade before the publication of Scott McCloud's *Understanding Comics*, predict McCloud's expansion of Marshall McLuhan's argument that comics are a "cool" medium—one that reduces everything from cars and buildings to facial expressions to a few expressive lines and thus demands of the reader a greater sense of involvement in order to fill in what that minimalism leaves out.[13] I prefer Miller's rhetoric to McCloud's, if for no other reason than it sets aside the historiographical problems that McLuhan's categories cause for media theory in favor of a more modest and medium-specific claim about readerly engagement with comics.

Miller appreciated "the architecture of genre" for the instructions it contained on how to strip a story down to its most basic elements. In genres, he told Groth, "there are certain presuppositions when you come in. And you can use them, betray them or turn them upside down. But it can be a working structure that's very useful."[14] For the Russian Formalist literary critics of the 1920s and the structuralist anthropologists and semioticians of the 1970s, genres like the folk tale or the Western are defined by their internal oppositions, in which a moral universe is constructed entirely out of the functions that characters and other conventional icons perform in relation to each other: the outlaw owes his significance to his opposition with the cowboy, the frontier derives meaning from the challenges it poses to civilization, and so forth. Against that backdrop, where secondary characters are more setting than psychology, the hero and the villain get to be a bit more complex than the rest, performing basic functions within the matrix of oppositions but also generating meanings that remain partly obscure. Characters must have goals to be genre *characters* rather than genre icons or mere genre furniture. No hero or villain in a Hammett story or an 87th Precinct novel by Ed McBain ever lives just to get by. Heroes and villains go after things, passionately. Yet their decisions and actions must remain within the boundaries delineated by the typed characters that surround them and the generic plots that generate them.

The parallel to classic hard-boiled fiction is instructive here because Miller understood his *Daredevil* as a crime comic. Later on, after beginning the *Sin City* stories, he characterized crime fiction as giving him "a chance to do stories with people, with motivations that were outside the norm of comic books. That is, people who would do things because of sex, for instance, or perversion, rather than it just being some mad scientist who wants to conquer the world, and doing the lonely, disenfranchised hard-boiled hero. . . . Superheroes stopped being interesting about the time they were deputized."[15] Matt Murdock may not have been disenfranchised or antisocial, but Miller hard-boiled the character anyway by using his blindness and heightened senses as structural factors, generic traits endemic to superhero comics, that isolated him. Miller also gave Matt a truly dangerous femme fatale in the form of Elektra, whom Daredevil is forever announcing must be brought before the law but is prevented by his obsession with their sexual past from doing anything about it. Like Philip Marlowe, Daredevil occasionally lets a bad one slide by out of optimism, nostalgia, or simple weariness with being the one and only person standing between the mean streets of Hell's Kitchen and an Armageddon of crime.

The remaining characters are as hard-boiled as they come, and like all good secondary genre personnel, they follow Foggy's and Heather's example by surrounding Matt/Daredevil with a network of social roles that allow Miller to define DD's role more clearly—an enforcer but not a cop, a fighter but not a killer, a man of compassion who plays the Mike Hammer part nearly to the hilt when he has to. Spider-Man was labeled a menace by the *Daily Bugle* newspaper, the Avengers were practically agents of the US government, and so forth, but Miller isn't all that interested in the roles attributed to Daredevil by other characters or the roles he consciously plays. He digs for the tacit, structural functions of the character the way a genre theorist looks for the structural functions of the cowboy in the dynamics of his relationships with Native Americans, lawmen, and female schoolteachers. In *Daredevil* #167, McKenzie and Miller introduce a police detective, Lieutenant Nick Manolis, who helps Miller develop DD's relationship with the New York Police Department as less antagonistic than Spider-Man's but still vexed in its own way. Daredevil turns out to be the more passionate defender of due process than Manolis, an honest but bitter cop straight out of Chandler's *The Big Sleep*. Manolis offers a preview of Murdock in old age, hard-nosed about justice but at once cynical and practical regarding how to dispense it.

Then there's Ben Urich, the jaded newspaperman introduced by McKenzie and Gene Colan in issue #153, just before Miller arrived. A chain-smoking investigative reporter who would fit right into the court pressroom of Howard Hawks's *His Girl Friday*, Miller's Urich functions as Daredevil's unofficial partner, giving the hero police-blotter data and researching the pasts of repeat offenders. He also acts as yet another mirror for Matt, this one reflecting Daredevil's detective skills while emphasizing the hero's courage and physical prowess in contrast to his own scrawniness and his impulse to run faster from dangerous situations than his smoker's cough allows. He digs courageously into the criminal underworld but stops short of risking his life. In #180, having nearly been murdered by Elektra in the previous issue for writing an exposé of the Kingpin's hand-picked mayoral candidate, he "spikes" the story: "It's not my fight. Not after what I've been through." There but for the grace of atomic fission goes Matt Murdock, whose heightened senses and fierce workout regimen give him the currency to defend justice so effectively.

Though Ben became a fan favorite rather quickly, and Miller did invest some well-articulated pathos into his marriage in #179, I don't experience him as a complex character because Miller doesn't seem to either. Ben's playful, artless, thoroughly believable flirting with Doris Urich in that issue makes it all the sadder when he has to leave to follow yet another hot tip and all the more horrifying when Elektra nearly assassinates him in #179's conclusion. But this is an isolated moment in Miller's run in which he exploits Ben specifically to expose Elektra's true, sinister colors and make Murdock's desire for her all the harder to take. For the remainder of Miller's *Daredevil*, he has one function, and he performs it well: to give Daredevil a confidant who will keep his secrets. Having Ben around allows him to discuss theories about where the Kingpin will strike next and air his feelings about his superhero role without forcing Miller to crowd the page with thought balloons. I'm not suggesting that Ben is a minor character or that his functions for Miller don't deserve more consideration, but following the criteria I have established in this chapter, he is, like the other secondary characters, no more or less than a thoroughly necessary plot device.

The *Daredevil* fan reading this chapter is likely getting impatient for something more than a gesture in the direction of Miller's key secondary characters, Elektra, the Kingpin, and Bullseye. But I'm simply getting the more "minor" characters out in the open now in order to clear a path for this triumvirate of villains. In order to better suss out their functions in the next chapter, however, I need to acknowledge something now about Miller's characterization strategy: Daredevil's villains resemble his friends in their flatness, but the villains' interactions with Daredevil generate more pyschosocial complexity. They function this way so consistently that I consider them costars rather than the ground to Murdock's figure. According to my schema, former secondary characters like Becky Blake, a legal secretary who uses a wheelchair and admires Matt from afar, must be demoted to tertiary characters, figures that lend the minimum verisimilitude needed to render convincing such key settings as the Nelson and Murdock law firm. Though the McKenzie issues spend a good deal of time airing Matt's worries that his secret identity endangers his supporting cast, again largely recycling Peter Parker's guilty anxiety attacks, this tendency fades once Miller takes over. Instead he makes the Daredevil identity into a welcome release from the restrictions of "blindness" and legal limits; Matt rarely worries over being Daredevil until his superheroic persona becomes a needle with which he can be pricked. Urich investigates Daredevil's secret identity and nearly goes public with it until he decides on the last page of #164 that Daredevil means too much to the upstanding citizens of Hell's Kitchen to reveal his secret and render him more vulnerable. And the Spider-Man theme of the hero endangering loved ones only comes into play when Miller's supervillain psychodrama demands it, as when Kingpin orders Elektra to kill Foggy Nelson in #180; the indirect result of Kingpin ordering that hit is Elektra's murder by the rival assassin Bullseye in #181, the defining moment of the entire run.

ALTER EGOS AND ALLEGORIES

Miller made another shrewd decision that humanizes Daredevil while placing himself at an ironic distance from the character: in spite of Miller's own atheism, he gave Daredevil religion. Though Daredevil's Christianity doesn't come to the foreground of the series until the "Born Again" arc that Miller coproduced with the artist David Mazzucchelli in 1986, Miller mentions it in interviews as early as 1981. As a devout Catholic, Miller's Murdock believes in the metaphysical thermodynamics of sin: the sinner is held to account by a higher power and must atone for each sin committed in turn by embracing Christ, admitting fault, and paying penance.[16] The result is divine absolution, the possibility of forgiveness after one atones, but for a staunch (stock) Catholic, once is never enough. Each new sin renews the need for confession, penance, and absolution by a merciful God who nevertheless keeps a strict set of books when it comes to human culpability. Daredevil plays the role of intercessor— the priest behind the screen in the Hollywood confession booth—for the criminals he captures, but with the impatience of a good police detective. Rather than waiting for guilt to propel the supplicant, Daredevil walks crooks to the stand to make their confessions. His priestly responsibilities, however, end there. He continually stops short of the line he has drawn between a suspect's capture and the enforcement of justice and rarely struggles with whether to cross it. Even as an attorney, Miller's Murdock sticks to the evidence that will exonerate or acquit defendants in court, no matter how loudly his gut might be telling him to fudge the details in the name of some higher justice that he feels is not his place to enforce. He is not God, only his servant.

Every once in a while, however, Miller turns a spotlight on that line

FIGURE 11. Frank Miller and Klaus Janson, "Devils," *Daredevil* #169 (Marvel, March 1981).

between legal defender and illegal enforcer. DD has a long exchange with Lt. Manolis in #169 at the hospital after Daredevil, having rendered Bullseye unconscious, plucks his enemy from the subway tracks to save him from an oncoming train. Earlier in the issue, suffering from a brain tumor that is only diagnosed upon his capture, Bullseye has committed multiple murders on the basis of a hallucination that *everyone* in Manhattan is Daredevil, costume and all. To concretize for readers just how mad he has become, Miller gives us the inside track on Bullseye's pathology by drawing everyone who walks past Bullseye in Times Square—slim, stout, tall, short, male, female, black, white—in a Daredevil suit (figure 11). Manolis fumes that Daredevil should've let the subway train pulverize him. After all, Bullseye is a lunatic whose mere presence on the streets guarantees the shedding of innocent blood. To make matters worse, Manolis points out, if Bullseye's lawyers give evidence in court that the tumor caused his rampage, "since we don't imprison loonies once they're cured, Bullseye will go free!" As they stand in an observation booth, watching doctors remove Bullseye's tumor in the surgical theater below, DD delivers Miller's first soliloquy on the costumed vigilante's role in the justice system:

> Nick, men like Bullseye would rule the world—were it not for a structure of laws that society has created to keep such men in check. The moment one man takes another man's life in his own hands, he is rejecting the law—and working to destroy that structure. If Bullseye is a menace to society, it is society that must make him pay the price. Not you. And not me. I—I wanted him to die, Nick. I detest what he does . . . what he is. But I'm not God—I'm not the law—and I'm not a murderer.

Daredevil delivers this speech over five panels, four of which are fairly typical head shots of the speaker, each one ending with a point, just as if Miller were narrating one of Murdock's closing arguments in a courtroom (figure 12).

FIGURE 12. Frank Miller and Klaus Janson, "Devils," *Daredevil* #169 (Marvel, March 1981).

Daredevil's ethical position could not be clearer: life-or-death decisions can never be left to individuals, and any equivocation about that state of affairs wears away at the social contract that makes the law objective, applicable to all. Yet the panels in which he speaks these words don't simply provide us with the obligatory talking heads. They weigh in on what is being said and what it means that Daredevil is saying it. In a single row of panels, Miller's picture plane shifts from a left close-up to a frontal medium shot, a frontal medium close-up, and finally a right close-up. Though panel borders separate them from one another, Daredevils proliferate on this page no less noticeably than during Bullseye's hallucinations in the first pages of #169. The panels, lit from underneath as though Bullseye himself were glowing like a white-hot isotope in the surgical theater below, cast this speech as an emotional boxing match Matt wages not so much with Manolis as with himself. The multiple DDs personify at least three distinct dimensions of Matt's strained relationship to the justice system, arguing with each other over whether the killer lying on the table below them lives or dies. There's the Daredevil who hates his enemy, the one who wants to protect Bullseye's future victims, and the one who believes that the laws must abide to prevent anyone, thug or cop, serial killer or the judge presiding at a murder trial, from becoming a law unto themselves.

Miller, however, takes the last word away from his titular character and hands it to Manolis instead: "He's gonna go free. He's gonna kill again. And next time it'll be your fault." Leaving the discussion hanging on that doubt emphasizes the insolubility of this superheroic conundrum. Which "greater good" is greater, preventing Bullseye from threatening more lives or guaranteeing his right to a fair trial? And Bullseye does survive to kill more people—many more—during Miller's run. The story ends, on the same page as Daredevil's speech to Manolis, with Daredevil, now a tiny silhouette at the bottom of the frame, exiting the room while a simple announcement pipes in from the surgical theater: "Gentlemen, the operation is a success. The patient will live." By the very next issue, Bullseye is back in business with a contract to kill the Kingpin under his arm. Miller never lets Daredevil, or us, forget thereafter that Bullseye is back to his old tricks courtesy of the Man Without Fear himself.

The ambivalence about due process expressed here stems in part from Miller's decision to make Daredevil a character whose convictions don't necessarily match his own: "I don't necessarily believe that Daredevil's right about everything he says. The character is built on very strong basic principles, and it would have been a terrible violation of those principles . . . to let Bullseye die. Daredevil has to believe that the law will work in every instance, but I'm allowed to believe differently."[17] Miller had much tougher critiques of Daredevil-style liberalism waiting up his sleeve, including the bleeding-heart psychiatrists in *Batman: The Dark Knight Returns* who claim that Two-Face and the Joker (the *Joker*, for crying out loud) can be rehabilitated and an unforgettable throwaway joke about liberal hypocrisy in the same book, in which a Central Casting suburbanite tells a reporter that he doesn't believe in Batman's brand of vigilante justice but then snorts that he himself would "never live in the city." But to paint Miller as a legal or social conservative would not be accurate, at least not at this point in his career. Satirically, in fact, Miller plays the entire political field, broiling John Ashcroft and George W. Bush in *The Dark Knight Strikes Again* (2001–2) for exploiting the Twin Towers' destruction to further their own political agenda (and while these men were doing exactly that in the aftermath of 9/11, no less). The *Daredevil* run, though, is less a satire of Matt's position, or anyone else's, than it is a Brechtian experiment in which Miller draws sympathy to Murdock's point of view while examining it with a microscope at the same time, pushing harder and harder on the question of whether justice is served if lives are left at risk, while putting just as much pressure on the opposing question of whether preventive justice deserves to be called justice at all.

Miller finally made public the circumstances of Matt's decision to become a lawyer—the "writing exercise" scene that begins with Matt being hit by his father and ends with him atop the Brooklyn Bridge, vowing to ensure that people keep following the rules—in issue #191, the final story of his *Daredevil* run. Looking back on the couple of years leading up to this climax, Miller used that turning point in Matt's young life as a divining rod for character exploration, as if this childhood event arrested Matt's emotional development, freezing it at the point where he might otherwise have begun to form "adult" psychological countermeasures to the problem of actual violence. Instead of recognizing his hatred of his father at that moment, he projects the scenario onto the world at large, setting himself up as the bigger, better

Father who will punish other, flawed patriarchs for committing injustices in private (or, rather, he sets himself up to symbolically punish his own father over and over again for hitting him that night). All the while he pretends that he hasn't internalized the violence himself but rather that he is somehow purging himself of it. The irony of committing new acts of violence against those who commit the injustices rarely, if ever, comes up—at least for Daredevil himself. For Miller and his readers, it's a different story.

BLINDNESS AND INSIGHT: ALL STICK, NO CARROT

The paradox of Murdock's use of violence to quell violence resonates throughout the world of *Daredevil*. Indeed, Miller uses Murdock's blindness and professional position to comment on how civil rights and the criminal code frequently crash into each other in a democracy. In Miller's calculus, crime is the ultimate test of individual liberty, where one's right to thrive without interference from others is violated by perpetrators who themselves exercise "personal freedoms" gone berserk. As the judicial arm of a representative democracy, the justice system in which Murdock participates (sometimes legally, other times less so) is intended to protect the innocent and punish the guilty, but in practice, upholding the authority of that system can mean letting violators of others' rights go free when evidence of a violation is lacking or insubstantial. The degree to which one receives justice, and how quickly it is administered, is unjustly linked to privileges organized by class, race, and gender and to how suspects and defendants alike present themselves, and are presented, to the court.

Miller tosses Daredevil with some regularity into such moral quandaries as the choice whether to save Bullseye's life, but never does Daredevil's fidelity to the law seem to backfire more explosively than it does in that case. Miller appears to be undercutting DD's position by putting Bullseye back in the assassination business the minute he recovers from surgery. If that is so, I have to wonder whether Miller thinks of vigilantism as a necessary correction to the criminal code, one that eschews the abstract generalization of rights when the situation demands it. In at least one crucial instance, Daredevil metes out punishment himself, as he does by dropping Bullseye from a telephone wire in #181, the second time he holds his enemy's life in his hands. Sometimes even those who deserve punishment the most don't go to jail because Daredevil makes an executive decision that the greater good can be served without the need for a single arrest. Rather than finding evidence that Randolph Cherryh, a candidate in the New York mayor's race, is in the Kingpin's pocket and delivering Cherryh straight to the cops (to be fair, he tries that first, in #178), in issue #180, Daredevil trades his knowledge of the whereabouts of the Kingpin's missing wife for the Kingpin's word that Cherryh will quit the campaign—which he does, on the very next page. In #190, DD makes another deal with Kingpin—at least the third deal he cuts with the crime lord during the Miller years—in which he roughs up some insubordinate Kingpin employees in exchange for the location of a group of evil ninjas known as the Hand.

The ethical experiments that Miller runs in such stories are part of a game he has played with readers throughout his career, the game of sponsoring a position without necessarily adhering to that position himself. Miller, himself either agnostic or atheist, refers often to Murdock as Catholic, or at the very least Christian (he sends Matt Murdock to confession at least once, but later, in the stand-alone graphic novel *Elektra Lives Again* in 1990). His reasoning is that Murdock's "concern is with the *victim* of crime, not with the criminal." To illustrate, he transforms a Silver Age supervillain called Gladiator from a remorseless killer to a legitimate hard-luck case: "The Gladiator's crimes—a series of really vicious, horrible acts—demonstrate [Murdock's Christianity]. . . . If the Gladiator truly wants to reform, then Matt will do everything in his power to help him."[18] In this scenario, the Gladiator/ Melvin Potter is a penitent convert to the straight and narrow, and Matt is the good Christian who forgives his sins to the point of defending him in court, where he successfully (and truthfully) enters a plea of not guilty by reason of mental illness. Matt's determination to forgive rather than prosecute whenever possible places Daredevil in a unique situation among comic-book vigilantes. Though spurred into heroics by the murder of his father, he's driven consciously by neither revenge (Batman) nor guilt (Spider-Man) but rather by the desire to see justice done.[19]

In #182–183, Miller puts even this least objectionable of legal standards under the hot lights. After Murdock clears a young boy of a murder charge, the prime suspect—Hogman, an angel dust dealer—denies the crime as the court police take him away, and Murdock, listening to

Hogman's heartbeat with his heightened senses, doesn't hear it accelerate, which in *Daredevil* means that Hogman is telling the truth. So Murdock decides to defend him, even at the cost of becoming a target of the Punisher, a vigilante who lacks Daredevil's scruples about letting violent criminals survive to stand trial. It turns out, however, that Hogman has a pacemaker, and not even telling a lie could force his heart to race. DD's heightened hearing underscores his uniquely embodied and affective relationship to justice, as ever, but in this case, the fallibility of bodies, human and superhuman alike, nearly makes a mockery of due process. The big question here is not only whether Daredevil erred this time in trusting his senses over clear forensic evidence but whether he's done the same thing before without ever learning of his error.

Until 1978, Matt Murdock's blindness—in its occasional moments of relevance—functioned primarily as a stock superheroic vulnerability and a reminder of the cost of his enhanced senses. As Miller points out in a 1982 interview, *Daredevil* had in the past crossed the line between thematizing blindness and stereotyping it for sighted readers: "If you do a story where Matt Murdock is in love with his secretary, but because he is blind, he can't tell her, because she'd have to pity him, you're saying something horrible about blind people. You're saying that they can only be loved as objects of pity. So there are certain implicit statements in whatever you do."[20] One version of Miller's professional autobiography claims Daredevil's blindness as an attraction: Miller told an interviewer in 2010, "I had done a couple issues of *Spectacular Spider-Man* and I looked at Daredevil, [who] was blind. All of a sudden I realized that I could do all my crime stories through this character."[21] He doesn't explain exactly what this means, but I think it must be connected to the metaphor of blind justice. Easy as it may be to dismiss *Daredevil*'s materialization of the metaphor as a clever pun, Miller changes it from a potential joke to the book's central source of tension. Matt is as literally blind as Justice purports to be figuratively but seldom is, as Miller continually reminds us. The parallel is not subtle, but it's a compelling one from which Miller farmed some moral quandaries that previous *Daredevil* creators had overlooked for nearly two decades.

Miller never neglects an opportunity to remind newer readers about the accident that gave Daredevil supersenses in exchange for his sight—sometimes employing expository ham-fisted enough to make a TV soap writer wince—but unlike his predecessors, he doesn't stop there. He employs Matt's blindness as a story element and as a tool for characterization by centering two major plot twists on Daredevil's hypersenses. In the first twist, Miller takes his radar away. In issue #174, Matt Murdock is under attack by the Hand, a fictional Yakuza-like criminal organization made up entirely of grim, faceless ninjas who never speak in contractions (this being Miller's way of signaling that English isn't their first language). They attempt to assassinate Matt by detonating a bomb in his apartment. Though to all appearances he is unhurt, he discovers that while his heightened senses remain, his radar is simply gone. Unnerved but undeterred, he tries to rely on his remaining hypersenses to compensate—listening for heartbeats, smelling the air, reading print by touching ink on a page, and generally just hoping for the best—but no amount of sniffing or listening can help maintain his traditional mode of superhero transport: jumping at high altitudes. In #176, he nearly dies trying to leap from Heather's penthouse apartment to an adjacent building. The only sensory element he has left to navigate by is the sound of the rain. Reading that story in the early eighties, I understood for the first time that the series's subtitle "The Man without Fear," by now just a motto that nobody paid much attention to, could mean something substantial and specific if put to the test.

To save Daredevil from his own stubbornness, Miller introduces his second major character invention after Elektra in #168: Stick, the foul-mouthed, pool-hustling American sensei. Matt tells Heather in #175 that Stick was his "mentor"—"who taught me how to live with my blindness before my radar fully developed"—before Jack Murdock's murder and even before he met Elektra at Columbia. As was the case with Elektra, introducing Stick as a character from DD's heretofore undocumented past helped Miller to take command of the character and its history with a freedom unrivaled by anyone since Lee, Everett, and Wood during the first year of the series. And like Heather, Foggy, and Manolis, Stick functions to sharpen Daredevil's characterization, this time by demonstrating something we would never recognize unless his radar evaporated: Matt's psychological dependence on it. Did I mention that Stick, too, is blind? Under Miller's pen, he's a masterpiece of efficient caricature, a bagman in a Holden Caulfield hat complete with flaps, his pupilless eyes staring out from under the brim of it like the white eyeholes of a grizzled Little Orphan Annie. In other words, he is the scariest old man you've ever seen and the last person one would expect to be one of the most powerful martial artists in the world.

Stick, as a blind man and (another) father figure, externalizes Matt's superego, giving Miller the opportunity to home in on less charted waters of the superhero genre, namely, the singular fears of the disabled hero. Matt's choice to become a masked man means, in the Marvel universe, that he can't tell anyone about his special abilities, and he must use his blindness as a cover for his secret identity. Up till now, his powers have rendered it more or less unnecessary to find a sightless community to empathize with his condition. With his radar sense gone, however, we learn that Murdock relies on his radar not only physically but also mentally. More than his heightened remaining senses, the radar keeps him from *feeling* disabled. In issue #176, he purges years of repressed anxiety in one big gush: "I'm blind, Heather! More blind than I've ever been. . . . My hypersenses just aren't enough by themselves. Without my radar, I'm—I'm helpless."

Stick's response to Matt's plight comes right out of the Spartan leadership routine of Miller's *300*, only with the argot updated a couple of thousand years: "Shaddup." Stick squeezes the self-pity out of Matt the way any good mentor would, by depriving him of sleep, testing his archery skills, and humiliating him. Matt gets nothing but Stick, without a carrot in sight. The nucleus of Miller's theory of heroism is embedded in this ordeal. It depends on the individual's aptitude for self-denial, as if one could only truly center one's ego under the threat of its destruction. If this isn't quite masochism, it is certainly a tribute to the old Nietzschean saw that the true font of strength is survival; all the phallic implications of the *Übermensch* ideal are laid out in plain sight. While the superego surrogate Stick whacks Matt repeatedly with his big, well, stick, Matt augments Stick's abuse by dwelling on past events, confrontations with his father and kids in the neighborhood that enraged and confounded him as a child and that now materialize aspects of his self-doubt. Miller takes a wholly subjective approach to representing these memories. First Matt stands, Lilliputian sized, before an enormous hallucination of his father, who chains him to a pile of books; when Matt goes outside, still proportioned like an adult, he is confronted by kids the same size as he but with proper kid proportions—big heads and hands and feet—who persecute him for carrying the very books his father forbids him to put down. How these memories get embodied so specifically and concretely in Matt's hallucinations is Stick's secret, but it is not difficult to consider Stick an ersatz Marvel archivist, a diegetic Mark Gruenwald who digs up formative elements from *Daredevil* #1 and tilts them toward the grotesque.

Backing all this pain and cruelty, surely, is a point about maturation, about learning to reject others' assessments of oneself rather than internalize them and to do so without hatred or anger. In the end, Matt succeeds in regaining his radar sense by quieting the white noise of his unacknowledged rage and learning to trust his body and his senses above all. At the same time, Stick's retraining regimen defines Matt/Daredevil as a product of abuse and isolation, whose only salvation rests with his ability to distance himself even further from the judgments of others. Though Matt wins back his indispensible sixth sense in the end, his struggle to regain it gives Miller the chance to explore the isolated, egocentric mind-set that a superhero might require in our own world, an attitude that regards all social relations as impediments to his goals. Attributing that mind-set to Matt is less a stretch than it seems. Writers dating back to Lee had portrayed Matt as capable of manipulating and even throwing away his friends if it served the survival of his vigilante persona. Using Matt's agility during the Silver Age at toggling between his Matt and "Mike" Murdock identities (not to mention his Daredevil persona) as fuel, Timothy Callahan claims that Matt Murdock has always been portrayed as "mentally unstable, perhaps bordering even on psychotic in his willingness to layer the fabric of lies in his relationships with others."[22] By the end of *Daredevil* #177, Matt has defeated his demons, but considering that his hallucination paints social relationships in general as one of those demons, this is at best a mixed victory. His final mental trial requires him to kill a giant talking rat that sounds suspiciously like Stick, a demonic predator combining his father's authoritarianism with the street kids' taunts. The rat's death doubtless represents Matt's triumph over his rage and fear, but it also drives home the narcissism of his heroic ideal, his impulse to distance himself from everyone, friend, foe, or mentor, in order to keep his identity as Daredevil pure.

Miller mucks with Daredevil's senses a second time near the end of his run. In #184, Heather begins to suspect that her family's high-tech manufacturing company, Glenn Enterprises, has come under corrupt management since her father's suicide. She discovers evidence that the CEO is building made-to-order bombs for an unspecified purpose. Foggy does some digging for her in #185 and finds that Glenn Enterprises produces these explosives for the Kingpin, the most powerful crime don in New York. Daredevil heads to the shipping docks to locate the bombs, but as he tries to prevent a crate of them from sinking into the harbor, one of the bombs blows up in his face. Instead of dissipating his radar this time, the accident expands the entire spectrum of his powers, heightening his senses to anguishing proportions. All the sensory data that his mind must constantly separate and orchestrate in everyday life suddenly becomes a hopeless cacophony, each bit of information in its turn distracting him from all the other stimuli for which he has to account.

Miller may simply be recycling his own earlier plot twist here, but structurally the second accident complements the first. For one thing, it demonstrates the opposite extreme of the mental labor necessary to manage Matt's hypersenses, the discipline he must maintain in order to cross the street without being overwhelmed by the sounds of car horns, whistles, shouts, and racing engines that ordinary city dwellers are able to block out over time. To hear heartbeats, coughs, and other involuntary signals of an adversary's location or secret intentions, he must increase their signal-to-noise ratio in his head, isolating the relevant sounds by sheer concentration. This second sensory crisis recontextualizes the first as only one stop along Miller's route of illuminating everything that Matt, and we, take for granted about his superhero career. The first accident establishes his tendency to live in his head, to relate to the material and social worlds primarily as elements to receive, categorize, and defend against. The second causes him to experience these worlds as sources of agony and requires him to push them even further away; this time Stick's solution is to put Matt into a sealed isolation tank where he can turn inward even more dramatically than before and coach himself to adjust to the higher amplitude of his sensory environment, just as he was required to do following the originary accident, the encounter with the isotope that gave him these abilities in the first place.

This plot expediency, Matt's need to distance himself further than ever from external experience, functions as a neat metaphor for his utter self-determination as a subject. The situation that develops with Heather after her CEO's treachery is discovered implies that, along with Matt's mechanisms for managing sensory information, he might take his own moral code too much for granted, as well. It is no coincidence that his senses go berserk in #186, the same issue in which he begins to psychologically torture Heather into seeing herself as a victim of her own incompetence. This new chapter in his relationship with Heather is more than just a troubling secondary plot, an expression of Matt's emotional and psychological suffering in the wake of Elektra's death in *Daredevil* #181. It portrays Matt's belief in his own moral superiority—a product of his tireless defense of the innocent in court crossed with his placing himself above the law as a costumed adventurer—as a trap or, worse, a tool by which he justifies even the most mercenary manipulations of others. In issue #186, when Foggy calls him, gently, on the strangeness of a public defender gathering a case to prosecute Glenn Enterprises for corporate malfeasance, he reverts to the argument that he—Matt, Daredevil, the man without fear and the unquestioned defender of justice—simply has a duty to the law.

At that moment, while Foggy looks on, Matt experiences his worst attack of supersensory overkill so far. Miller represents the episode by making Foggy's words burst their balloons to become larger and larger block letters, signaling their transformation from language to noise. Matt's heightened senses have long made the physical world less important to him than how he processes its data. Now it asserts itself as something independent of him. In the following issue, #187, Daredevil staggers through a Manhattan crosswalk, dwarfed by street noises that finally crowd everything but his body out of the frame (figure 13). He can no longer count on his senses even to navigate the crosswalks of his beloved city. Matt's submission to it here and during his argument with Foggy sheds a bit of allegorical light on the graver flaw he exhibits regarding Heather, his legalistic self-righteousness. As his hypersenses have always rendered reality little more than an obstacle course, so his overconfidence in his own moral rectitude has, until now, rendered transparent to him the murky realm of right and wrong. But now even that realm has turned on him. This new chapter in his relationship with Heather is more than just a troubling

FIGURE 13. Frank Miller and Klaus Janson, "Overkill," *Daredevil* #187 (Marvel, October 1982).

secondary plot, an expression of Matt's emotional and psychological suffering in the wake of Elektra's death. It portrays Matt's belief in his own moral superiority—a product of his courtroom defense of "his" clients crossed with his paternalistic, extralegal defense of "his" city— as a trap or, worse, a crutch he uses to justify each action he takes, including being cruel to lovers and friends.

Matt's reaction to the death of Elektra is to bully Heather into the submissive role that Elektra couldn't play. Miller attributes to Matt not a single thought balloon to suggest that he is aware of the toll his bullying takes on her, while Miller continually draws the reader's attention to that toll via Matt's glib condescension and Heather's devastated reactions to it. The soundness of Daredevil's judgment is now more questionable than ever. Does his heroism stem from a neurotic urge to control everything around him, and is that neurosis reaching a tipping point? After all, we see him suffer a nearly dissociative breakdown when he convinces himself in #182 that Elektra somehow survived her own murder. The splash page of that issue still chills me with its full-face close-up of Matt in a cold sweat, staring into our eyes, as if pleading with us to believe something we know to be utterly false just because he believes it: "SHE'S ALIVE." By #189, only seven issues later, his demeaning paternalism has driven his new fiancée straight to the bottle.

In spite of the ugliness of Matt's abuse, and the emphasis Miller places on that ugliness, it's difficult for me to decide whether terrorizing Heather this way makes Daredevil less heroic or more heroic in Miller's definition. Miller has often spoken about the archetypical hero as something other than human, as dismissive of what others think they need as Matt is of Heather's feelings. When Miller discusses *The Dark Knight Strikes Again!*, which he and interviewer Gary Groth agree is nearly a parody of superhero comics, he emphasizes Batman's abstract quality, born of the kind of social isolation that Stick enforces on Matt: If Batman's "motto is striking terror" into the hearts of criminals, then "Batman can only be defined as a terrorist. . . . I don't want you to like this guy." "My feeling about Batman is that he's similar [to James Bond] in that you'd want him to be there when you're being mugged, but you wouldn't want to have dinner with him. The way he cheers Hawkman on as he crushes Luthor's skull . . . For me, [such scenes demonstrate] the idea [of Batman] coming into its own without the bullshit on top of it being a socially acceptable role model and all of that."[23] Matt's disregard for Heather's emotional state during the Glenn Enterprises affair further clarifies Miller's sense of the heroic impulse: it is prosociety but deeply antisocial, convinced that Right and Wrong are real and unchanging standards but dangerously solipsistic in its interpretation of how to achieve Right at the expense of Wrong. The true hero, according to Miller, is, compared to "normal" human beings at least, a pathological narcissist. Daredevil, with unwavering faith in his own judgment, performs "necessary" services for a culture whether it asks for them or not, while those who are under his protection see him as unfathomable at best and terrifying at worst. But even if Miller thrills to his own extrication of the "lies" and "bullshit" from the Batman persona a few years later, in *Daredevil* he employs dramatic irony to relate the high cost, to both individuals and their community, of the uncompromising, take-no-prisoners heroism that Americans think they want. "Dirty Harry . . . is a profoundly, consistently moral force," Miller tells Kim Thompson, but that wouldn't keep him out of jail for "administering the 'Wrath of God' on murderers who society treats as victims."[24]

In an authoritative study of Jack Kirby, Charles Hatfield has suggested that Marvel Comics distinguished itself in the 1960s in part by placing new stress on the tension intrinsic to superhero comics between the hero's desire for justice and the extralegal means by which she or he pursues it.[25] I would add that Marvel's Silver Age stories place the stress primarily on the plotting opportunities provided by this tension, as in the case of Spider-Man, whose good deeds only draw the ire of a public (understandably) suspicious of ununiformed law enforcement. Miller further develops the "upstanding vigilante" paradox from a cliché of the genre into a philosophical dialectic that, though sometimes decried as fascistic, cannot be reduced to an unironic plea for authoritarian rule. The superheroic fantasies on display in *300*, the *Sin City* graphic novels, *The Dark Knight Strikes Again!*, and even the controversial *Holy Terror* cast a clear eye on the paradox of the specifically American fascination with the superheroic ideal. All pose to the reader the implicit question, Is this *really* what you want? Considering the consistency of this theme dating back to *Daredevil*, I think of the pre-9/11 Frank Miller as less conservative than libertarian, a posthippie refugee of the 1960s who disdains the everyone-is-special

relativism of grade-school participation trophies and liberal humanism but shares with the conscientious objector and the bra burner a
fervency for personal liberty: "I'm no middle-of-the-roader, but I find
that people who tend to follow any party line, of the left or right, tend
to all end up saying the same thing, which is 'Do what I tell you.' Quit
those habits I don't like, don't use the words I don't like, don't draw
the pictures I don't want my children to see. . . . So yeah, I have a
very jaundiced view toward most authority."[26] In any event, Miller's
focus on Daredevil's unflagging moral code, and his attention to how
a relentless diet of violence might change that code into an ideologi-
cal prison, allows him to explore the upstanding vigilante figure from
multiple angles—the broadly liberal defense of constitutional protection for criminals and victims alike; the broadly conservative ideal of
defending one's own body, family, and property without impediment
from the state—without readily disclosing his personal politics.

The arc of Matt and Heather's codependency in *Daredevil* #184–189
all but undermines our willingness to root for the titular hero of the
series. For this reason, I suspect, Miller finally backs Matt away from
the psychological precipice by staging an intervention. In the end,
Heather is saved—as is Matt, from becoming even more monstrous—
by a split mirror image of Matt/DD himself: his law partner teamed
with another costumed hero. Filling in for Matt's absent superego,
Foggy and the newly returned Black Widow force Heather and Matt
apart by forging a couple of blunt, uncompromising breakup notes.
In a two-page sequence in issue #189, in which Miller arranges the
pages to run across from each other (such placements were not easy
to organize in the newsprint era of comics publishing, when issues
contained more advertising than story pages and ad placement was
sometimes inflexible), Heather reads a note "signed" by Matt breaking
off their engagement, followed by a similarly sparsely paneled page
in which Matt reads nearly the identical note "signed" by Heather.
The layout that Miller constructs here not only renders a plot event; it
provides a kinetic expression of the emotional landscape. On the first
page, Heather's phone rings repeatedly as the framing of each successive panel distances her from the picture plane, suggesting how her
pain at reading the note causes her to recede from the sensory world.
On the second, a similar series of panels reverses the direction of the
first by creeping into a different apartment, gradually revealing that

FIGURES 14 AND 15. Frank Miller and Klaus Janson, "Siege," *Daredevil* #189 (Marvel, December 1982).

Matt is the source of Heather's phone call, and allowing us to "hear" the ringing phone as the pulsing buzz he hears at his end of the line.

White space dominates both pages, rendering the panels as sparse as the terse Dear John letters each lover holds. This page spread riffs on the cinematic convention of changing scenes on a straight cut between similar close-ups by beginning and ending on the letter(s) instead of the usual faces and "cutting" instead, at the page break, on long shots of Heather and Matt (figures 14 and 15). This tactic gains Miller the effect of two filmic long takes—a track-in/graphic match cut/track-out sequence that uses the existence of the second letter to make clear the provenance of the first and employs the neat and precise graphic match between the nearly identical phony letters to emphasize with a little dramatic irony the chaotic, distraught feelings of the couple whose engagement has been brought to an end.

Miller gives Matt a dose of his own medicine here. When DD extra-legally stops, holds, and delivers suspects to be booked for alleged crimes that sometimes only he has witnessed (if he witnesses them at all), he upholds justice at the abstract level. At the same time, however, he takes the freedoms of others into his own hands without anyone's permission, while giving himself an unfair advantage as an attorney if he participates in the suspects' trials. The Foggy/Widow letter conspiracy is similarly compromised, for it protects an innocent but is also unquestionably unethical. It renders Matt's and Heather's rights superfluous, thus preventing Matt from doing Heather further harm but leaving him just as tormented, and probably as pathologically unsympathetic toward Heather, as before.

The agonizing sensitivity of Matt's senses during this final Miller arc makes our hero's lack of sensitivity to Heather's pain all the more ironic. Without excusing his treatment of Heather, however, Daredevil's crisis invites us to feel pity for Matt the relentless idealist. Isolated by his secret, his heightened perception, the trauma of Elektra's murder, and the knowledge that he could save neither her life nor her soul, he has reached a point where he no longer knows how to engage friends and lovers without grabbing the rudder and steering these relationships by himself, no matter what the consequences. Few superheroes have ever seemed so ill equipped to continue their own civilian lives. Brian Michael Bendis presses this point even more relentlessly in his *Daredevil* run with the artist Alex Maleev in the early nineties, by making Matt give up nearly everything and everyone he cares about just to save his secret identity from public knowledge. True to Miller's model, this iteration of Matt Murdock fails even at that. The Bendis/Maleev run ends, in *Daredevil* volume 2, #81 (March 2006), with Matt being arrested, arraigned, and hauled off to a cell block filled with Daredevil's arch nemeses. The FBI agent who nabs him arranges his incarceration this way in hopes that Murdock and his enemies will all kill each other. Bendis reports that in 2003, when *Daredevil* won him a Will Eisner Award for Best Writer and another for Best Continuing Series, Frank Miller was the first to congratulate him: "Actually Frank took the Eisner away from me and said, 'You know this is mine, right?' And I held up my hands and genuinely offered back, 'Yeah, I do. Take it.' He smiled drily and handed it back, just goofing with me, but I was glad that he knew I knew that without him, nothing we did would have existed."[27]

The moral complications and gray areas of Miller's *Daredevil* days are seldom on display in his most recent work. The figuratively black-and-white moral universe of his literally black-and-white series *Sin City* leaves no room for such ambiguities. Marv, *Sin City*'s sociopath with a heart of gold, presumably kills only people who deserve to die, but we are forced to take Miller's word for it; in any event, he gives Marv's victims no personalities that would allow even our superficial judgment of their guilt. The Miller of *Sin City* places himself at odds with his own past self as a storyteller whose unique point of view derived from his hyperawareness of the grander costs of living the heroic ideal. It's as if Miller has gone figuratively blind to the truism of realist fiction that he once held dear: to paraphrase a line from Jean Renoir's film *La règle du jeu* (1939), "good" and "evil" can never be cut-and-dried categories because, sadly, everyone has their reasons.

In Miller's final issues as writer and layout artist, Stick reveals to Daredevil that his powers are not superhuman at all but basic potentials that everyone possesses. The accident that triggered his abilities did not mutate his senses or load him up with radar sui generis. It merely heightened these latent potentials temporarily, giving Matt an opportunity to recognize them and control them even after their moment of greatest intensity had waned. This is where Miller leaves Daredevil: aware at last that he is not unique and stripped of whatever part his physical singularity played in his faith that he and he alone is above the law. Self-awareness is a liberty he has had to sacrifice in order to fight crime on the streets of New York in a red suit rather than a blue one. But the climactic moment of the "Elektra: Resurrection" story arc, which takes place in issue #190, suggests that in spite of the havoc Daredevil's arrogance wreaks, he is better off naïve. After watching one of Stick's inner circle bring the stone-dead Black Widow back to life by "moving energy around," Daredevil attempts to render moot the Hand's plot to resurrect Elektra as a mindless killing machine by bringing her back to life himself. He fails, of course, as Stick's ninja colleague Stone predicts, but after the battle is won, Stone is surprised to find that Elektra "is clean!"—meaning, apparently, that while her body is dead, her soul has been purged of its overarching bitterness by Matt's unreasonable but unstinting optimism that Elektra could be reformed. Whatever the cost, Miller prefers Matt's idealism to the praxis of abandoning crises to the "proper" authorities.

This idealism cuts both ways, however. Daredevil's optimism about saving Elektra's soul is the same idealism that moved him to save

Bullseye from the subway tracks, an act that allowed Bullseye to kill many more crooks and civilians between issue #169 and his incapacitation in #181. As Miller puts the finishing touches on the ethical universe he constructed for Daredevil, he leaves us pondering whether he has really given us what we wanted out of a superhero comic. After Miller confronts us with the dehumanization that hides in plain sight within the superheroic ideal, do we like what we see? Or do we want our old fantasies again, with the lies crammed back in?

THE UNHOLY THREE

The Kingpin, Elektra, and Bullseye [were] three elements that developed very quickly and I felt that I wanted to take that group somewhere. I figured my options were simple: I could either take a limited number of characters and put them through a variety of situations, or a variety of characters and put them through one situation, and I decided to take these [three] characters for all they were worth.

FRANK MILLER

Perhaps above all the changes Miller made to *Daredevil*'s cast, none pulled more forcefully against superhero conventions than Miller's reduction of Daredevil's rogues gallery to essentially three: the Kingpin, Elektra, and Bullseye. (My chapter title actually refers to the band of unremarkable goons wearing animal suits who act as Death-Stalker's evil henchmen in *Daredevil* #158, but they're not unholy so much as goofy looking, so I pinched their team name for a more deserving group.) None of the three possess superpowers in the sense that Spider-Man or Iron Man does, nor do they have the extra mechanical arms or electrically charged battle suits of Marvel's garden-variety supervillains. Keeping superpowers out of the equation was part of Miller's plan. He had nothing against Kirby and Ditko or the comics of his own youth in the seventies, and he published fan letters in various Marvel comics in the 1970s to prove it (one in *Amazing Spider-Man* #169 commending the penciler Ross Andru, another in *Claws of the Cat* #3 cheering on the development of more independent female characters). When the writer Roger McKenzie was fired from *Daredevil*, however, Miller took the opportunity to transform it into the kind of hard-boiled crime comic he had written and drawn for his high school newspaper back in Vermont. This does not mean that he threw out the theatrical fight scenes and impossible feats of physical strength and skill that Kirby had made into standard Marvel fare. But he chose these three nemeses carefully, made them sustaining (and competing) elements in *Daredevil*'s ecology of crime, and effectively built the melodrama of his entire run around the challenges they posed to both Matt Murdock's faith in the law and his faith in himself.

THE KINGPIN

Importing the Kingpin of Crime from *The Amazing Spider-Man* series was a risky move. Fans of the Marvel universe can get possessive about supervillains, expecting heroes to fight villains whose powers parallel or directly counter their own, and enjoying the tension as grudges develop over repeated matchups. If you expect parochialism from your bad guys, you might feel affronted were you to open a copy of *The Avengers* and see them taking on Baron Mordo from *Doctor Strange*. Some villains just wouldn't belong anywhere but the series that spawned them. Galactus, the Fantastic Four's gigantic world-eating nemesis, would have looked ridiculous outside those few books like *Fantastic Four* and *Captain Marvel* that were "cosmic" enough to make him an appropriate adversary. (Just imagine Daredevil whapping Galactus on the nose with his billy club or Matt Murdock suing him in civil court for committing planetary genocide.) These concerns have faded in twenty-first-century fandom, though twinges of them linger for longtime readers, myself included. In spite of the Green Goblin's development into a company-wide baddie since the turn of the millennium, I was a little disappointed at the end of Marvel's "event" miniseries *Siege* (2010) when someone other than Spidey took him down. After all, he did murder Peter Parker's beloved Gwen Stacy back in 1973.

To add to the risk of a fan revolt, the Kingpin was the silliest looking villain in the entire Marvel stable. When Stan Lee's plotting notes for *Amazing Spider-Man* #50 called for a gangster character called the Kingpin, John Romita Sr. drew him as a monstrously obese bald man wearing a white tux jacket, a diamond-studded ascot, and purple pants apparently on loan from the Hulk (sans the post-Hulkification rips and tears). Miller once called the Kingpin as originally conceived "the

Jackie Gleason of supervillains." "He might as well have been called Fat-Man."[1] Though he looked "merely fat," readers were constantly reminded, he was an agile martial artist whose bulbous girth was, somehow, all muscle. But the cartoonishness of his body made it hard to accept his status as a crime lord whose icy glance struck fear into even his most hardened cronies. Not that any of Spider-Man's flashiest baddies seem any less silly from an adult perspective. Doctor Octopus has four long, skinny metal arms sprouting from his chunky torso; the Green Goblin wears a purple stocking cap over a scaly, green rubber suit and rides a bat-shaped glider; Electro fires countless amperes of energy from his fingers while wearing a mask that looks like an electrocuted starfish from a SpongeBob SquarePants cartoon. But at least those villains' nefarious superpowers worked as science fiction. Kingpin was just a tub of lard with a "head . . . shaped like a piece of cake."[2] To top it all off, Lee made him speak Evil English, the quasi-Elizabethan dialect most favored among sixties supervillains: no contractions, frequent use of archaic insults like "cretin" and "jackanape," and alliterative threats that would have made William Safire natter with glee.

Miller's only stated reason for pinching Kingpin from *Amazing Spider-Man* was that he "needed a ganglord," and I assume he wasn't keen on inventing too many characters that would belong to Marvel, rather than to him, the moment they appeared. He could certainly have chosen a different Marvel-universe mob boss, though, one that would not require much of a makeover. My guess is that Miller was intrigued by the challenge of transforming this cake-headed blimp into a noir villain. He wasted no time in changing Kingpin's specific threat from physical to psychological and organizational. This new and improved Kingpin resorts to physical violence only rarely, and when he does, the display serves some larger purpose of plot or characterization. In *Daredevil* #171, Kingpin's second appearance in the series, Daredevil attempts to subdue him by force and effectively knocks himself out in the process. This clear mismatch renders all but moot the question of future physical tussles between the two and helps establish their true battlefield as one of wits, bluff, and influence.

From that point forward, Kingpin's body becomes a shape Miller utilizes for expressive effect. To a cartoonist with expressionist tendencies, the Kingpin must have seemed irresistible. There's a cockeyed brilliance about Romita's original design, which brings to mind nothing so much as a crooked millionaire from a Depression-era political cartoon, his sheer size and comically oversized head evincing his rapaciousness and overconfidence. Miller made him even bigger than Romita did, towering a good meter or so above the heads of his capos as they stand around his office awaiting their orders and hoping to God that the boss is in a good mood.

It takes only one issue, #170, for Miller to shift the character's gears, and he does so gradually, acknowledging the old and justifying the new in turn. The Kingpin, a.k.a. Wilson Fisk, having exiled himself to Japan for legal reasons, is performing his familiar Silver Age workout routine of throwing his bodyguards around in a big gym and getting vicious when one of them says the wrong thing in front of him. Before this, the wrong thing to mention was usually his wife, Vanessa, a gentle, regal woman with stripes of silver in her dark hair and doubts about her husband's profession. This time, however, the unlucky tough guy remarks on how unstoppable Fisk used to be "when he was the Kingpin!" It seems that Fisk has given up the life for Vanessa and agreed to provide evidence against former associates to the FBI, and he doesn't appreciate reminders of past glories. He lashes out at his employee, apparently breaking his arm. When Vanessa appears on the scene, he does what he has always done in this situation: he lies to her, claiming he was merely helping a workout partner who has "dislocated his shoulder."

So far this is the Kingpin we've always known and been indifferent to. But then Miller throws us a curve ball. Concerned to protect himself from prosecution when he returns, Kingpin sends Vanessa to New York to (what else?) find a good lawyer, and when she arrives at (where else?) the offices of Nelson and Murdock, rival gangsters kidnap her to prevent the Kingpin from testifying against them.

Then it happens. In the final pages of #170, the rival gang's assassins hunker down in an open field near a barn, awaiting the arrival of the Kingpin's private plane, but then the "retired" don makes his move to thwart the ambush. This time he doesn't break somebody's arm. Instead, he does what any good criminal bureaucrat would do: he solves the problem by remote control. The plane lands by degrees over a series of time-lapse frames, but it is empty—save for a bomb that detonates upon landing, killing the thugs who lie in wait. As the smoke clears, one panel at a time, Miller brings another plane—the Kingpin's real plane this time—into view moment by moment. Its slow descent, foreshadowed by the same sound effect that announced the decoy's arrival, is a small masterwork of timing via layout. The repetition of a landing plane and of Miller's accompanying sound effect provides a sense of destiny, implying the inevitability of Kingpin's victory thanks to his skill at thinking several moves ahead of his opponents. At the bottom of the page, in a third row of time-lapse panels, the Kingpin lights a cigarette—and suddenly he is illuminated by directional lighting as stark as a noir cinematographer's fever dream. Miller says this reintroduction was the *X-Men* and *Fantastic Four* storyteller John

FIGURE 16. Frank Miller and Klaus Janson, "The Kingpin Must Die!," *Daredevil* #170 (Marvel, May 1981).

Byrne's idea. Upon learning that Miller had decided to poach the Kingpin for himself, Byrne "took [Miller] aside one time" and said, "'You know what you gotta do: You draw [Kingpin] the way he's [always] been drawn for the whole first issue he's in. . . . Then, you turn him into a Frank Miller character. Light him. You're the guy who does the lighting.'" "And all of a sudden," says Miller, "he was mine" (figure 16).[3] Alan Moore argues that the Kingpin's real metamorphosis actually occurs in a five-panel "track-in" sequence that appears an issue later, in #171, after "an explosion that has apparently claimed the life of his wife. . . . In the five brief panels that make up this sequence the Kingpin is transformed in Miller's capable hands from the podgy, pompous buffoon of the early Spiderman [*sic*] appearances into a man who has buried his humanity under a mountain of iron resolve as vast as his physical body."[4]

While Moore makes a compelling point, I favor Miller's version of when and how he claimed the Kingpin, because that final sequence from #170 establishes not just a new mode of lighting him but also a new mechanics for the character. It is no longer what we see but what we don't see that makes this Kingpin dangerous. He reserves his physical presence for specific occasions, moments when the invisibility of his looming threat needs an icon to freshen up its impact. This Kingpin commands fear and respect not because he loses his temper at the drop of a hat but because he restrains himself. Miller lets his size represent potential, not actual, destruction as he purrs laconic orders from the shadows. If you thought the Kingpin was dangerous in a fist-fight, just wait until you can't even see him throwing the punches.

Miller uses Kingpin sparingly after that, but we never forget he's out there somewhere, waiting just out of frame for the right moment to pounce. Like the classic film noir villain Whit Sterling from *Out of the Past* or a more obvious visual precedent, the rotund Kasper Gutman from *The Maltese Falcon*, he appears primarily when it's time to make plans or time to cash them in, a strategy that simultaneously acknowledges his power as a behind-the-scenes player and gives him an aura of omnipresence. Indeed, regardless of his size, you can hardly see him even when Miller plops him right in front of you. His office is always lit low-key, with deep blacks obscuring three-quarters of an implied space that seems to be all walls, the details stripped down to a window, a chair, and a desk illuminated by a single rectangle of light. The Kingpin's office is drawn not as a realist space but as a sketch of the impression it makes on a visitor familiar with Kingpin's ruthlessness and invulnerability. It also conveys Miller's editorial view of crime in general as a void to which its overlords sacrifice their humanity in order to retain their empires. The Kingpin's storehouse is always full of ill-gotten contraband, but parasite that he is, he produces nothing but carnage. To show for it, he has no friends, no personal effects, not even a potted plant in his suite to recycle the ruined air.

Among *Daredevil*'s impressive lineup of patriarchal figures, good and bad—Jack Murdock, the Fixer, Stick—the Kingpin most nearly reaches the level of the fantastical Oedipal father. He controls everything. He has moles in the police force, a syndicate that runs the length of the East Coast, and the liquid assets to get anything he requires, from the murder of an enemy to a handpicked mayoral candidate with poll numbers that render his competitors toothless. The Kingpin opposes Miller's Daredevil so successfully, I think, because whereas Daredevil ostensibly cares about the victim more than the criminal or the crime, the Kingpin's rapacity for profit and power evacuates his victims of any significance whatsoever. To him they are numbers to crunch, distractions to eliminate, advantages to gain. Enemies and innocents alike are dead to him from the moment he orders their elimination. Kingpin is ultimately defined less by the enormity of his actions than by his ability to think multiple moves ahead on the chessboard of organized crime, a skill he wields so expertly that the consequences of his moves, and everyone else's as well, are all in his favor. Worse still for Matt Murdock, Kingpin keeps a tight grip on evidence that might incriminate him, from fingerprints, shell casings, and witnesses to receipts, tax records, and offshore accounts. Nothing could possibly unnerve Murdock more than a criminal who so completely controls the narrative of his career that he is, for all intents and purposes, above the law.

In this sense, the Kingpin justifies Daredevil's existence. But he also kicks up more dust around the paradoxical nature of Matt Murdock, his desire to enforce the rule of law, and the denial of that very rule inherent in his vigilantism. When the puzzle at hand is how to catch a known crime lord who operates unhindered in plain sight, the logical solution (in a comic book or an action movie, anyway) would seem to be an enforcer who is no more restricted by the law than his adversary: Daredevil can spy, confiscate evidence, do whatever he must to defeat the Kingpin. It's a liberating fantasy, one that differs little from the fantasy provided by Batman and other action heroes. Unless comics readers are lawyers or judges or police detectives themselves, they are unlikely to worry over issues of legal verisimilitude, questions like whether the evidence the hero collects against the villain passes the Fourth Amendment's legitimacy test. In Daredevil's case, though, it's tougher to ignore the irony. Here is a prominent attorney who effectively runs his own rogue justice system with a police force of one. As I've established, Miller is fully aware of the defining strangeness of Daredevil's premise, often embracing it for philosophical purposes, though at least once he sidesteps the shaky legal status of vigilante-collected evidence to keep a good plot humming. In issue #178, a teenage kid named Sheldon somehow acquires a briefcase filled with canceled checks that represent Kingpin's "donations" to the Cherryh mayoral campaign, which is coasting to a big victory, and tries to sell them to the *Daily Bugle* newspaper. Nobody questions how he got the checks or whether they're legitimate; in their comic-booky way, they just are. But ultimately, the checks are simply the McGuffin that made the plot push forward. When Kingpin's cronies attempt to kidnap Sheldon, their ensuing scuffle with DD and the "Heroes for Hire" Power Man and Iron Fist accidentally opens the briefcase, spilling the checks into the middle of a ticker-tape parade on a windy day.

In issue #180, left without even circumstantial evidence of the Kingpin's wrongdoing, Daredevil, champion of justice, resorts to extortion to get Cherryh off the ballot. To accomplish this little masterpiece of table-turning, Miller brings the Kingpin's kidnapped wife back into the spotlight, and it hits us: Miller has been carefully setting things up for this moment for ten issues, since the kidnapping occurred in #170, the Kingpin's debut issue of *Daredevil*. Thought to have been killed in an explosion by the Kingpin's (former) chief lieutenant, Vanessa eventually turns up living in the sewers of New York, brain-damaged and enslaved to the King, a pasty-white behemoth who is a dead ringer for the Kingpin himself. With the help of the reporter Ben Urich, Daredevil finds her, retrieves her, and as I've discussed, supplies Kingpin with her whereabouts in exchange for pulling Cherryh's campaign. Placing the climax of the Cherryh-Vanessa story line in the New York sewer system is a blunt but brilliant bit of commentary on the legitimacy that Kingpin attempts to cultivate for his "business" by installing a puppet mayor. Though the Kingpin can keep his criminal underworld looking spotless, he can't fool Miller, who creates its mirror image in a literal underworld filled with garbage, wasted souls reduced to pure want—"Money for food," they chant mechanically, like zombies demanding quarters instead of flesh—and an ersatz king whose gleeful acts of physical violence materialize the hidden brutality of the Kingpin's bureaucratic regime. The sewer is the Kingpin's realm as Daredevil sees it, for what it is—an expressionist doppelgänger for the Kingpin's obscene world of office buildings with torture chambers in their basements. But true to Miller's tendency to out Matt's internal contradictions, there's an unexpectedly subtle parallelism here. Dare-devil deflates the Kingpin's ambitions by the same shady, remote-control methods employed by the Kingpin himself—and thanks to the terms of Daredevil's deal, the Kingpin loses the mayoral race but escapes the legal punishment he richly deserves. I, for one, never saw that one coming.

The scary thing—when the Kingpin gets Daredevil where he lives—is when he returns a "favor" for Daredevil in #190. Daredevil has to find the members of the evil Hand before they resurrect Elektra to serve as their lead assassin. He goes to the Kingpin, whom he con-vinces to help him because "if she returns, she'll serve the Hand," not her enormous former boss. The Kingpin promises to find them, but in a close-up that frames him from slightly above, his face disappearing into an attached shadow, Kingpin tells Daredevil, "there is something you must do for me, in return." That shadow, the product of Klaus Jan-son's brimming inkwell of crosshatch effects, is also the ethical shadow that haunts this deal—the shadow of Murdock's compromising him-self to the criminals his methods make him resemble. Daredevil takes out Injun Joe's gang for Kingpin—"The police get these men, as we agreed"—and the Kingpin offers his thanks by using one of his lieu-tenants to feed Daredevil the location of the Hand. Once the site has been located, DD, Black Widow, and the ninja Stone are fighting off hordes of agents of the Hand when suddenly shots ring out and the Hand assassins fall. It's the Kingpin's men to the rescue, delivering via gunfire a most unexpected second thank-you note. Having thus thwarted the resurrection of Elektra, Daredevil leans against a lamp-post scratching his chin when the Kingpin rides up to the street corner in his limo to get the last word:

You wonder why I saved your life, do you not? Consider it an illustration—of the true nature of our relationship. Your attack on Injun Joe has served to quell a mutiny in my organization. It demonstrated to the mobs that you are a common enemy, against whom they need protection—protection that I provide. Consider also, Daredevil, that when you needed to find the hide-out, you did not contact the police. You came to me. We need each other, Daredevil. We are partners, after a fashion. We are the power in this city.

You could've knocked me over with a feather the first time I read those words—the last lines Miller wrote for the Kingpin during this run—in the fall of 1982. It meant that DD and the Kingpin had each served their own ends through precisely the same means, with the Kingpin gaining advantages in the deal that undercut Daredevil's mission both now and in the future. The Kingpin, by submitting his own men to be roughed up by Daredevil, strengthens his grip on his organization, thereby transforming DD into nothing more or less than the Kingpin's primary enforcer, a boogeyman to keep the wayward in line even as he climbs a few notches on the syndicate's enemies list. Janson colors the Kingpin exclusively in street-lamp yellow for this scene and, in a final extreme close-up, uses wash-like Zipatone swaths to sculpt his face into the most human expression ever attributed to him; he smiles, almost kindly but with an eyebrow slightly arched, as though he's calling Daredevil not only his partner but his trusted (because malleable) ally (figure 17). Murdock's freaky behavior after Elektra's murder and his all-out assault on Heather's self-esteem already had me worried that the character had not gained the self-knowledge Miller claimed for him in interviews. Before the arc's climax, Stone himself wonders at one point whether DD's obsession with Elektra will cause him to betray Stick's good ninjas to the Hand. Now I had to ask myself if he had sold his soul to the Kingpin just to boost his paternalistic ego.

FIGURE 17. Frank Miller and Klaus Janson, "Resurrection," *Daredevil* #190 (Marvel, January 1983).

Miller, following his noir instinct to court moral ambiguity wherever possible, leaves the point dangling right there when he departs the series after the very next issue. The possibility that the existence of Daredevil worked to the Kingpin's advantage clouded every Daredevil story Miller had told up to that point for me and every new Daredevil story I was to read thereafter. Before I read *Daredevil* #190, I was a teenager who enjoyed superhero comics without feeling any need to understand the attraction. This issue, however, made me question exactly why I still biked to the comic shop every week, if what it gave me was not the triumph of good over evil but a genre-driven acknowledgment of their symbiotic relationship.

Thus, a character that could have been a mere villain-of-the-month or a plot device to motivate Daredevil's confrontations with Elektra and Bullseye becomes a formidable deus ex machina, amplifying the run's implication that Comic Book Good and Comic Book Evil are not opposites but poles of a spectrum, the extremes separated by a few scant gradations of gray. Evil and crime in Miller's New York are as indestructible as heroism, not so much because human nature is despicable as because crime now takes the same modern form as any other kind of controlling power: white-collar bureaucracy. The Kingpin's approach to crime is indistinguishable from crony capitalism, in which a smart stock trader or shell-company executive can rook the system just by riding its tide with an eye trained to recognize opportunities—to take advantage of market trends or corporate deals ripe for hijacking, to route the passage of inside stock information so intricately that the Feds can't track it, and so forth. Few things could be less flattering to the superheroic ideal than a successful attempt to put the bad guys down that actually benefits organized crime. It's as if Miller is telling us that nothing Daredevil has done since issue #158 affected the big picture of crime's hold on New York or, maybe even worse, that his small victories may change the forms crime takes, who gets hurt and who doesn't, without altering a whit the infrastructure of big crime and big money. Vigilantism, even the rough-and-tumble, justice-loving kind practiced by Daredevil, may be the equivalent of using a popsicle stick and a Band-Aid to set a broken back. Today I wonder whether Miller's Kingpin symbolizes the rich and indifferent "1 percent" as Miller perceived it when he was a younger man with fewer resources, long before he accused the Occupy Wall Street movement of wasting its energy protesting corporate power instead of training to fight terrorism. But that's a historical plot twist energized by Miller's more contemporary motivations, one to which I return in the conclusion.

ELEKTRA

In 1973, a fifteen-year-old Frank Miller got the following letter published in an issue of *The Claws of the Cat*, a short-lived series about a female superhero: "Wonderful! At last a woman character with character. I, for one, am sick of the helpless-female types [that] have cluttered up comics for so long. While I do think they are necessary and nice to look at, they don't have to be the only kind. . . . Keep it up!"[5] In *Daredevil* #168, his first issue as writer-penciler, Miller kicked off his epic analysis of Daredevil's internal conflict by introducing a "woman character with character" of his own named Elektra Natchios. Elektra's laconic speech, her athletic, eroticized body (the trade press critic Larry Rodman has described her as a "psychotic swimsuit model"),[6] the daddy complex reflected by her very name, and the phallic threat posed to Daredevil by her martial arts skills and her twin *sai* (Japanese short swords) place her in a long line of film noir women who exist primarily to be destroyed or redeemed by the beleaguered male protagonist. But it's not hyperbole to claim that there had never been a superhero comics character like her before. Together with Claremont and Cockrum's Phoenix, the near-omnipotent reincarnation of the X-Men's former hostage-in-waiting Jean Grey/Marvel Girl, Elektra made female empowerment both a plot turn that the rest of the comics industry scrambled to emulate and a new wrinkle in the fabric of superhero masculinity.

Elektra represents Miller's most dynamic revision of the Daredevil mythology. By shoehorning her (and later Matt's pre-Daredevil martial arts teacher, Stick) into Murdoch/Daredevil's past via flashback, Miller injected instant gravitas into the character. However, as a retcon (short for "retroactive continuity") character, one invented in the present but projected back on an earlier moment in Daredevil's timeline, she was also the riskiest. Back then, Marvel fans like me could be pretty unforgiving when creators took liberties with a character's history. Introducing a character from Matt's uncharted past, however, was an opportunity to make the character Miller had been drawing for more than a year into *his* Daredevil, and he was not about to miss it.

One dank, film noiry day in Hell's Kitchen—the kind that dumps rain in sheets and makes all but the nearest streetlights, trash cans, and bums impossible to see—Daredevil approaches a blind pencil seller who turns out to be Turk in disguise and starts shaking the thug down for information he needs to turn the wheels of justice: Turk's employer, an assassination specialist aptly named Mr. Slaughter, is hiding a witness to a murder for which an innocent man is about to be convicted. Rattled by a Molotov cocktail thrown by another crook, Daredevil chases down the bomber only to be ambushed by a woman wearing a red leotard, head scarf, and gloves and boots that are less worn than wrapped like scarlet ribbons around her extremities.

We see Elektra before DD senses her presence. Miller positions the viewer behind her as she perches on a line peering down at DD and the bomber, three-pronged sword in one hand. "Daredevil?!" she thinks. "What is he doing here? He could ruin everything! I cannot let that happen." The next page bursts with violence more wrenching than the explosion a couple of pages before. In three skinny panels that span the page from left gutter to right, the butt of Elektra's sword whizzes from frame right to hit Daredevil's neck in a close-up; a medium shot shows the booted, curvy leg of his assailant kicking DD in the teeth from right to left; and finally, the woman in red, her face nearly visible, completes the vector by throwing the sword frame right, where it bounces off a wall, "smashes [the] unprotected jaw" of the bomber, and hangs suspended at the panel's center. Miller uses no more setting here than he has to—there are walls in the second panel only because the sword has to bounce off something—thus making it impossible to concentrate on anything but the disorienting dynamics of the sword's force, until the three horizontal panels give way to four equally skinny vertical ones, offering us disorientingly "brief" shot/reverse-shots at a moment of high tension. It's an effective layout style, particularly here, at a moment of double revelation: the readers see the woman's face for the first time, and Daredevil, initially lying face down on the pavement only fifteen feet from Elektra and the bomber, suddenly pulls himself up long enough to express the last thing readers expect: recognition. "That voice—Elektra?!" he blurts out before dropping back to the sidewalk in the page's final panel.

Miller can't disguise his status as a first-time writer. The third-person box narration is melodramatic and verbose, even more laden with modifiers than McKenzie's *Sturm und Drang* scripts. (Daredevil's face plant motivates a verbose, seven-page expository flashback—overlong by any standard—that slows the momentum to a near halt.) But now that Miller has full control over words and pictures, from #168 on, he is free to experiment even more with the zigzag motion he has learned to force on the reader's eye, to give it significance beyond its visual dynamism. The shifting lines of sight generated by this first Elektra-Daredevil fight sequence offer us comics narration as double take, a visual metaphor for Matt's pain and bewilderment. Several rows of horizontal action panels yank the eye left to right and back again, then a stutter of skinnier and skinnier vertical panels spits DD's climactic recognition at us only to hang us from the cliff of the last panel, helpless to do anything but turn the page as quickly as possible to find out who this "Elektra" is and why Matt knows her well enough to let out that agonized cry. As we have already learned, she's a bounty hunter looking for the same witness Daredevil wants to haul before the judge, and she states calmly that she will either get help from the bomber or kill him. Where could straitlaced Matt Murdock, pure-hearted champion of the oppressed in the court-room and on the streets, possibly have met *her*?

Even fans who hated retcons (which were still relatively rare in 1980) had to contend with the sheer force of Elektra's introduction, which Miller charged up with Oedipal complications to spare. Elektra's origin story, told in flashback while DD lies unconscious, resembles Daredevil's in all but its outcome: it, too, involves the violent death of a father (hence "Elektra" was Miller's shorthand for the Electra com-plex, which Freud theorized as the girl's version of the boy's Oedipal complex but later disavowed—not exactly an obscure subtext) and the child's turn to violence as a coping mechanism. Matt had known Ele-ktra in law school after the accident that gave him his supernormal abilities but before his own father was murdered. He falls in love with her instantly and reveals the secret of his augmented senses, but after a "euphoric" year of necking on the Columbia University green, her father, a Greek ambassador to the United States, is kidnapped and held captive in the school's administration building. Matt attempts to free him, wrapping the red scarf he'd bought for Elektra's birthday around his eyes as a makeshift disguise and practicing some proto-Daredevil martial arts moves on the kidnappers, but it's in vain. Then, like Jack Murdock sometime in the near future, Ambassador Natchios is shot— but not by the kidnappers. Rather, a trigger-happy policeman outside the building sees a thug being flung through a window, assumes the kidnappers are killing hostages, and takes a shot that kills Elektra's father instantly. But Elektra "doesn't cry. Not then. Not later," even at the funeral, displayed from the point of view of the open grave as Matt and Elektra watch shovelfuls of dirt cover the body for good. Then she drops out of law school and disappears. "There is no other way," she tells Matt. "I cannot continue to study laws in which I no longer believe." To make peace with his own father's loss and teach the world to follow the rules, Matt chooses the law as both profession and extracurricular activity. But Elektra chooses to defy the law, whose enforcers effectively punished the prey instead of the predator when they accidentally shot and killed her father. She expresses that defiance by becoming a contract killer—the quintessential thief of the legal rights to life and liberty that Daredevil is pledged to protect. For the first time since Karen Page's exit, the series has a solid, clear emotional center, only this time, that center rests not on interpersonal dynamics but on internal conflict, the continuing torture of Matt Murdock as the woman of his dreams proves herself his mortal enemy.

Miller labors, perhaps too heavily, in #168 to construct Matt's former lover as his evil twin, shredded-looking red ninja costume and all. But reeling out the exposition so thoroughly gives Miller the freedom to get down to the fundamental conflict between the former lovers all the sooner. And for all the flashback's overeagerness as a first-time writer's show-and-tell project, it slyly withholds exactly how Elektra transformed from a shy international student into a hired killer with bone-crunching martial skills. That tale would have to wait for issue #190, nearly three years down the road; in the meantime, we have only her origin story and our inferences about her to guide us.

"Elektra" also pays homage to one of Miller's heroes, the Golden Age artist, comics entrepreneur, and educator Will Eisner, with whom Miller struck up an abiding friendship. The story is at heart a retelling of Eisner's "Sand Saref" from *The Spirit* Sunday comic strip (actually a comic-book-sized supplement) that first appeared in newspapers January 8 and 15, 1950. "I steal from the best," Miller once quipped.[7] Where Miller's tale differs from Eisner's is in how it connects the dramatic conflict between Daredevil and Elektra directly to the conflict between personal feelings and public responsibility that focus Miller's development of Matt Murdock. Eisner's Spirit, also a masked crime fighter, is a cypher, less a dramatic protagonist than an excuse for the stories that Eisner wanted to tell. The Spirit had been a cop named Denny Colt who, left for dead in a pool of chemicals after a solo run-in with gangsters, cheated death and nabbed his assailants. Thereafter Eisner had him endlessly shot, beaten, stabbed, and blown up only to drag himself back up like a crook-eating zombie that only a taste of justice can satisfy. But for all his mystery, wit, and charm, he was primarily a vehicle for Eisner's experimental comics narratives, which ranged from hard-boiled crime tales to Aesopian yarns about the plight of everyday people in a violent and indifferent metropolis. "The main thing that interests me" about Eisner's work, Miller said in 1982, "is the way he makes the words and pictures act together. That's very, very rare. [He is the] one man [in comics] with complete command [of both drawing and writing] and what makes his stuff so magical isn't the quality of his writing or the quality of his drawing, but it's how he combines them."[8]

Sand's "return"—for she, too, is a retcon character, installed in the Spirit's past to allow Eisner to tell a story about lost love and generosity—leans hard toward the noirish end of the genre spectrum, complete with a complicated flashback and a climactic escape attempt at the docks. Sand is as beautiful as she is deadly and bold enough to use her attractions to satisfy her uncontrollable desire for riches. She is Brigid O'Shaunessey to the Spirit's Sam Spade, a beguiling woman who grew up crooked in the same slum where Denny Colt was raised arrow-straight by his policeman father. Elektra draws from the same tradition, up to a point. Like the noir femme fatale as E. Ann Kaplan's *Women in Film Noir* defined her decades ago, Sand is ruthless in her pursuit of money and her refusal to depend on anyone or be defined by anything other than her own needs.[9] From the Lacanian feminist perspective of Kaplan's collection, the femme fatale is a projection of the postwar American woman as fully modernized, unwilling to give up the independence that many women experienced during the Second World War working, earning their own money, and pursuing their own lives rather than being defined by marriage and family. Sand's story offers this "dark lady" in shorthand but puts a twist on the usual noir conclusion of punishing her for breaking the rules of patriarchy. The Spirit, usually Spade-like in his ability to resist most sexual come-ons, decides that there's hope for her yet and allows her to escape (figure 18).

Like Sand, Elektra combines the vicious but irresistible femme fatale with the equally exotic fascination of chop-socky martial arts movies, of which Miller had become an avid fan while living in New York. "I deliberately picked up on the 'ninja' thing as soon as I saw it coming and worked it into *Daredevil*, partly because . . . I got into the fad, and partly just to see what would happen," Miller told the *Comics Journal* in 1981.[10] What happened, as it turns out, is that Miller's introduction of Elektra and the horde of ninjas who pursue her (and

FIGURE 18. Will Eisner, "Bring in Sand Saref," *The Spirit* (newspaper supplement, January 15, 1950).

the hero of Miller and Chris Claremont's 1982 *Wolverine* miniseries) incited a ninja-mania that hit independent American comics like a ton of bricks in the early 1980s. It's rarely remarked on now, but before the Teenage Mutant Ninja Turtles became Saturday-morning cartoon stars, they were characters in an indie comic that simultaneously parodied Miller's *Daredevil* and Claremont's teenage mutant series *X-Men* and *New Mutants*. (The Turtles' martial arts *sensei* was a crusty sewer rat called Splinter instead of Stick.) If a dame with a rod is like a guy with a knitting needle, as an unwittingly Freudian gumshoe puts it in Jacques Tourneur's film noir *Out of the Past* (1947), then Elektra is a girl with *sai*—a three-pronged weapon of Oedipal one-upmanship if ever there was one. Miller chose *sai* because "the power of almost every karate blow can be amplified with it," giving her an edge against larger, stronger assailants.[11] He and Janson also made her beautiful and exotic looking—one image of her in *Daredevil* #190 is clearly swiped from contemporary photographs of Bo Derek, onetime star of sex comedies, soft-core movies, and *Playboy* magazine—without giving her the supermodel voluptuousness that John Byrne gave Phoenix and Storm of the X-Men. Rather, he based her body on that of Lisa Lyon, the champion bodybuilder and favorite photographic subject of Robert Mapplethorpe during the four years that Miller drew *Daredevil*. Basing a beautiful new comic-book villainess on photos of a professional weightlifter taken by a gay male artist may be the most brilliant prank Miller ever played on his adolescent male readers.

In Elektra's case, however, the bodybuilder trope is as much about sexuality as strength. Miller has frequently called out the comics industry on its tendency to give male superheroes unsuper girlfriends and trudge them both through dull domestic situations. Superheroes' costumed careers allow them to perform epic acts of physical prowess. Why not make their sexual lives just as superhuman, with all the bombast of leaping tall buildings in a single bound? Miller even calls the fierce battle between Elektra and Daredevil in #179 an example of "what superhero sex would be like."[12] Elektra was Miller's first attempt at hooking up two superbodies and probably his most important turn thus far away from Marvel's Silver Age signature, the hero as a nebbishy reflection of his readership. Why should extraordinarily powerful people like Superman or Spider-Man date normal humans like Lois Lane or Mary Jane Watson? Why wouldn't they look for their physical equals and pursue sex lives that bristle with the intensity of their heroic exploits? Miller is not vying for superverisimilitude here; rather, he appeals to a precedent outside comics altogether. By making Elektra a Greek warrior, Miller alludes to the sexual escapades of the heroes and gods of classical mythology and the unselfconscious acts of heroism that mark both the Homeric epics and the histories of Sparta that Miller pored over when planning *300*, his tribute to the Spartan army's final battle at the Hot Gates.

When Miller talks about Elektra this way in the context of superhero romance, however, he seems to be projecting his more recent fascination with supersex onto his earlier choices regarding Elektra. He is describing less the Elektra of Daredevil #168 than the Elektra of Miller and John Romita Jr.'s 1993 miniseries *Daredevil: The Man without Fear*, a revised and expanded treatment of DD's origin story that Miller had prepared for a proposed television series. This later incarnation of Elektra was not the demure, trusting persona that dies along with her father. Instead, she begins *The Man without Fear* as an Amazon, bounding around Manhattan from building to building wearing a maniacal grin, nearly killing people just for the thrill of it, while Matt, mesmerized by her prowess, mostly goes along for the ride. In the face of this Revised Standard Version of Elektra and of the Wonder Woman who wallops, bites, and then has violent, midair sex with Superman in Miller's *The Dark Knight Strikes Again!* (2001–2), it's easy to forget that in the beginning, Miller characterized Elektra's battles with Daredevil as necessary evils that pained them both, not rapturous moments of release. But it would be equally incorrect to assume that Miller made the early Elektra more vulnerable, like the typical girlfriend of a male superhero. Rather, he needed her to seem vulnerable in order to lead the reader to mistake her for a more conventional villainess/love-interest type, the good girl gone wrong—the Batman's Catwoman or Spider-Man's Black Cat, both sexy teases with hearts of gold, in a red head scarf. Elektra was "designed to get as much sympathy as possible from the audience, [but] appearance by appearance I've been trying to make them like her less," Miller said in 1981.[13]

Miller's emphasis on Elektra's cold efficiency during her first appearances, her lack of mercy or remorse when she kills her prey, probably looks anything but subtle to first-time readers now, but Miller managed to sneak up on his readers by relying on their expectations of a good-bad girl to distract them from the mayhem she caused. Another comics convention, violence without permanent consequences, also allowed him to hide her bloodthirstiness in plain sight as the body count continued to rise.

Elektra presses on the central paradox of Murdock's character harder than anyone else in the series. She is a serial murderer who profits from her cold and deliberate crimes, and when DD first encounters her "again" in #168, he reacts as we would expect him to. He stands in the storm-drenched street, rainwater running down his cheek like tears, and thinks to himself that he must "hunt Elektra down . . . and bring her to justice!" But he never does bring her in, despite all his opportunities during her fourteen-issue life span, and the fans noticed the discrepancy. "Not in my copy, he doesn't," wrote a reader of *Daredevil* #168 whose letter was published in #170, She goes on to say that she "bristled at DD's 'wonderfully' chauvinistic explanation for Elektra's 'life of crime'": that is, without her father's tempering influence, she couldn't help herself. There's more to this "chauvinism" than Elektra's Electra complex, however. Ultimately, Elektra exists to sharpen Miller's definition of Matt, as surely as the classical Hollywood action director Budd Boetticher used female characters merely to give the men something to save, argue about, and prove themselves over; "in herself," goes Laura Mulvey's infamous Boetticher quote, "the woman has not the slightest importance."[14] Or as Miller puts it, Elektra "test[s] how good Daredevil is."[15]

So is Elektra a "strong woman" or a castrating, misogynist stereotype? Sure, she kicks Massive Quantities of Ass, and if we judge the
autonomy of female comics characters exclusively on superhero comics' terms, perhaps there's not much else we can expect. And she does
foreshadow other determined female characters in Miller's oeuvre,
most notably Martha Washington, the African American freedom
fighter of his Dark Horse Comics series *Give Me Liberty* and its sequels
(Martha may be Miller's most psychologically complex character in
spite of her largely symbolic functions in the books). At the same time,
of course, Elektra once lures Daredevil into a punch with the promise
of a kiss and nearly chops off his foot in a power play, the Freudian
implications of which Miller himself describes as difficult to miss.[16] If
the phallus signifies not just male sexual potency but also the supposed
biological basis of male dominance, and in the Oedipal imaginary,
dominance is a zero-sum game between men and women, then all the
metal phalluses in the world would never give Elektra the advantage.
She has to possess Matt's, too, or demonstrate that she already controls
it, that he is "utterly helpless" against her as she puts it in #179, gloating
while he lies locked in the bear trap's grip. Even then he can't exile her
from his mind and heart and therefore can never defeat her. Like any
femme fatale, however, she's only dangerous insofar as she can resist
her own palpable desire for Matt, which Miller repeatedly represents
as a weakness more or less intrinsic to her femininity.

Miller doesn't reserve such character dynamics for women, of
course. He once grumbled that all it takes to peeve feminists is to create a female character who isn't a feminist role model,[17] but to be fair, he
never introduced a secondary character in *Daredevil* that didn't have
defining Matt as its ultimate function. Miller plays it coy with Elektra
at first by convincing us to root for her, and against Matt's conscience,
in hopes that her apparently positive qualities will eventually reform
her. He keeps us going on that ever-thinning hope for more than a
year. Time and again between her first appearance and her death in
#181, she nearly kills Matt or nearly leaves him to die or nearly skips an
opportunity to intervene and save his life—but stops herself. To goad
us further, Miller's third-person narration boxes relate her desire to
protect him in spite of herself, even to the point of leaving Japan for
the United States in *Daredevil* #174 when she overhears he is targeted

for assassination. Surely she still loves him, we think. She actually cries on the last page of #168 when she discovers that this nut in the devil suit, this man who has saved her life and now walks away with her would-be killer slung over his shoulder, is Matt Murdock, the man she used to tumble with on the Columbia lawn. She never cries, Miller has made a point of telling us in the flashback, not even when her father is laid to rest—until now.

All the buildup to Elektra's final appearance in #181 constructs an ethical trap for the reader. Gradually, Miller makes Elektra's behavior less and less redeemable, and then, just before Elektra's fatal battle with Bullseye, Miller springs the trap. In #179, Matt gets into a tussle with Elektra that his reporter friend Ben Urich, the issue's guest narrator, describes in terms of the contrast between the brutality of their fight and the agonized look on Daredevil's face: "He wants to make every part of her soft and loving." But it's that very hope that makes it possible for her to lure him into a more literal trap, the bear trap she has set to hold his foot, painfully, rather than sever it (figure 19). "With the bear trap there was some pretty vicious symbolism going on," Miller says; "that was meant just to be a horrible sequence. In a way I was trying to capsulize their whole relationship."[18] The battle concludes with Miller drawing an even bolder line between them. Upon hearing the hidden Urich hack up a lung from the shadows ("Ben, you've got to stop smoking those cigarettes. They'll kill you," DD tells Urich earlier), she flings one of her *sai* without hesitation, running Urich straight through the chest. "Lousy cigarettes," he chokes in one last narration box before a final, blackened panel apparently marks his death. Trap sprung. Angry letters poured into the Marvel offices castigating Miller for killing Urich, who suddenly seemed to be everyone's second-favorite character behind DD himself. (Urich turns up alive in the very next issue. Miller is playing his readers for suckers here.) I have to wonder if fan resentment at Ben's skewering was equally spurred by readers' disappointment at the simultaneous revelation that Elektra was beyond redemption.

Why manipulate readers this way? Why trick us into sympathizing with a character, even wishing for her reconciliation with Matt, only to reveal that she is nothing but a monster? Like the Hitchcockian "spectator trap" described by Robin Wood, Miller's reader trap presses us to acknowledge that we are the real sadists here, we spectators who derive voyeuristic pleasure from the havoc that fictional villains wreak on fictional bystanders.[19] To make the trap all the more insidious, Miller invites us to sympathize with Elektra's situation as a devastated daughter lashing out at the world, but in doing so, he shrewdly places us not in Elektra's perspective but in Matt's. Matt's faith that Elektra might be redeemed has caused him to set aside his responsibility to her victims, and if we sympathize with her along with him, we abdicate

FIGURE 19. Frank Miller and Klaus Janson, "Spiked!," *Daredevil* #179 (Marvel, February 1982).

the desire for justice that we, as avid superhero fans, supposedly share. In other words, Murdock's unbreakable duty to justice can still be bent in half when the law runs counter to his personal needs. If Daredevil is justice personified, then justice is more than blind; it's blinded by its own need to deny the reality right in front of it.

Stereotypical though Elektra may be, the larger dynamics of Miller's run make the gender politics of Elektra's love-hate relationship with Matt seem more self-conscious than, say, the kill-her-before-she-kills-you threat presented by Ava, the femme fatale in Miller's *Sin City: A Dame to Kill For* (both the 1993–94 comics series and the 2014 film). Tourneur's *Out of the Past* pits a modest, adoring blonde against the thieving, killing, exciting brunette in a typical noir bid to make male-affirmative femininity as distinct as possible from the desiring (and thus, goes the logic of film noir, castrating) kind. Bucking that trend, Elektra's competition is Heather Glenn, a sexually and financially independent brunette who desires Matt without threatening his masculinity. She dates other men occasionally but apparently in reaction to his inattentiveness (that is, his perpetual call to arms as Daredevil) and in hopes of making him jealous. The twisted joke of the final year of Miller's run, as I discussed in chapter 2, is that Murdock *makes* Heather into a punishable femme fatale, the corporate boss too ditzy to perform her duties, whom Matt leaves no options for the future save becoming Mrs. Murdock. In issue #186, Heather's response when Matt tells her he's preparing an incompetence defense for her is, "All right, Matt. I'll marry you," delivered with her head tilted downward, face completely lost in shadow. In film noir, the shadows that encircle the femme fatale are as much a projection of the male protagonist's misogyny as they are an expression of the woman's deceit; the difference between *Out of the Past* and this *Daredevil* scene is that Miller and Janson leave no doubt that Heather is the victim here. Their use of shadow to swallow her as she relents openly acknowledges that Matt is projecting on her the role he needs her to play.

Against the example of Matt's perverse urge to punish and control Heather, Elektra nearly seems a satirical figure, part of Miller's plot to undercut the myth he had cultivated so carefully of Matt the grown-up superhero, the stable, confident reverse image of Spider-Man. As with the secondary characters on Matt's side of the law, Elektra represents one of Matt's roads not taken. An orphaned adult like him, she is a dead ringer for Matt if he had let his anger at Battlin' Jack's death take control: while Elektra's ego is driven mad by grief, her id uses the father's death as an excuse to grab all the leash it wants. She is angry, vengeful, acting out her resentment against the law enforcement system that got her father killed, the same system that Matt superseded to find and punish his own father's killer. But there is also a messier Oedipal narrative on display here that reveals a masochistic shade of Matt's career as Daredevil. For Elektra is not just avenging her father; she is avenging her lost self, the possibility of a mature and self-determined identity she lost when her father died. She takes life and treasure ruthlessly, hysterically, as if the entire planet were the father from whom she must prove her independence by punishing him, breaking his laws, showing him who is really in charge now—all feats of self-assertion that his death renders moot. Matt goes about avenging himself in the opposite way by upholding the law, his shield against the pain his father caused him, but he cannot conclude the work of distanciation and defiance any more than Elektra can finish her own Oedipal conflict and move forward. He is doomed to repeat this battle endlessly, up to and including the pursuit of Elektra to punish or reform her: not only does he not believe she is dead and spends all of issue #182 maniacally trying to prove it, but he attempts to resurrect her by sheer force of will in #190.

In Miller and colorist Lynn Varley's 1990 graphic novel *Elektra Lives Again*, Miller at last makes the terms of Matt's obsession explicit. Haunted by what he believes are Elektra's attempts to reenter the world of the living, he temporarily loses the ability to distinguish between dreaming and waking and finds himself fighting by her side against the undead hordes who attempt to claim her for good. In the end, however, the soul of Elektra pleads with Matt to let her go; she "lives again"—against her own wishes—not because she is haunting Matt but *because he is haunting her.* Suddenly their entire relationship as delineated in issues #168 to #181 snaps to grid. Elektra is not an independent subject but Daredevil's projection of himself, the insatiable avenger of the violent crime that enforcers of the law committed against the father. So much of the saga is hooked to Matt's perspective that we cannot tell for certain whether we know her primarily by her own lights or whether what we have come to know as "Elektra" has actually been a representation of Matt's relationship to her as seen by him and only him. The real Elektra, if there is one, wants to be free to pursue something she can never have in Matt's presence: her own life, of which she is the author, and her own death. Miller has always said that he wanted Elektra to stay dead, a desire that Marvel has not honored since the writer D. G. Chichester and the artist Scott McDaniel resurrected the character in the mid-1990s and threw her back into the Marvel-universe continuity.[20] Still, I think of Miller's own quasi-resurrections of the character, first for the "prequel" *Elektra: Assassin* (1986–87), an eight-issue miniseries (with art by Bill Sienkiewicz) that takes place after her father's death but before her return to New York in *Daredevil* #168, then for *Elektra Lives Again*, as second chances Miller seems to feel he owed the character—chances for her to slip the noose of Matt's projections and become a character in her own right.

BULLSEYE

Despite Elektra's popularity and her importance to Miller's definition of Daredevil, Bullseye is the one indispensible playing piece in Miller's character study. DD had adversaries, many of whom held grudges after past battles, but as I've suggested, neither the villains nor the grudges added up to much reader interest. Bullseye is different. He is smart and amoral and loathes Daredevil far more bitterly even than DD's earliest adversary, the Owl—and let's face it, the Owl was a cheap knockoff of Spider-Man's foe the Vulture overdubbed with Doctor Doom's cackle. And the Owl just wanted to get rich; the source of Bullseye's indefatigable rancor is Oedipal hysteria. A dozen issues before Miller's debut, in *Daredevil* #146 (June 1977), the writer Jim Shooter's DD turned Bullseye into a cowering basket case simply by refusing to back down when held at gunpoint; then, on Miller's watch in #169 (March 1981), he saves Bullseye from being flattened by a subway train. To Bullseye, who had never been defeated by anyone besides Daredevil in any form of combat, this last is an insult that no retribution short of killing his savior can avenge.

In the Silver and Bronze Ages, Marvel villains differed from DC's traditional villains in that they tended to be damaged goods, as sympathetic in their way as the nebbishy heroes who battled them. They seesawed between the extremes of blood-and-thunder stage melodrama: either they were flat-out types, determined to rule/destroy the universe just because the casting call required it, or they were as abused and misunderstood as Frankenstein's monster and had to be saved from themselves. Often they were both at once, as was Doctor Octopus, the brilliant cyberneticist whose personality was corrupted by the same explosion that fused his mechanical arms to his torso, or Doctor Doom, another nonphysician mastermind who, for all his cruelty and ambition, was a tortured, disfigured, sometimes sentimental tyrant who always kept his word.

Miller took a second-string assassin and made him both dangerous and a primary threat to Daredevil's idealism. For Marv Wolfman, who introduced the character in issue #131, Bullseye was cruel but mostly in it for the money, and he spoke like Snidely Whiplash (or the Kingpin as written by Stan Lee). He continued to spout supercilious threats and insults through his McKenzie-Miller appearances, which otherwise paint him as a generic bad guy. The first line of dialogue that McKenzie writes for him in *Daredevil* #160 goes like this: "Good evening, Natasha Romanoff. A lovely night for murder, isn't it?" He sounds like a radio actor rehearsing an episode of *The Shadow*, fastidiously mentioning the first and last name of his quarry so the audience at home gets its expository fix. The rest of the story is just as conventional, climaxing with Natasha nearly getting cut in two by a roller coaster after Bullseye—apparently picking up a cue from Snidely himself—ties her to the tracks. As if to drain the last drops of plausibility from the story, Bullseye has actually tied down a dummy, thus giving DD the chance to use his hypersenses to determine that the roller coaster is not really plummeting toward a human being, which in turn gives Bullseye the chance to scream, "He knew! Somehow . . . some way . . . he knew!" like the dutiful stock villain McKenzie tried to make of him. It turns out that Bullseye is letting an evil, knife-throwing carny use the Black Widow for target practice somewhere in the bowels of the amusement park, which naturally take a while because the carny really, really enjoys throwing knives that barely miss his target. The arc of Bullseye's evil scheme has all the finesse and poise of a cliffhanger from an Adam West *Batman* episode.

Already, though, Miller transcends the material by formal means. He manipulates the reader's access to key plot information. He conceals Daredevil's realization about the Widow decoy until Bullseye knows that he knows, making us wonder momentarily whether DD, who first rushes to save Natasha but suddenly turns tail, has decided to chalk her up to collateral damage when in reality his hypersenses have determined that the dummy Black Widow doesn't have a heartbeat. Graphically, Miller makes the roller-coaster trap scary, much scarier than the silly Rube Goldberg traps perpetually bested by Batman and Robin on the TV show. The roller-coaster car's path to the Black Widow dummy is mapped onto a two-page spread that emphasizes the height and expanse of the tracks, how it outscales the tiny body tied to them, all from a canted bird's-eye perspective that characterizes what we will come to know as Bullseye's mental take on the proceedings according to Miller. It's all fun and games for him as he looks down his nose at his victims, treating them like the insects he believes they are. His victims deserve to die because they are weak—and because they aren't him.

The psychotic narcissism that Miller grants Bullseye in #169 is revving up already before Miller even picks up the scripting duties. This quality wouldn't distinguish Bullseye from the megalomaniac villains of the thirties pulps except that Miller and McKenzie give him a nervous breakdown at the end of #161, brought on by Daredevil taunting him with the fact that though they have sparred at least three times before, Bullseye hasn't managed to kill him yet. Bullseye is reduced to sobs. The reduction of Bullseye to a basket case is over the top, to be sure, but this competitive twist to the Daredevil-Bullseye relationship seems to be what Miller needed to make him a real menace. Now, as characters in eighties action movies used to say, it's personal.

When Miller brings Bullseye back in #169, it's as an escaped mental patient whose hunger to kill Daredevil has driven him over the edge on which he had teetered since his last defeat. Now he sees everyone in New York as Daredevil, and Miller lets us view this delusion through his eyes, cementing his characterization as psychotic but also overlapping his insanity in a startling way with the creative powers of the cartoonist, not to mention the spell that superpowered wish fulfillment holds on its readers. Miller draws a Daredevil costume onto everyone walking through Times Square as Bullseye shrieks in paralyzed terror; and then, once readers are standing in the trap of enjoying Bullseye's delusion (bulky, boom-box-bearing guys and petite women both look pretty funny wearing devil suits), Miller again snaps it shut when Bullseye begins killing them one after another, sometimes a couple at a time. Funny stuff, right? Miller may as well tell us up front that we are the disturbed ones for enjoying stories that depend for dramatic conflict on the villain torturing the hero's body. *Is this why you keep reading issue after issue? To see the villain try endlessly to murder the good guys?* Miller seems to ask. *Let's see how you like it when it happens two or three times in each panel, and the villain happens to succeed.*

With Miller egging on Bullseye, the character became the most cold-blooded asshole in comics. I use "asshole" in the most technical sense, as defined by the philosopher Aaron James; no other descriptor does justice to Bullseye's sense of entitlement and his total lack of obligation to the needs of anyone besides himself.[21] Not all supervillains are assholes. Doctor Doom would kill thousands to serve his cause, but he never breaks his word, even if it means scrapping the cause altogether. Doc Ock takes life lightly and is a bit more of a thug than Doom, but he doesn't go out of his way to kill if he can make good on his larger plan without doing so. Bullseye doesn't even hate anyone, perhaps not even Daredevil. He just wants to make people suffer and then stop breathing. He would do or say anything for the opportunity to follow through on that hobby, and while he recognizes others' desire to survive, for him that desire only serves as leverage for getting something else he wants, often the whereabouts of someone he has been paid to kill. I think Miller isolated and amplified the asshole in Bullseye because, as a creature of chaos, he presents a better foil to Daredevil's legal idealism than does the Kingpin, who at least has respect for a formidable enemy, or Elektra, for whom Murdock still carries a torch. Bullseye has no hidden pain to sympathize with, either, as does Kingpin in his worship of Vanessa or Elektra with her tortured feelings for Matt. Because Miller makes Bullseye a total waste of carbon and water, he puts to the ultimate test Daredevil's passionate belief that everyone is innocent until proven guilty in a court of law. When it is unclear whether Bullseye is responsible for the murders he commits while suffering from a brain tumor, Daredevil chooses to assume his innocence and let the legal system decide his fate in due course. Though he lives to regret it, Miller's Daredevil would not, could not have made any other choice. In the 1982 *Comics Feature* interview, Miller says that "Murdock's concern—and Daredevil's concern—is with the victim of crime, not with the criminal. And someone falsely charged with a crime is a victim of the crime, as well."[22] The toll on Matt's conscience would doubtless have been greater had he allowed Bullseye to die without standing before a jury of his peers.

There's a curious way in which Bullseye acts as DD's doppelgänger over the course of Miller's run. Thirty years ago, I wasn't able to get a handle on what the nature of this twinning might be. I loved the drawings (despite my serious problems with the execution, as I explain in chapter 4), but I loved them as drawings, for what they showed the artist could do. And I went through *Daredevil* so quickly every time I read and reread an issue that I doubt I could have uncovered anything beyond the most superficial similarities. As I wrote this book and considered Daredevil's radar sense as a formal device, however, I noticed something that my younger self couldn't slow down long enough to catch. The similarities begin with the costume designs, and once the figures are in motion, the parallels only get clearer. They wear similar bodysuits, they share similar physical strength and similar fighting skills, and they are both disciplined to a fault. And the target pattern on Bullseye's uniform—concentric circles decorating the forehead of his mask and circling his shoulders, as if his head were the target's center—is identical to Daredevil's radar sense as visualized by Wally Wood. Marv Wolfman and John Romita Sr., who according to Wolfman designed Bullseye together,[23] had visualized him as the perfect nemesis for Daredevil, an assassin whose sheer accuracy could turn those figurative rings around Daredevil's head into a nearly literal bull's-eye. It's an alarming graphic reversal, an icon for how Daredevil's greatest asset as a fighter meets its match in a fighter with similar, even superior abilities to locate adversaries and pinpoint their weaknesses—something like the demonic mirror image of Daredevil's radar sense, a lizard-brain GPS unencumbered by Daredevil's conscience or the sightlessness for which Matt endlessly overcompensates. And while Daredevil focuses tirelessly on justice, Bullseye has an equal and opposite urge for anarchy, for decimating the rights of others just to see what will happen.

All these startling similarities have their basis in Romita's visual design and Wolfman's intentions for Bullseye as depicted by Wolfman and the artist Bob Brown in *Daredevil* #131–132. Nevertheless, Miller made the character his own for as long as he wrote the series. Simply by existing, his Bullseye poses a question rarely asked in superhero comics before Miller: To what degree do we gauge the greatness of our heroes by their adherence to the law? To become monumental, bigger than life, can they stick to legal remedies, or must they step beyond them? Bullseye's utter dedication to mass murder—his decisiveness, his ability to turn thought into action instantaneously, his unflinching faith in the inferiority of his victims—makes him closer to Miller's hero ideal than Daredevil is, at least where instincts and drive are concerned. Miller's "true" hero, for better or worse (and Miller recognizes both sides of this coin), does not truck with communal human standards, no matter how rightly or convincingly one might criticize the hero's actions according to those standards. This is not to say that Miller paints Bullseye as heroic but rather that, like the Joker, the arch nemesis of the Batman, Miller's Bullseye forces Daredevil to question whether the law is always adequate to the cause of justice. By Miller's definition, the most heroic act Daredevil performs in this run comes at the end of issue #181, when DD, hanging from a telephone wire, releases Bullseye's hand just as the assassin moves to stab his would-be savior and says, "You'll kill no one—ever again!" with the matter-of-factness of a judge meting out a death sentence. Here Daredevil's Christian charity gives way to ruthlessness, perhaps to avenge Elektra's death, perhaps for more lofty reasons regarding the safety of innocent citizens. Miller never lets us know for certain which motivation won out.

Whatever Daredevil's reasons, for at least this moment, his evolving sense of justice places him, in his own mind, above the law. Miller does leave open the question of whether dropping Bullseye is simply an instinctual act; Elektra's own *sai*, the one Bullseye killed her with, is now on its way to Daredevil's throat when DD lets his enemy drop, shattering his spine and rendering him a mind trapped in a paralyzed shell of a body. But motive or duress aside, the act itself is indistinguishable from one of Bullseye's murders in that one person, without legal oversight, is commandeering the life or prosperity of another. No wonder that for much of this final, climactic struggle, Bullseye and Daredevil appear only as indistinguishable silhouettes.

Miller had the good judgment to raise more questions than he answers regarding what U.S. comic-book readers really expect of their heroes. In hindsight, the entirety of Miller's run reads like a continuous story thread in which Daredevil faces a series of challenges to his determination to remain, somehow, right on the line between law and lawlessness—challenges that come primarily in the form of these three villains. Each encounter with them, each epic labor strips away more of Murdock's ability to ignore his own defiance of the law. All the while, and in spite of the physical and psychological damage he sustains as a result, Matt remains blind to the walking contradiction he has become until the very end, in #191, when he faces Bullseye for the final time in Miller's run. I'll wait to discuss that ending until we get to where it belongs, at the end. But I'll offer a hint: Miller's *Daredevil* is the only creator run I can remember on a comic book in which the ultimate climax hinges not on the hero saving the world but on the hero realizing who and what he really is beneath his own idealism. Forgive me if I don't want to spoil the outcome just yet.

COMICS FOR COMICS' SAKE

Frank Miller was probably Marvel's most prolific cover artist during his *Daredevil* years, next to Dave Cockrum, the cocreator of the New X-Men. I was eleven and had never been to New York when Miller's cover for *Daredevil* #163 (cover dated March 1980) swallowed me into Miller's vision of Hell's Kitchen, metonymized by a dingy alley filled to bursting with a monstrous threat (figure 20).

Two things stood out about the cover of #163: blood and the Hulk. Let's begin with the Hulk, the Frankenstein's monster of the Marvel universe and, at the time, a prime-time star with his own live-action series on CBS. The Hulk never laid claim to my imagination the way Spider-Man did. Hulk stories of the early 1980s rarely strayed from a single bait-and-switch routine: somebody is kind to the Hulk or his "puny" alter ego, Bruce Banner; somebody else kills or otherwise messes with the kind somebody; Banner gets really, really mad and changes into the gigantic, universally misunderstood Hulk (somehow without rendering his human-sized pants unwearable); the Hulk beats the bejeezus out of the evil somebody else while destroying real estate and yelling "Hulk smash!!" and other epithets in which he names himself in the third person; the Hulk gets chased by the military; Hulk transforms back into Banner, whose shredded pants *still* fit, and wanders off in a daze; we beg our psychiatrists to increase our dosages of Paxil in anticipation of it all happening again when the next issue hits the spinner rack at the neighborhood QuikTrip.

Miller's cover defined the Hulk not by these conventions but by the dynamic between him and Daredevil, while audaciously leaving four-fifths of the Hulk's body out of the image. Both heroes are clearly

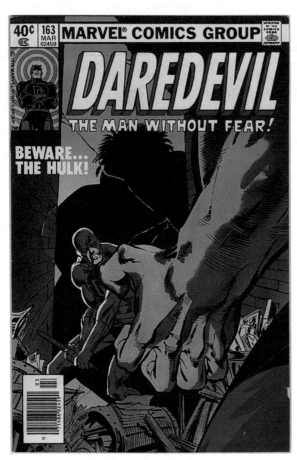

FIGURE 20. Frank Miller and Josef Rubenstein, cover to *Daredevil* #163 (Marvel, March 1980).

"there," the latter named explicitly in a familiarly terse hunk of Marvel boilerplate—"Beware . . . the Hulk!"—but we only get a clear look at the one in the red tights. To put the Hulk across, Miller and inker Joe Rubenstein render nothing but a giant green arm jutting into the frame from the top right, its fist dominating a quadrant of the cover, and a massive shadow of a fright-wigged head looming on the wall behind Daredevil as the Man Without Fear stands in the alley, teeth gritted in concentration, pain, or both, gripping his billy club low like a National League pitcher waiting to bunt.

And then there's the blood. In my childhood experience, Marvel characters routinely got beaten with fists and blunt instruments, kicked with metal boots, dropped from great heights, and sometimes even shot, but they rarely bled. Wounds and bruises looked like spotty black ink or scratchy crosshatching, and gunshots usually doubled people over, conveniently obscuring their painful and deadly gut wounds (the bloodless, contorted death of Betty Brant's brother in Ditko and Lee's *Amazing Spider-Man* #11 from April 1964 being the Platonic ideal of that trope). When characters died, as they did on occasion, they had never looked better; one need only glance at the last couple of pages of *Amazing Spider-Man* #121 (June 1973), featuring the stylishly dressed and coiffed body of Gwen Stacey just after she dies of a broken neck, for a representative image of Marvel mortality in the 1970s. But Daredevil is *bleeding* right there on the cover of #163. Blood pours from his mouth and nose in a suspended cataract of black ink (not red; the Comics Code had to draw the line somewhere). In spite of what both Daredevil and readers know about the gentle and just nature of the Hulk's soul, the cover defines this issue's protagonist-antagonist relationship in terms not of sympathy or mere sparring but of violence with consequences—violence that, the giant shadow portends, will only get more deadly. The frame angle and level at which the drawing places viewers helps develop this dynamic even further. At first it appears to position viewers at knee level looking up, the better to symbolize how outmatched this normal-sized hero is compared to Marvel's "Green Goliath." Then, after a moment, we register that we are seeing from knee level all right, but it's the Hulk's knee level—no low-angle framing is necessary to incite the usual low-angle sense of dread. The shadow the Hulk casts does not exaggerate his height at all. Instead it issues a warning: *In a moment, this monster will land the last punch against a determined, strong, but hopelessly normal man in a brawl that only someone expecting to die would willingly join.*

Something about the drama Miller injected into this cover without even showing me the antagonist's face made #163 worth my forty cents. Part of my attraction, I'm certain, derived from my desire to draw comics myself. For several years, my brother and I had produced our own version of *The Amazing Spider-Man* on our father's used typing paper, which we glued together and stapled into comic books that featured the *Spider-Man* daily comic strip, my brother's parody comic "Spider-Hag" (premise: what if elderly Aunt May, not her nephew Peter Parker, had been bitten by the radioactive spider?) and my own attempt at a "serious" Spidey strip, an endeavor mostly cobbled from layouts, poses, and plot bits plagiarized from Silver Age *Amazing Spider-Man* pages by John Romita Sr. and the late 1970s Pocket Books reprints of the first dozen or so Ditko stories. By the end of 1979, when this Hulk cover appeared on the stands, I was a little disappointed by current comics. I had a dim sense that the Bronze Age Marvel heroes were just the Silver Age versions driven into cul-de-sacs of plot repetition and character self-loathing, with a different villain every other month to spruce things up. Miller's cover didn't look like a retread of anything, though. For the first time since I began reading comics that didn't star talking animals or a happy-go-lucky phantom who looked like, as Bart Simpson once put it, the ghost of Richie Rich, a cover drawing had caught my attention irrespective of the characters in it. The cover radiated real menace and real violence, both of which were in short supply in the Spider-Man and Fantastic Four comics I was reading. I wasn't hooked, not yet, but at last I had glimpsed a forbidden image of mortality, something I'd never known I was looking for in a comic book.

At this point, before Miller had even begun to script *Daredevil*, he was already giving the series something it hadn't had in years and badly needed: a sense of danger, the possibility that anything could happen and the creators didn't care who knew it. I had learned only a little about Daredevil from reading *Son of Origins of Marvel Comics* (1975), the second volume in a compilation of Marvel origin stories, and thumbing through random issues at a friend's house, but I hadn't been much interested in the character until #162, a filler issue (a stand-alone story that waits in an editor's file until a series's regular creators need time to catch up on their deadlines) with cover and interiors by Steve Ditko. So I lied: I *had* chosen at least one cover for the drawing alone before #163, because I knew Ditko's *Spider-Man* and was thrilled to find he was still drawing Marvel comics. Like Miller's Hulk cover, Ditko's cover for #162 swipes a moment of plot the way a well-chosen excerpt from an epic poem can narrate a specific event while always keeping our minds on the big picture—the Trojan War, the wages of jealousy, the loyalty of dogs, and so forth. Daredevil, standing ready at the left with his head cocked toward his shoulder, senses a leopard leaping on him from the right. Ditko renders Daredevil's perception as it had been rendered for more than a decade, as concentric circles emanating from Horn Head's head. The difference in my attraction to the two covers is that I chose Ditko for style and Miller for storytelling. What Ditko's cover doesn't do, and Miller's does, is announce something more profound about the character than his generic readiness for action. Each cover shows him in danger, but while Ditko does a serviceable job of showing Daredevil threatened by a surprise attack, Miller portrays him facing risk head-on, planting his feet and steeling himself for impact.

The choice of the Hulk as Daredevil's adversary also reflects Miller's determination to look to the beginnings of the series for fresh perspectives on the character. The referent for this story, and the tension it creates between the superhuman adversary and the all-too-human hero, is Daredevil's tangle with the Sub-Mariner in *Daredevil* #7 (April 1965), by Stan Lee and Wally Wood. There Daredevil, refusing to submit to a powerhouse who had fought the entire Fantastic Four to a standstill, takes one terrible beating after another but keeps getting up to try again. In the end, the Sub-Mariner, awed by Daredevil's dedication, decides to let New York alone. Miller says that his pitch for the Daredevil-Hulk standoff became "an office joke: Daredevil fights the Hulk—what happens in panel two?" But being allowed to do the story also allowed Miller and the writer Roger McKenzie to strip back the character: "The Hulk story was in fact an attempt to reestablish what the Sub-Mariner story established about Daredevil to begin with. He is capable of losing, but he doesn't let that stop him. I find him to be much more heroic than most of the superheroes because of that, because the odds are certainly against him. I mean his outstanding quality is a handicap, and I think the [Sub-Mariner] material related to that."[1] The character implications of this mismatched fight are deceptively simple. Daredevil, "the Man without Fear" as the book's masthead reminds us, will defend Hell's Kitchen even if he has to street-fight a nine-foot green Yeti to do it. And he'll do it without his vision, the one sense without which even a fair fight is nearly impossible for most of us to imagine. This is a hero who willingly jumps into the abyss, confident in his abilities and, more, sure of his reasons, his moral code of action.

This cover distills the argument of this chapter: Miller not only wrote *Daredevil* first and foremost as a character study; he drew it that way, as well. The pose of determination that Daredevil strikes on the cover of #163, the many drawings in the issue itself of the Hulk towering over DD by more than a yard—Miller made these choices on the basis of the character's mission, the personality traits that complicate the ethics of that mission, and the social Darwinist urban environment that circumscribes the work he does as a costumed vigilante. What I really want to establish, though, is the approach to superhero drawing that Miller introduced with *Daredevil* and how his style complemented his creative agenda on the series. Style in comics is notoriously hard to discuss—Charles Hatfield reminds us that for the comics giant Will Eisner, style in art "is our failure to achieve perfection"[2]—but in the narrative (or at least serial) image media of film and comics, we can probably agree that *style* refers to certain technical choices that become staples of a specific creator's work. It also demarcates the idiosyncratic, excessive quality of these choices, their occasional resistance to economical storytelling, their irreducibility to narrative functions. Well-known characters are often the litmus test by which readers discern the presence of a particular artist's style or the absence of any such thing. For example, though Rich Buckler's Marvel and DC covers of the seventies were about as dynamic as covers drawn by the equally prolific Neal Adams, Buckler's renderings of characters looked like templates, model sheets for artists learning to draw a certain character; I can never identify a Buckler cover unless I'm close enough to see the signature (though these days, lack of stylistic identity has now become a marker of "Buckler" for me). Miller is on the opposite end of the style scale from Buckler. Whether I'm looking at a Miller drawing of Daredevil or Bullseye or a minor character's face or hand or a cityscape or even a table lamp, the provenance of the drawing is never in doubt, and that's part of the story of how Miller, a creator with very little visibility before this, made Daredevil *his* character.

As I've suggested, style is by no means synonymous with rendering skills. In a review of the first issue of Miller's six-issue miniseries *Ronin* (DC, 1983–84), Miller's first major work after *Daredevil* and *Wolverine*, the late Kim Thompson praises DC Comics for giving a creator near-complete freedom in everything from editorial control and color separation to fine details of the printing process. Further raising expectations, DC published *Ronin* on high-quality Baxter paper using far better presses than those used to produce newsprint comics, resulting in finer line reproduction, more uniform areas of black, and a much-broadened color spectrum that gave the colorist Lynn Varley unprecedented freedom to experiment. Then comes the bad news. Miller's draftsmanship, Thompson argues, is objectively terrible. He criticizes Miller's grasp of linear perspective and human anatomy but reserves his real ire for Miller's handling of "action":

> The artwork [in *Ronin* #1] is thoughtfully designed and meticulously executed, and virtually none of it is any good. Miller still

draws the human body very badly; his characters never balance or move correctly. Now, in a book that is mostly composed of fight scenes, it would seem quite a liability to have an artist who doesn't draw action well. In a sense, though, Miller doesn't draw action at all. I had begun to notice this in *Daredevil*, and it is even truer of *Ronin*: Miller's panels, individually, are usually immobile. They display people posing before and after the action; every movement happens *between* the panels. Significantly, the few panels where the characters actually *do* move are among the worst constructed and least convincing.[3]

Thompson makes a few claims here that are hard to dispute. He argues that a relevant percentage of comics artists, notably such stars as Marshall Rogers and Jim Starlin, perfected their signature styles before they learned to draw the human figure (or anything else) correctly from life and subsequently missed their chance to learn to represent what they see with any degree of realism: "[Miller] seems totally unable to *translate what he sees* onto the page. Somewhere between his eye and his hand, reality runs afoul of his technique."[4]

Looking at Miller's *Daredevil*, even the later issues of his run, it's not difficult to see where Thompson is coming from. Anatomically, some of Miller's drawings are just plain bad. I used to go through issues #163 through #165 in particular and wonder, enviously, how he even got a foot in Marvel's door if he couldn't draw convincing facial expressions or proportions: hands were too small for bodies, legs were impossibly long or looked as though they were about to shake right off their pivots, objects were four times the size they ought to have been. I've collected a few of my favorites here. Call it "Mood-Breaking Loopiness for the Soul," my personal collection of examples where Miller's plastic approach to physical reality made *Daredevil* look like a Daffy Duck cartoon with low-key lighting:

- Matt, having just defeated his personal demon and regained his radar sense, smiles a stoned, toothless smile like James Franco's *Freaks and Geeks* character after getting a C on a quiz instead of the expected D– (figure 21).
- Matt touches the Rushmore-sized face of Elektra's corpse with his teeny-weeny hands (figure 22).

 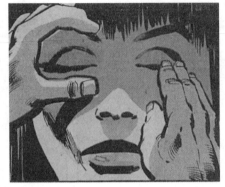 

FIGURE 21 (LEFT). Frank Miller and Klaus Janson, panel from *Daredevil* #177 (Marvel, December 1981). FIGURE 22 (MIDDLE). Frank Miller and Klaus Janson, panel from *Daredevil* #182 (Marvel, May 1982). FIGURE 23 (RIGHT). Frank Miller and Klaus Janson, panel from *Daredevil* #173 (Marvel, August 1981).

- Betsy, the Gladiator's parole officer, prepares to defend herself against an assailant by grabbing a knife with equally teeny-weeny hands that would look perfectly appropriate on Kristen Wiig's potty-mouthed "Judice" character from *Saturday Night Live* (figure 23).
- When discussing Daredevil's secret identity, Bullseye gets an extreme close-up in which he suddenly has a huge nose and a toothy smile that makes him look like Milton Berle—though to be fair, Miller never publicly recognized Uncle Milty as his photo reference for the world's deadliest assassin (figure 24).
- The mouth of the slimeball drug dealer Hogman, disembodied by an extreme close-up panel, eats spaghetti with a fork the size of a large toothpick (figure 25).
- At a picnic, Heather slams an apple into Matt's mouth at a velocity usually reserved for dunking a basketball, somehow leaving his teeth intact (figure 26).

My brother Tim and I used to point at these pictures and guffaw like rubes at a freak show. Not only is Hogman's fork tiny; it looks like the copyeditor scratched it in at the last minute with a ballpoint pen! Did the head of Elektra's corpse swell to twice its original size while it lay in wait for Matt's Lilliputian hands to cradle it? Why does

FIGURE 24 (LEFT). Frank Miller and Klaus Janson, panels from *Daredevil* #181 (Marvel, April 1982). FIGURE 25 (RIGHT). Frank Miller and Klaus Janson, panel from *Daredevil* #184 (Marvel, July 1982). FIGURE 26 (ABOVE). Frank Miller and Klaus Janson, panel from *Daredevil* #171 (Marvel, June 1981).

overcoming his demons cause Matt to grin like the wake-and-baked subject of a K-Mart portrait photograph? Tim and I couldn't see these images as anything but bona fide errors, even though we knew something of how strict the editors at Marvel and DC were about things like proportion and perspective. But consider the era as you mull our reactions. The Bronze Age was a literalist period for comics art. The influence of Neal Adams, a late addition to the Silver Age Marvel stable, still saturated the market. Adams was a stylist, certainly, but he worked on the "realist" end of the scale. The bodies he drew were not bulked up like Kirby's New Gods, but they had muscles—hundreds of them, more than most comics fans knew the human body had; and Adams drew them all from angles that no one else in comics had bothered to attempt. The difference was that he knew how to draw them accurately from any point of view without sacrificing the dynamism that readers expected.

Under Adams's influence, caricature and symbolic gesture were gently pushed out the window of the superhero business in favor of delicately rendered bodies that were always in motion. If Kirby centered his heroic anatomy on characters' legs, Adams focused on arms, snaky but uncannily real-looking appendages that turned conversations and arguments into some of the most energizing images on a given page. His X-Men were skinny figures who expressed themselves in spidery gestures, often with hands jutting out to the reader in forced perspective compositions that nevertheless had all the depth cues necessary to convince readers that Adams drew them from life while peering through wide-angle camera lenses. Nothing was rushed, nothing accidental. Adams's influence dominated the field for a long time to come; even the brilliant Bill Sienkiewicz, who later flouted the flatness of comics by using impasto and gluing physical objects to his pages for Chris Claremont's *New Mutants* and Miller's own *Daredevil: Love and War* and *Elektra: Assassin*, joined the first *Moon Knight* series in 1980 as an Adams clone. There was room for many such clones in the industry, especially after Adams, an early crusader for the creators' right to own the characters they invented, pulled out of Marvel and DC altogether.

The dominance of writer-editors over artists in the Marvel comics of the early seventies, a point made definitively by Sean Howe, didn't make it any easier for artists to set themselves apart from the pack even if they had wanted to.[5] In addition, the Marvel method was still in full force, and while it had clearly augmented the quality of some series depending on the artist doing the plotting and character design (Kirby on *The Fantastic Four* and Ditko on "Doctor Strange" in *Strange Tales* representing its creative zenith), historically the method had not been kind to *Daredevil*. In the early seventies, Gerry Conway, the first writer to have the misfortune of following Stan Lee on *Amazing Spider-Man*, was also writing *Daredevil* and seemed determined to cycle Peter Parker's anguished mental tirades through Matt Murdock. In the meantime, Gene Colan was still drawing his pages for the book before the script was fully written, plotting out the story from action to action, which would likely have looked just fine had Conway's dialogue and captions stuck closer to the storytelling. As Colan's drawings show Daredevil fighting for his life against the Minotaur and other baddies, Conway's thought balloons have Daredevil agonizing over his fear of committing to the love of his life, Karen Page, and wondering whether he makes like a superhero primarily to avoid the question. The result for the reader is something like trying to listen to two vivid pop songs—an original, catchy tune and a hackneyed knockoff of last month's Top 10 hit—simultaneously. In Daredevil's case, the disjunction between word and image is particularly alarming because he, of all heroes, seems to require preternatural focus to get through brawls like these. How does this man, who relies entirely on a nuked-up amalgam of his remaining senses to survive and even win his battles, manage to subdue supervillains twice his size when he's mentally trashing his own motives all the while?

And that was just the *early* seventies. Now, in 1979, the writer-editors, though their day was waning, dominated the bullpen, and Lee's vision of characters defined by neurotic self-doubt seemed ineradicable. And however unique, the styles of Bob Brown and such short-timing *Daredevil* pencilers as Kane, Colan, Heck, the DC expatriate Carmine Infantino, John Buscema, Buscema's younger brother Sal, and Jim Mooney were fresh to nobody any longer. As one of the industry's few writer-artists, the relative newcomer Jim Starlin had done remarkable things with floundering characters like Captain Marvel and Warlock by raising the superheroic stakes from protecting the innocent to defending solar systems, thus porting Kirby's cosmic scope into the psychedelic, post-Vietnam era. Changes in aesthetic approach—chances taken with style, story, and hoary old character patterns—seemed unlikely to occur without infusing this or that series's creative team with similar energy, and that meant shaking up personnel.

Miller and his upstart generation of fans-turned-creators showed up at Marvel at just the right moment. However little Marvel's creators appreciated Jim Shooter at the end of his tenure as Marvel's editor in chief, at the end of the 1970s, his rise to the position coincided with the end of the writer-editor system and the recentralization of editorial control.[6] While centralization might sound stifling to creative freedom, its effect at Marvel was in part to hand more control over characters and their series back to the artists, and in this case, doing so meant giving a break to the new class of young pencilers who ached to draw their favorite characters. Around 1976, he joined an amateur press association called APA-5, a group of young creators who circulated work to each other by mail; there Miller tried his hand at crime and suspense stories rather than superheroes.[7] As he has often mentioned in interviews, he also began carting his portfolio to New York to ask advice from the industry legend Neal Adams, who would rip his work to shreds and send him back to Vermont to try again. He got his first major work at several different companies in anthology books, long a testing ground for new talent but by no means a guaranteed springboard to success. Moving to New York with no resources except his battered portfolio and the ability to stomach ramen noodles for weeks at a stretch, he freelanced on anthology series: issues #84 (June 1978) and #85 (July 1978) of Gold Key's *Twilight Zone* series (figure 27) and DC's *Weird War Tales* #64 (June 1978) and #68 (October 1978).

That early work is recognizably Miller's, but recognizability isn't necessarily a compliment. It showcases technical choices and tricks that he would capitalize on later but lacks the compositional rigor of his later work. Characters have the same eyes Miller draws to this day, eyes that are too large for the faces that bear them, with lids stylized to look more like parallel lines than ovals or almonds. They stare wide, sometimes without seeming to have any consciousness behind them except a kind of hollow terror. Compositionally, panels are resolutely rectangular, but the images they contain veer off in all directions. The diagonals prioritize movement within the panels, the better to keep our eyes off the awkward perspective and the mostly empty backgrounds. Inking his own pencils for Gold Key (something he did infrequently enough at that stage that he singles out a black-and-white Elektra story for *Bizarre Adventures* #28, October 1981, as nearly his first attempt)[8] allowed Miller to distinguish his art by preserving its inherent cartoonishness, with gestures and emotions resembling the idealized boilerplate drawings that accompany dictionary definitions (*grimace, fist, tooth*).

DC's *Weird War Tales* specialized in throwaway shorts about possessed superior officers and infantrymen who sell their souls to Satan in exchange for survival on the battlefield. Pat as they are, such stories offered amateur cartoonists something that Denny O'Neil once bemoaned as a lost resource, the chance to draw brief, low-stakes tales for a major publisher and make mistakes without jeopardizing their futures.[9] In spite of the low risk, however, *Weird War Tales'* editors seemed unwilling to take chances on Miller's unusual style. Here his drawings were subjected to Danny Bulandi, an inker who approached artists' figures the way a steamroller approaches gravel, flattening every dynamic point to the same level of torpor. Still, Bulandi may

FIGURE 27. Frank Miller, "Royal Feast," *The Twilight Zone* #84 (Gold Key, June 1978).

actually have helped Miller by exacerbating his difficulties with drawing the human figure in repose. Or perhaps the real problem was that Miller hadn't learned Lee and Kirby's lesson that superheroes should never stand or walk undynamically; *everybody* had to look as though they were leaning into a punch it took all their strength to throw.

In 1978–79, Miller also drew shorts and full-length stories for Marvel, minifeatures buried in the back pages of series annuals and a few issues of second-tier series like *Marvel Two-in-One*, a team-up book featuring the Thing from the Fantastic Four and a rotating lineup of guest stars. Of all the mainstream books Miller had worked on up to that point, however, *John Carter, Warlord of Mars* seemed to suit him best. Neal Adams's turns with Batman, Superman, Deadman, Green Lantern, and other DC heroes in the early 1970s had made "realistic" anatomy de rigueur for superhero comics, with results that Miller has described as both rejuvenating and restrictive for the next generation of cartoonists: "By following in [Adams's] footsteps, [comics artists] have restricted themselves a bit as to what can be done with drawing and what can be done with caricature, and there are other ways to work."[10] The issue of *John Carter* that Miller drew (#18, cover date November 1978), in which four-armed Martians battle to the death, gives him license to try one of these "other ways." He makes the alien bodies look plausible while still playing around with their expressive possibilities, like a political cartoonist trying his hand at rendering *Conan*-era Barry Smith characters—barbarians, aliens, statuesque women wearing steel bikinis—rather than caricatures of politicians.

When Miller started drawing *Daredevil*, his skills hadn't progressed much past the awkward character anatomy that marked him as a fan artist. His first issue, #158, is a step beyond his *John Carter* work, but not by much. The cartooniness hasn't diminished from his pair of *Twilight Zone* stories from the previous year, but there's also a grimness on display that feels both overstated and, for lack of a better descriptor, attractively raw. Miller makes the panels extremely busy, cramming them with superfluous details and fussing interminably over minor elements that drive young artists crazy, like the Black Widow's strappy heels on the splash page. He appears to be proving to the readership that he can draw, that he can lay out pages in a way that keeps the eye darting, and most of all that that he's worthy of a regular assignment on a superhero book published by the top comics publisher in the United States. Some of the unrealistic foibles from his first assignments—the occasional impossibly planar jawline, the arms long enough to reach the figure's shin while standing upright—fight against this superheroic version of "serious" realism or hyperrealism in favor of something more Kirbyesque, in which, as Charles Hatfield puts it (citing Tom Crippen), a realism of volume and definition, "by weight of contrast," gives the fantasy elements of superhero comics "some ballast, some sense of solidity and grandeur."[11] The realities of human movement are not kind to Miller. Once in the issue, he draws multiple, translucent Daredevil

FIGURE 28. Frank Miller and Klaus Janson, "A Grave Mistake," *Daredevil* #158 (Marvel, May 1979).

figures representing multiple stages of movement in the same panel— a convention established for Daredevil by Colan and developed by Brown, Carmine Infantino, and Gil Kane—but he flubs the physics: Daredevil sails into a gravestone head first, then rebounds away, also head first, from the same stone as though his head were light and pliable enough to bounce off granite yet heavy enough to drag the rest of his body behind it wherever it flies (figure 28). Such drawings, crummy as they are, radiate an enthusiasm for drawing that gets ahead of itself. That quality alone shoots Miller past the Don Hecks and Bob Browns of the industry, workhorses who had their inspired moments but treated every assignment as a job of work, not an opportunity to make a reader's head explode the way Kirby or Ditko did. Miller doesn't simply draw action here; he draws an *idea* about action that requires that the reader's eye be engaged by the entire page. The implausible action taking place in individual panels is primarily a means to that larger, more ambitious end.

Planting motifs in a story—images, angles, or panel shapes and patterns that can be repeated for emphasis—is also on Miller's to-do list, and he is just as eager to harvest them. As early as *Daredevil* #160, his page layouts offer details that foreshadow coming events; whenever he draws settings, he simultaneously establishes certain mise-en-scène elements as a precondition of turning them into props. In that issue, Bullseye, undergoing psychotherapy in a prison hospital, recounts how he murdered his own father. Over three panels, he uses the microphone cord of a tape recorder, a perfectly benign object in the first panel, to strangle the psychoanalyst; no mention of the action appears in the narration boxes or the dialogue (figure 29). Such dependence on the image to tell the story can falter when comics get produced the Marvel way, for it's difficult to predict whether the dialogue writer and editors will pick up on this even if the artist points it out, especially when the artist is as new and unimportant as Miller was. By contrast, his writer-artist stint always feels unified in a way that the Marvel method rarely managed: everything planned ahead, seeds planted early on in a story or an issue that bear fruit only much later. Miller rarely presses us to notice his cleverness on this count, in part because he conceives image and text in tandem, complementing each other. Miller's skill at communicating that conception remains mostly latent in *Daredevil* #160: the most important object in Bullseye's encounter with the psychiatrist, the tape recorder, never fully registers in the reader's mind because Miller plants it deep in the mise-en-scène for only a single panel before Bullseye uses it as a murder weapon, and he never once offers a close-up. Still, the scene portends things to come. It lets a visualized plot point go unmentioned in the dialogue rather than the other way around.

In issue #166, a similar attempt fares better. Daredevil fights a massive villain called the Gladiator in a miniature coliseum at a museum, beneath a statue of a Roman emperor with its thumb pointed downward. The Gladiator, while hallucinating that he is an actual gladiator

FIGURE 29. Frank Miller and Klaus Janson, "In the Hands of Bullseye," *Daredevil* #160 (Marvel, September 1979).

of ancient Rome, interprets the thumb as the living Caesar granting him permission to kill Daredevil, and at that moment, Miller offers us a perspective from above and behind the giant hand as if we have taken Caesar's position, reminding us of the Gladiator's insanity by using objective reality to nod in the direction of his fantasy. A few pages later, however, the Gladiator, in his own moment of defeat, interprets the same thumb as Caesar's judgment against him, and Miller offers us the same statue's-eye-view perspective. The first moment nicely resonates with a narrative junkie's Freudian instinct that psychotic episodes force people to interpret their surroundings in terms of their delusions, but the second moment expresses something I wasn't sure I had seen outside the relatively complex novels I had begun reading for junior high English class—a sense that organizing a story may not be simply a matter of one damned thing happening after another. Structuring a comic book like this meant, among other things, choosing setting and props as potential icons to be aggregated, explored, and revealed in their full significance when required; it meant waiting patiently to reveal the meaning of the iconography and even then having the modesty to mute the revelation and leave the rest to the reader;

it meant offering the reader the satisfaction of having paid attention to parallel moments and harbingers of plot turns to come without necessarily being able to predict them, the way Hollywood screenplays did during the heyday of film noir.

Miller emulates classical Hollywood in other formal ways, particularly in how his panel-to-panel flow mobilizes frames ("shots") to imply collectively spaces that couldn't exist in physical reality yet makes these spaces plausible in the medium-specific terms of plot action, genre, and graphic design. As a film studies scholar, I find fascinating the challenge of unpacking what it means to label Miller's run "cinematic," especially considering that compared to Colan's *Daredevil*, Miller's drawings progressively become as minimalist as his writing, thick with attached and cast shadows that complement the book's other nods to noir (hard-boiled dialogue; a deterministic perspective on New York City as an urban wasteland crawling with crime). This is the issue that made me recognize that comics, at least comics made with ambitions of exploiting the form's possibilities, required preplanning. Miller's line quality and compositional mind-set drew from many more influences in comics and film than I recognized back then, but the sheer amount of work he had to do before actually drawing the pages just about blew my head off. Where did this guy come from? What else was I missing?

Consider the climax of the origin story in issue #164 and the decisive functions of Miller's choices there. The plot has Daredevil chasing down Roscoe Sweeney, a.k.a. the Fixer, and the Fixer dying of a heart attack brought on by the combination of physical pursuit that his body can't handle and his fear of bodily harm or death when DD catches up with him. Our eyes must not resist the torrent of action moving from left to right, and to ensure this movement, Miller increases the size of figures across the page to increase the sense of proximity; he moves the picture plane slightly to the right with each new panel; and he employs the EKG wave representing the Fixer's heartbeat as a kind of arrow pulling the action forward—anything to keep the action tumbling over itself to its conclusion with his death. All along, Miller also uses individual panel frames to give a rhythm to that movement. The panels get narrower and narrower throughout the second row of the page, each frame offering something like a film frame, an isolated microsecond of movement cut apart from its larger action. Scott McCloud attributes to panels like these a "moment-to-moment" form of closure: each represents the same space from the same angle, with only the figures changing position.[12] I will not resist the temptation to compare this tactic to Eadweard Muybridge's protocinematic experiments, his "motion studies," for Miller too supplies us with serial images that primarily signify the larger action. Unlike Muybridge, however, Miller chooses his frozen moments on the basis of their ability to heighten the drama: one frame of the Fixer running full steam ahead, one of him trying to run but glancing back to see his pursuer, one of him clutching his chest, and a final panel showing him writhing in pain, head thrown back as his last word, "devil . . . ," escapes his lips.

"We need people [in comics] who think like painters," Miller told Kim Thompson in 1982. "We need people who think like cinematographers."[13] And Miller was never one to shrink from taking his own advice about borrowing from other media traditions to find untested potentialities in comics. He takes a recognizably cinematic approach to representing time's passage as early as #158. One fight page, which occurs two pages earlier than the bouncing-head page I described earlier, is dominated by two horizontal, gutter-to-gutter panels stacked atop each other (a pattern to which Miller adheres pretty faithfully for the entire second half of the issue). These panels function to make the blows landed during Daredevil's battle with Death-Stalker seem lengthier, more painful, and more dynamic. Below those panels on the same page lie four moment-to-moment panels, during which, by stages, Daredevil enters the same pose he strikes on the cover, crouching before a gravestone just as Death-Stalker floats above him to spring the trap (figure 30). It's an experiment in temporal expansion, a test to see what sorts of things can be done with it. Here it produces a nice contrast of verticality with horizontality, like columns holding up the top panels. Within a few issues, though, Miller makes it a signifier of monumentality and expanded time that has less and less to do with motion as the series continues.

The problem with calling this style "cinematic," however—and in fact, it's only in writing this study that I've learned to articulate the distinction between these panel breakdowns and such cinematic manipulations of time as slow motion—is that Miller actually borrowed the technique from two cartoonists for the infamous EC company: Bernard Krigstein, whose work I discussed at length in the introduction,

FIGURE 30. Frank Miller and Klaus Janson, "A Grave Mistake," *Daredevil* #158 (Marvel, May 1979).

and Harvey Kurtzman, best known as the creator of *Mad* magazine but also the creator-editor of *Frontline Combat* and *Two-Fisted Tales*, perhaps the most critically revered of all US war comics. Krigstein, a fine artist working in comics to pay the rent, did so much moment-to-moment comics narration in the 1950s that, taken together, it begins to look like conceptual art. At Atlas/Marvel, he would regularly derive more than three times as many panels as other cartoonists (Ditko, Kirby, Heck) from four-page Stan Lee scripts. That decision resulted in full-blown experiments in arresting the passage of time in comics, of making even the slightest figural movement—the gesticulations one makes while speaking, for example—into an event that the frame line divides into discrete actions, events unto themselves as vivid as a single frame from a Muybridge motion study. Krigstein's "Master Race" pulls time apart in the most dynamic way possible while keeping the line work minimal, thus conveying the energy and desperation of the chase without diminishing the bleakness of the subject matter.[14]

Kurtzman, too, breaks up time into incremental panels, often retaining the same point of view from panel to panel. Yet Kurtzman's rhythm is completely different. According to Thierry Groensteen, rhythm on the comics page depends on the reader's attentiveness and speed as much as it depends on the cartoonist's breakdowns.[15] In "Corpse on the Imjin!" (*Two-Fisted Tales* #25, February 1952), Kurtzman gains control of our reading speed rather sneakily, by attempting to bore us to death visually for the first couple of pages. Kurtzman's panels depict a US soldier waiting for the enemy, listless, looking around for something to pay attention to in order to break the monotony. If Krigstein gives the effect of slow motion—the stretching of a few seconds into a long row of images—Kurtzman uses nearly identical-looking transitions to produce ellipses, giving us the impression of excruciatingly long cinematic takes. The gutter between panels implies unrepresented moments of boredom that we have been spared by the storyteller but that we still experience as a signifier of the character's listlessness as time creeps by. When the soldier is suddenly forced into hand-to-hand combat with an enemy soldier, Kurtzman's temporal strategy more closely resembles Krigstein's, but Kurtzman's lugubrious setup—the soldier's boring wait—ensures that the drama still lies in the ellipses, not in the minutiae of discrete, deconstructed moments: like the soldier who holds his adversary under water, we too must wait for the

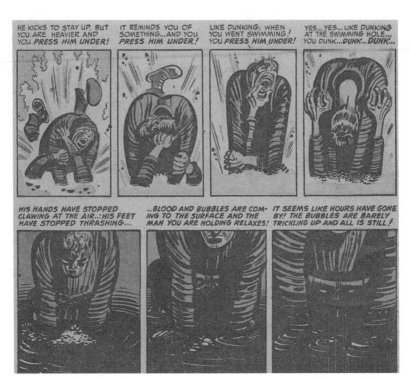

FIGURE 31. Harvey Kurtzman, "Corpse on the Imjin!," *Two-Fisted Tales* #25 (EC, February 1952).

enemy to drown. The picture plane moves closer to the water's surface over three panels, like jump cuts that abbreviate the agony of waiting for a man to die—a man this man is killing—while forcing us to recognize that that wait, for all its abbreviation here, was interminable for the soldier and his enemy. Kurtzman's narration boxes augment that sense of frozen time simply by causing us to remain with each panel long enough to read the text; their function is both to dramatize the moment and to protract it as painfully as possible (figure 31).

Miller acknowledges the difference between these influences by employing similar-looking panel series in the distinct ways Krigstein and Kurtzman did. At least once, he manages to exploit both temporal effects at the same time. The last page of *Daredevil* #165 (July 1980) contains a three-frame "zoom in" on the figures of Daredevil and Heather kissing, in silhouette, while behind them, the Black

Widow—shown behind the silhouettes but drawn in greater detail—
looks sadly on and decides to give up on Matt's affections (figure 32). If
Miller is inviting readers to project assumptions onto the gutters in the
process that McCloud calls closure, the assumptions in play are both
textual and metatextual. Collectively the panels suture us into second-
by-second spatial continuity like Krigstein's motion-study series, but
they also imply a slower and more deliberate movement, not of the
characters but of the point of view. This maneuver carries an unusual
Gestalt effect, inverting the usual emphasis on the area of action nearest the picture plane. By showing Heather and Daredevil in silhouette
while fully rendering the Black Widow (albeit abstracted somewhat
by Zipatoning and monochromatic coloring), Miller directs our eye
to the Widow's unhappy realization while simultaneously communicating the lovers' absorption in each other and symbolically emphasizing the Widow's alienation from Matt. The final panel in that row
repeats the size and shape of the other three, but this time the Widow
appears alone in a medium close-up and in full color, her mouth partly obscured by her hair as if to allow her some privacy as she contemplates her loss. All the while, the visual emphasis of the four panels
tends gradually toward the right, giving an impression of inevitability

FIGURE 32. Frank Miller and Klaus Janson, "Arms of the Octopus," *Daredevil* #165
(Marvel, July 1980).

to the Widow's loss that Miller supports by shading her brow and giving her eyes an expression of resignation.

On the last page of #164, just after the Krigstein homage, Miller offers
a landmark rendering of the Kurtzman approach. The reporter Ben
Urich has discovered Daredevil's secret identity and has spent the issue
interviewing him about it in the hospital as he convalesces after battling
the Hulk. DD has just finished recounting the death of his father's murderer. Now comes the moment of truth when Miller releases the tension
he introduced at the beginning when Ben reveals what he knows: will
Ben publish his story, putting Matt Murdock in danger and probably
ending Daredevil's career? Miller unfurls the moment in what Benoît
Peeters calls the rhetorical mode of panel arrangement, in which "the
whole page layout is placed at the service of a pre-existing narrative for
which it serves to accentuate the effects."[16] The panels begin tall and thin
and progressively get even thinner, stressing the brevity of each moment
as Krigstein does, but also stretching that moment out to communicate a subjective experience of interminable time as Kurtzman renders

FIGURE 33. Frank Miller and Klaus Janson, "Exposé," *Daredevil* #164
(Marvel, May 1980).

it in "Corpse on the Imjin!" (figure 33). The dramatic effect of Miller's sequence is not to underscore the development of the moment of truth but to impede that development, to slow down its rhythm by forcing us to wade through the same image over and over.

I used to get impatient with panel rows like this one. How could a "real" professional cartoonist, someone whose job it is to draw, get away with photocopying his own panels as Miller did, albeit adjusting the drawings slightly to convey the passage of time? Perhaps I felt I wasn't getting enough manual labor out of Miller for my forty cents. But I could not mistake the intended impact of the moment. Ben is giving up his chance at a Pulitzer Prize for the sake of keeping Hell's Kitchen a little safer, and Miller's layout choice lets us experience Ben's selfless act as he himself presumably does: nearly stopping himself at every moment, he finally burns the story with his cigarette lighter and then accepts the consequences in a new panel configuration, a narrow horizontal panel that gives us time to digest this impossible choice. By placing Ben's tiny figure in the back of the frame, facing away from Daredevil (in the foreground, facing away from us in turn), Miller leaves it to readers to imagine the look on his face as he speaks the story's refrain for the last time: "This one's for you, Matt." I soon found myself willing to wade through oceans of Xeroxed panels so long as dramatic visual payoffs like this one waited on the other shore.

COMICS AS CINEMA

Miller disavowed any interested in the work of his predecessor Gene Colan in the 1982 *Daredevil Chronicles* interview,[17] but Colan's remarks about page layout for a *Comics Journal* interview nevertheless offer a useful insight about Miller's own approach to his medium:

> Well, the biggest complaint that Stan [Lee] ever had about my work was that he didn't have an easy time understanding what I was drawing. There's a lot of confusion about my work. [*Laughter.*] And I meant it to be a little confusing. You don't always understand what you're looking at even when [you look at] a photograph. [Think of] a room with many things on a desk. You can only identify a few of the objects but you can't say what they all are. Some books might be there, an inkwell might be there. . . . It all lends to the authenticity of what you're looking at. In life,

you don't notice everything at one time. Certain things—and the rest you don't know. You don't even think about. So I try to do that. If there's a fight scene, and it's in the dark, I try to confuse it so that you see arms and legs but you don't know who they belong to. A fight is a confusing thing to begin with. Tables and chairs are overturned. You shouldn't be defining everything for the reader. The reader is not an idiot. He gets out of it what he wants to get out of it. And if it thrills him to see all these puzzling pictures, then I've accomplished something. At least that's how I viewed it anyway, personally. Someone would say to me, "Yeah, but, who does this belong to? Whose leg is that?" I said it isn't important. Put any connotation you want on it.[18]

Colan emphasizes that such stylistic idiosyncrasy would have been impossible at rival company DC with its strictly enforced "house style." Even at Marvel, however, making it difficult to perceive who punched whom and from what direction surely didn't please everyone, and it's a cinch that readers expecting relatively objective narration in their comic books would not consciously grasp the purpose of Colan's impressionism, his attempt to use mise-en-scène and page layout to convey a first-person experience of a fistfight.

In the documentary *The Men without Fear*, in which the late Colan also appears (and gives a condensed version of the statement just quoted), Miller says of his *Daredevil* run, "I came in wanting to make comics more cinematic. I stay in wanting to make them less so." Miller stakes out territory on each end of that spectrum in *Daredevil*. Where Miller's *Daredevil* may be most self-consciously "cinematic" is not in its representations of time but in its expressionism. Colan's statement well summarizes *Miller*'s demonstration that in comics, subjective effect *is* realism. Miller's Times Square is, according to the artist himself, the one the tourists would recognize as such—the glaring marquees, neon signs, and filthy streets of the *Taxi Driver* era, all crammed together into single, stifling panels, not the "real" Times Square of a detailed map or an architect's orthogonal drawing.[19] This is an aesthetically arresting choice for *Daredevil*, a cartoon strip starring a hero who doesn't see anything, whereas we the readers want to see everything. We devour the action with our eyes, recombine it, and process it in constant tension with the dialogue and narration boxes.

Miller was one of the only writer-artists in the superhero business when he took over the scripting of *Daredevil* with issue #168 (January 1981). His new autonomy allowed him to get around the limitations of the Marvel method. In the Sanderson interview, as Miller looks back at his first year of writing his own scripts, Miller breaks down his creative process into three distinct tasks: writing, illustrating, and direction.[20] *Direction* purposely evokes the tasks of the film director in the sense that she or he oversees editing, cinematography, and performance, organizing the visual track and combining it with the soundtrack to produce unified effects. Miller credits Marvel editor in chief Jim Shooter with teaching him how to "direct" by dragging him through the same Jack Kirby story over and over again, from expository and character introduction to confrontation and resolution, panel by panel and conflict by conflict. But Miller is also a cinephile, a haunter of New York repertory theaters who once called François Truffaut's interview book *Hitchcock* "the best book [he'd] read on doing comic books."[21] Whoever acts as director of a comic, whether writer or illustrator, chooses the angles on the action in each panel, keeps track of temporal and spatial relationships between one panel and the next, and determines the focal points of panel and page.

The value of using cinematic style as a creative guide for comics is a subject of debate, to be certain. Narrative cinema's focus on sequential storytelling doesn't leave much room to consider the unique possibilities of comics layout, as evidenced by the pages from Miller's *Spectacular Spider-Man* #27 I discussed earlier. The Atomic Age cartoonists that Miller most admires, including Will Eisner, Krigstein, Kurtzman, Johnny Craig, and Wallace Wood (about whom Miller famously quipped "he could draw a half-dissolved Alka-Seltzer or a dog turd, and they would be the most beautiful things you'd ever seen in your life"),[22] all experimented with expressionism to powerful effect. Eisner reshaped physical reality for multiple purposes, from turning tenements or billboards into splash-page logos to making the Spirit's body look as liquid as the rain that pounds him as he lies unconscious in a gutter. True to Miller's fascination with crime fiction and film noir, his expressionism leaned toward the dynamic, even frenetic end of the spectrum. When he discovered that New York's Rikers Island penitentiary looks "like a grade school," he chose to invent his own Rikers for *Daredevil* #181.[23] Miller's version does not look the way Rikers looks to the eye or the camera

FIGURE 34. Frank Miller and Klaus Janson, "Last Hand," *Daredevil* #181 (Marvel, April 1982).

but rather the way Bullseye experiences it: "What a prison was to Bullseye is bars—that's all there are. There's no toilet in his cell, no door, just bars for the walls, floor, and ceiling"[24] (figure 34).

Ironically, of course, Miller joined the industry at a moment when cartooniness—the caricatural quality that makes comics comics to McCloud—was, if not forbidden, then certainly frowned on in the superhero business. Miller learned his expressionism from film directors who used the camera not as a faithful recorder of physical reality but as a tool for transforming it. Orson Welles, Fritz Lang, and Alfred Hitchcock—all avowed influences on Miller—played with light, shadow, and camera angle to produce a shadowy, angular style that became a herald of American film noir, in which low-key lighting and compositionally bold camera angles translate the desolation, confusion, and powerlessness of a central male figure faced with a postwar environment poised to unman him in every possible way. Miller and Janson's stated precedents go back even further to the German "expressionist" filmmaking of 1920s. Janson tells Peter Sanderson that he transmits the sadness of a character by making even the desk he sits at look lonely, saggy. In the same vein, he congratulates Miller for making a particularly expressionist choice in *Daredevil* #181:

The whole page is just Bullseye thinking, and in the top panel is a whiskey bottle that he has obviously pretty much emptied and the whiskey bottle is out of proportion to him. It's much too big. So I noticed this and I said to myself, does Frank want this bottle as big as this, and I thought, yes, and I agreed with him that this was a use of expressionism to show how much alcohol he had devoured, how important alcohol is to him and to make sure that the reader sees it. . . Again, it wasn't a slipshod thing that we had done that was a mistake. It was something we thought about and went ahead and did—it was true expressionism.[25]

And indeed the bottle's disproportionate size communicates with marvelous economy the fact that Bullseye is drunk as he flips through photos of his next targets and laughs uproariously at the sudden thought that blind Matt Murdock might secretly be Daredevil (figure 35). I can only add that by dividing this full-page rendition of Bullseye into several discrete panels, Miller and Janson avoid even a realist's criticism that the bottle is out of proportion in the first place. While the multiple panels appear at first glance to show everything on the page from the same distance, in fact the panel show-

FIGURE 35. Frank Miller and Klaus Janson, "Last Hand," *Daredevil* #181 (Marvel, April 1982).

ing the bottle simply frames a closer view than the remaining panels do. Strictly speaking, Miller has not distorted visual reality at all, yet he achieves the intended subjective effect just the same.

Miller goes along with Janson on these points during the Sanderson interview, but with a drollness that implies he takes expressionism for granted as a technique. He gleefully speaks of borrowing everything he could from Hitchcock, John Ford, Stanley Kubrick, Lang, and even D. W. Griffith and puzzles over why he didn't have more company in grabbing at the low-hanging fruit of cinematic style: "By following in [Neal Adams's] footsteps, people have restricted themselves a bit as to what can be done with caricature, and there are other ways to work. I'm astonished that there is as little reference to film expression[ism] as there is because it seems a natural leap to make. We have more freedom to do that than the film directors do."[26] In another interview the same year, he expands on the thought by naming German expressionism in film as a major reference: "I've been watching some German Expressionist movies, and I've found that the way they create sets just for psychological purposes is something that comic-book artists could do a hell of a lot more with than they do. Instead of doing rooms, they could do the state of mind of the person who's in them as a room. The first place I was able to apply that was in a scene in prison where the prisoner's narrating the story."[27] Following this logic, the relative size of Bullseye's whiskey bottle is a moment of rhetorical emphasis indicating its subjective importance.

We might look back to my favorite "bad" Miller drawings as examples of just this kind of emphasis. Hogman's Lilliputian fork pushes the idea that he is all mouth and foreshadows the revelation that he lied on the stand and is in fact guilty of murder (his steady heartbeat, augmented by a pacemaker, had convinced the unwitting Murdock to defend him). The giant smile also becomes a productive motif of the story. The repetition of gutter-to-gutter horizontal panels featuring Hogman's grin in *Daredevil* #183 and #184 comes to a satisfying end when Hogman is convicted and that mouth twists into a similarly exaggerated frown. In #182, Matt's tiny hands touching Elektra's giant face offer multiple expressionist readings: Matt finally accepts that Elektra's death is real; the size difference visualizes the ontological distance between the living and the dead, an idea furthered by Elektra's bluish-white skin; and hands as expressive barometers in such

German silent horror films as F. W. Murnau's *Nosferatu* (1922) and Robert Wiene's *Das Cabinet des Dr. Caligari* (1920) inevitably shrink before the intractability of mortality. Whereas many of Adams's acolytes seemed determined to evacuate cartoonishness from their work, Miller manipulated angle, the relative sizes of objects, and page layout and composition to make the physical world legible in ways that neither words nor facial expressions could accomplish on their own.

NIGHT AND THE CITY

I used to think Miller was fluffing his reputation when he told interviewers that, by the time he broke into comics, he had given up reading comic books for prose crime fiction and had come to see the latter as his vehicle for delivering the former. Was he denying his comics fanhood to pick up cultural clout for his comics work, I would wonder? But I'm much less certain of that now. For one thing, at the risk of repeating a cliché, Miller's *Daredevil* made New York into a character. Marvel's founding its "universe" in a fictional New York City was its way of claiming greater realism over DC Comics, where heroes defended fictional towns with names like Metropolis, Gotham City, or Coast City. Janson, when explaining why he decided to return to *Daredevil* when Marvel offered him the job of inking Miller's pencils, credited Miller's urban sensibility: "I said [to myself] well, he does a lot of buildings, and I like to do buildings, so okay, I'll give a crack at it."[28] New York (and San Francisco) had played picturesque roles in the series over the years, as cityscapes always had in *Amazing Spider-Man*. The buildings and water towers that Spider-Man swings past during Stan Lee and Steve Ditko's inaugural run, however generic they may look, serve as constant reminders of the risks he takes fighting levitating criminals like the Vulture or the Green Goblin far above the city and the exhilaration that the buttoned-down teenager Peter Parker feels whenever he takes to the sky with only a skein of artificial spiderweb to support him. Yet as centered on New York as Spider-Man has always been, the city contributes to his stories mainly as an obstacle course or a catalyst for occasional walk-on appearances by celebrities. In *Daredevil* before Miller's time, it would have been difficult to say the city had much of a role to play at all.

In Miller's *Daredevil*, however, New York functions as an urban jungle right out of film noir. Though Miller denied that he intended to portray New York City as a trap, he perpetually painted it as an unavoidable obstacle, alternately an urban frontier land and a claustrophobic cage. On one page, Daredevil might bound between building tops and swing from flagpoles to let off steam, the city his playground, while on the next, he might find himself tied up and stuffed into a sewer pipe by a couple of thugs. Of the first fifteen issues that Miller wrote as well as penciled, ten of them open with characters in typically urban locations and situations: in the street or on the sidewalk, on a bridge, in a phone booth, perched on a window ledge, in an alley, and, in three instances, soaked in garbage. Even when we can't see the street in a panel, we're always conscious of its presence and the myriad dangers that accompany it. The first scene of issue #175 (October 1981) ends with Daredevil being flung through a closed high-rise window by his former lover Elektra and saving himself by grabbing a window ledge behind his back.

Miller doesn't draw the city so much as he caricatures it in what he calls a "compressed" manner that stands somewhere between a metonymic form, in which tall buildings signify "city" with all the connotations of excitement and danger the word conjures in crime and adventure fiction, and a subjective form of realism that reflects the experiential memory of an observer of the city, particularly one overwhelmed by its scope, activity, and noise:

> [Something] done very consciously at the layout stage is that I see the city as a series of rectangles encasing organisms. We are soft little creatures that walk around these big concrete rectangles. One of the things I do is to use the shape of the page and the shape of the panels to emphasize that, often to make it more claustrophobic. I have not yet come to a situation where I would use a tilted border between panels. I don't believe I'm likely to . . . because part of what makes the art successful is that the rectangles get so extreme and they so dominate the overall look of the book, that that says many things about the city and how the characters relate to it that don't have to be in words or illustrations.[29]

In an early example of formal self-consciousness, Miller says in 1982 that he rarely works from photographs of New York because city photographs look airy and open and thus cannot communicate the claustrophobic experience of a city as he intended to communicate in *Daredevil*. Instead, he moves the buildings closer to one another. Now he's definitely in film noir territory, where cities act as literal mazes and figurative prisons, expressionist dreamscapes where a simple tilt of the camera can make clean, modernist perpendiculars into webs of intersecting, conflicting angles.

Some of *Daredevil*'s noir experiments are more successful than others. Thirty-odd years after the fact, I read *Daredevil* #172 (July 1981) for the first time after filling a few gaps in my run. I was surprised to find narration boxes—the equivalent of a cinematic voice-over—offering a running spiel about how the city takes care of its own, but only if one watches one's step, in six page-length vertical panels scattered about the story. Rendered typographically rather than by the issue's letterer, Joe Rosen, and written in a Noo Yoakah slang that brings to mind a hustler showing a fellow grifter the ropes, this commentary never gets attributed to a character, but it's not the voice of God either. The diction reads like Georg Simmel posing as a stereotypically loquacious homeless man, relating his enthusiastic ambivalence about the city to anyone who will listen. Its blatant sourcelessness has the uneasy effect of taking me out of the story, disconnecting events from the cause-and-effect plot and rendering them instead representative of something else that I can't quite determine. And yet, very much in the classical noir tradition, it enlists artful language as a hedge against urban trauma, a mental shield against violence that also functions to process the noir antihero's craving for it, as proof that he still exists.

The horrible, exhilarating city offers the noir filmmaker, and the noirish cartoonist, endless icons of modern experience as a disaster waiting to happen. There are, for one, the anonymous crowds in which Bullseye psychotically mistakes everyone around him for Daredevil and begins killing civilians at random. As in such classic films noirs as *Detour*, *Murder My Sweet*, and *Dark Passage*, what we see in the panels is what Bullseye sees in his head. We are implicated in his madness first by his point of view, then by the absurdity of his killing Daredevils all along the perimeter of Times Square; Miller challenges us to remember that we are watching innocent passersby be executed by a madman simply for walking down the street. Miller does not limit the expressionistic subjectivism to a lunatic's perspective, of course. He daubs every issue with city streets represented by turns as rain-soaked wastelands, neon jungles, and refuse dumps in which heroes and villains alike find themselves mired (see issues #171, #172, and #176). But noir would not be noir without the pulsating energy it attributes to the city, and Miller gives us that too: utopian flashes of Daredevil using the city as his playground, showing off for civilians by running up a bridge rather than over it (#170) or expressing his love for New York on a "gorgeous morning" by bouncing from roof to roof like an Olympic gymnast (#178). Ultimately, the city acts as the hero's expressionist mirror, reflecting Murdock's optimism or pessimism back at him. Miller marries his representations of the city as threat or playground to Murdock's passion to save it when it needs saving and to his joy in celebrating it when it doesn't.

Daredevil also parallels film noir in its examination of the romanticism of urban violence. Miller explicitly hits this note when Bullseye and Daredevil stumble into a repertory screening of John Huston's *The Maltese Falcon* (1941) in *Daredevil* #169. Miller develops the scene through the setting in a moment of metacommentary worthy of a Robert Crumb comic with the volume turned down. Kurt Olsson praised Miller in 1981 for planting in the audience two movie buffs who comment on the "frightening, yet attractive nature of violence" in film noir while Bullseye and Daredevil duke it out to the death (figure 36). By contrasting the screen violence with the (comic-book version of the) real thing so directly, "Miller show[s] the reader that violence may be frightening, but it certainly isn't attractive."[30] But the comparison drawn by the scene is not so simple, because Miller depicts the hero-villain battle as a veritable ballet of punching, ducking, throwing, falling. What could possibly be unattractive for the average reader of superhero comics about the violence in this scene? When Bullseye pegs Daredevil with the knife, the latter falls as gracefully as an Olympic diver in Leni Riefenstahl's *Olympia*. Rather than exposing the ugliness of violence, the scene exposes the degree to which representing violence unavoidably aestheticizes it, no matter what the style, the level of detail, or the medium. In particular, it discloses how the hard-boiled aesthetic of exposing the real in all its ugliness both recognizes the horror of violent crime and romanticizes it with terse, tough-guy dialogue and narration. Deadpan description of violent acts, literary naturalism's gift to modernism and hard-boiled fiction alike, has long been a kind of contest in which the spoils go to the writer who makes violence the prettiest while pretending to hate it the most. Miller may not have walked away from that contest without playing, but he certainly makes us aware of what's at stake in participating.

The series's most blatant visualizations of subjective experience come when Daredevil uses his hypersenses. I would not want to call Wally Wood's concentric circles and EKG lines expressionist, exactly, for they add visual information to the mise-en-scène rather than distorting preexisting settings and objects from *Daredevil*'s diegetic world. In the 2011 reboot of the *Daredevil* (volume 3), Mark Waid and Paolo Rivera change the trope into

FIGURE 36. Frank Miller and Klaus Janson, "Devils," *Daredevil* #169 (Marvel, March 1981).

something more explicitly expressionist by linking Matt's subjective experience directly to the environment. Rivera transforms bodies and spaces into topographic maps whenever Matt uses his radar, thus managing to represent what he experiences visually without rendering moot the material, physical terrain without which there would be no such experience. Though I admire Waid and Rivera's experiment, I prefer Miller and Janson's method of keeping us attached to Matt's perspective. By this I don't mean their adoption of Wood's concentric circles, which they use less frequently as their run continues, but their more subtle, blanket approach to representing *Daredevil's* world: subjectify everything through expressionism, all the time, even when Matt isn't present in the diegesis. Miller gives us a universe already filtered through some consciousness that limits its meaning, by which I mean that consciousness continuously interprets it—as Murdock must by necessity, and as we all do, however subconsciously compared to a blind man on the prowl for bad guys and evidence to use against them.

Aesthetic risks like this seldom paid off in mainstream comics at the time. Miller calls artists like Frank Robbins dangerous not only because they buck industry trends but because they don't even acknowledge them and instead follow their own vision—be it anachronistic, ugly, whatever, so long as it has impact.[31] Looking at Miller's own work on *Daredevil*, the "danger" that Robbins represents may also connote the expressionist's way of challenging or even endangering the reader's comprehension and endangering sales along with it. Not many comics artists have been dangerous in that way for long without shifting gears or getting the ax. An example of a cartoonist who did get away with dangerous expressionism in the sixties is Steve Ditko, whom Miller has praised for his ability to "cartoon a character or situation from an emotion, from an intellectual or moral abstraction."[32] Ditko began drawing gruesome horror comics for the poverty-row company Charlton Comics at the end of the 1940s but survived the Comics Code purge by drawing toned-down horror, suspense, and science-fiction strips for such defanged horror anthology books as Marvel's *Tales of Suspense* and Charlton's not-coincidentally-titled *Strange Suspense Stories*. After creating the superhero Captain Atom (the character that Alan Moore and Dave Gibbons molded into Dr. Manhattan for *Watchmen*) at Charlton in the late fifties, Ditko began to focus on Marvel superheroes, most famously Spider-Man and Doctor Strange. Ditko created these characters in collaboration with Stan Lee but designed them himself, with a little help from the shrewd eye of the colorist Stan Goldberg.

Ditko's drawing style is one of the most singular styles in comics history, so singular that by the end of the seventies, he was struggling to find an appreciative audience. I will doubtless fail to get across exactly how and why his drawing style stands out from everyone else's—I have never seen it done very well—but it's worth attempting for what it could teach us about Miller's unlikely mainstream appeal. Ditko's anatomical drawing is usually accurate to a fault where muscle groups and figure balance during activity are concerned, but something is always a bit uncanny about those bodies: hands, legs, and especially eyes have a supernatural intensity generated by intense, concentrated rendering and slight but recognizable contortionism. In Ditko's revisionist physics, everything from bodies to venetian blinds looks kinetic, and yet nothing appears to move. Objects and people remain forever frozen in midmotion, no matter how dynamic the angles of the drawing. Choices like this rendered his style singular enough to turn off some of Spidey's earliest fans, and yet he was responsible for making the character unforgettable; no one had a half-formed opinion about his drawing. Ditko's people's bodies didn't look quite like they belonged to them; their fingers and legs got away from them as though he had built splints for all his models that made their limbs longer and bonier and pointed them at slightly off-kilter angles. These were perfect stylistic hooks for a horror cartoonist, and indeed Ditko weaved in and out of horror anthology series at Charlton, Marvel, and DC many times during the course of his long career. His characters disappear into pools of shadow, not because their identities had to be hidden from readers (though Ditko did pull that trick for the Green Goblin in *Spider-Man*) but because their dark intentions or the bleak fates that awaited them were integrated into the image.

Miller's drafting style resembles Ditko's in that both can make anything look otherworldly, repellant, and yet fascinating. He learned a trick or two from Ditko about signifying a place without drawing it accurately, like Times Square or a New York office building:

The comic books that I grew up on and loved for their New York material were Steve Ditko's, but when I investigated New York rooftops, I discovered that they don't quite look the way he drew them. Details were very different. He probably operated from memory; he certainly converted the details to his style and made them more suitable for his purpose. The point is, they worked for me when I first read them. I want to be able to deal in emblems that well, to be able to manipulate them skillfully enough so that my New York will be convincing but serve my purposes. I almost wish I was doing Gotham City instead of New York, because then I would have total freedom.[33]

Considering the consciously emblematic approach Miller exported to *Daredevil* from his favorite cartoonists, Ditko especially, I've always been puzzled by the claim that Miller brought a new realism to super-hero comics. By the middle of Miller's stint, fans began pointing to the new hard-boiled *Daredevil* as evidence that comics had the potential to become a "serious" art form, with "real" violence and "real" death, but the implication always seemed to be that to live up to that poten-tial, comics would have to stop being comics in the sense that comics by their nature take liberties with physical reality. Miller's *Daredevil* did quite the reverse: it never let you forget you were reading a comic book. Miller never treated the character as anything but a cartoon fig-ure in a cartoon world. Arguably, he has never done any differently in any genre, even his interpretation of the Spartans' last stand at Ther-mopylae, *300* (1998). He is not drawing Scrooge McDuck here, to be certain (in spite of his remark that superhero comics are "only a few steps away from funny-animal drawing"),[34] but his cutthroat version of Daredevil's beloved Hell's Kitchen is nearly as fanciful as the exotic locales Carl Barks invented for his ducky explorations and is crafted just as unapologetically to serve the cartoonist's story.

THE VIRTUE OF BOUNDARIES

Miller has made a career of embracing the pliability of comics while at the same time accepting its parameters as productive limitations. His interviews since the early 1980s continually express his desire to use the limits and conventions of comics as spurs to creativity. Thompson's scathing review of *Ronin* offers a key to both the attractions of Miller's drawings and the role of limits in their execution: they don't move because their purpose is to arrest movement at some moment use-ful to his storytelling, and highlighting "befores" and "afters" allows him to exploit the very immobility of the comics medium to sug-gest more than he shows. Really, the complaint that Miller's images are "immobile" seems an absurd one to lodge against any cartoonist. Comics break time down into individual frames that seem to freeze a moment in the story. Surely Thompson is not disputing that comics are a still-image medium. What could his critique mean? What both-ers Thompson, it seems, is the method Miller chooses to represent action unfolding in time. He draws the titular hero of *Ronin* "posing" as he prepares to swing his samurai sword, then shows the poses of attacker and attacked resulting from the sword strike, but he skips the moment of impact in between. Regardless of whether this approach undermines the visual accuracy of the art, Miller approaches action precisely as something that the comic-book panel cannot capture. This is not, I imagine, because he can't draw action (whatever that means) but because the theory of temporal narration that he used *Daredevil* to develop requires him to portray a given action—and allows him to demur a bit on the graphic violence—by concentrating on its run-up and its effects. If Miller doesn't draw action in the usual sense, it's because he aims to emphasize something that film has no need for: the vectors of action, the movement of fist or weapon toward and away from the point of impact. This decision functions like a handicap on Miller's *Daredevil* pencils, a limit he imposed on himself. Such a limit acts as the equivalent of a generic convention—a boundary within which one has to work and solve problems if one is ever to learn what to do with the freedom that working on a second-tier character, or a wide-open project for that matter, offers.

Another limitation that Miller takes productive advantage of is rhetorical page layout. Thierry Groensteen, following Benoît Peeters, defines *rhetorical* as a layout format in which (in Peeters's words) "the dimensions of the panel submit to the action that is described";[35] as a technique, it functions to "mol[d] the shape or size of the panel to the action that it encloses: a vertical frame for a lone, standing character, a wide frame for a crowd scene, and so on."[36] Certainly Miller uses this logic for framing different types of objects in unobtrusive ways, such as horizontally oriented panels for landscapes, vertical ones for skyscrapers, and so forth. However, whereas Groensteen seems to mean by "mold[ing] . . . to the action" that the rhetorical panel takes the shape of an object or setting involved in a discrete plot event, Miller's frame shapes adjust to accommodate physical motion. As early as his first issue, #158, Miller stages fight scenes in horizontal, edge-to-edge panels that accentuate the impact of kicks and blows by sending the recipients (and the perpetrators, for that matter) flying in all directions. In this, he was probably borrowing from Goseki Kojima's *Lone Wolf and Cub*, for which Miller drew covers and wrote glowing prefaces when First Comics reprinted a chunk of the series in English in the mideighties (figure 37). Similarly, he employs rhetorical panels to frame falling people or objects. When an assailant with a flamethrower

FIGURE 37. Kazuo Koike (script) and Goseki Kojima (art), "The Assassin's Road," *Lone Wolf and Cub* #1, translated and adapted by John Bruno, David Lewis, and Alex Wald (First Publishing, June 1987): 27.

falls to his death in *Daredevil* #170, Miller's vertically oriented panel gives the fall a certain monumentality by including as much of the motion as possible in a single frame and adding an extra bit of finality to the figure's downward vector by making him smash into a sidewalk that is also the horizontal bottom frame of the panel. Narrating vertical motion in the midst of a suspenseful sequence usually leads Miller to take up an entire panel row with similarly narrow, vertical frames that often employ the Krigstein maneuver of breaking motion into increments. In the same issue, when Bullseye kicks DD through the Kingpin's penthouse window, the skinny panels that follow show the hero making futile grabs first at a flag and then at a gargoyle to break his fall, until his fall is finally broken by a conveniently placed garbage-truck trailer.

The engagement that such sequences require of the reader differs somewhat from what McCloud describes as closure, where the gutter between panels cues the reader to infer whatever part of the action is missing from the panels flanking it. Closure, McCloud writes, is the "phenomenon of observing the parts but perceiving the whole."[37] "Comics panels fracture both time and space, offering a jagged, staccato rhythm of unconnected moments. But closure allows us to connect these moments and mentally construct a continuous, unified reality." This process demands active "participation" by the reader to "simulat[e] time and motion."[38] The unusual frequency of panel-to-panel temporal series in *Daredevil*, however, actually reduces the reader's participation. It muddies the line McCloud draws between moment-to-moment and action-to-action panel series, effectively defining every microsecond in one of Miller's Krigsteinian panel-to-panel sequences as an action—not necessarily a story action in a cause-and-effect chain so much as an open act of storytelling along the lines of a musical composition: a beat, a series of accents that meticulously paces our reading speed. If we define our role as readers here as providing closure, we really don't have much to do. Does that mean we're not participating in the reading process as actively as we might when engaging with a more conventional storytelling mode?

I wouldn't say so, but describing how our engagement with Miller's distended action sequences differs from closure requires me to theorize readerly "participation" a little differently. McCloud's notion of participation as involving mental visualization of what "happens" in the gutters between panels is too limiting. As I discussed in chapter 2, McCloud here calls on McLuhan's theory of cool media, in which low-definition information requires readers or viewers to do more cognitive and imaginative work to absorb themselves in the text at hand. As a result, he shares cool media theory's disadvantage of somewhat ingenuously placing the responsibility for constructing the story largely on the reader. It's true that if one panel presents a medium shot of a man chasing another man with an ax, and the second panel cuts to an extreme long shot of a visualized scream next to a darkened building (this is McCloud's perennial example for describing closure as participatory visualization), readers may infer different versions of how the murder occurred, but in my experience, visualization is neither inevitable nor necessary to the inference. In other words, you need not mentally "see" the murder at all in order to deduce its occurrence and get on with the story. Soviet cinematic montage theory, though it doesn't apply to comics on many counts, seems a more appropriate way of describing how the reader engages with Miller's incremental storytelling. Soviet montage juxtaposes shot A and its subsequent shot B to generate abstract meaning that we might call more thematic or metaphorical than strictly diegetic. This meaning depends on the viewer not filling in mental pictures between the filmed shots but instead surmising what is *signified* by the cut or the "missing" image whose placeholder is the gutter.

Whereas McCloud suggests we project mental images onto panel gutters in order to fill in the narrative blanks, what Miller invites us to project there (stressing the metaphorical nature of the projection) more closely resembles Soviet montage's guided, abstract inference. What we experience in those gaps are discursive acts we attribute to the artist, as if narration boxes stating "time has elapsed" (in elliptical sequences of panels) or "the murder was too horrible to look at" (in McCloud's example) have been squeezed into the gutters themselves. If we do see anything in our imaginations, the gutter is that image's trigger, not its screen. When Miller breaks down Daredevil's descent from the Kingpin's tower into one try after another at breaking his fall, keeping the angle on the action consistent from attempt to attempt, he is scarcely distinguishing between the temporality of such action-to-action sequences and that of moment-to-moment sequences in which Urich holds a photo in front of Daredevil or the wounded Daredevil stands suspended for two identical (photocopied) panels before collapsing in a heap (#187). The primary function of those gutters is not narratively connective but rather a matter of aesthetic emphasis. Such incremental panels discourage the reader from envisioning *anything* in between. Perhaps the abstract concepts that the gutter could catalyze in such instances are effectively reduced to one: *Miller is the one telling this. Shut up and let him drive.*

Miller's experimentation with the gutter has forced me to rethink my assumptions about the relationship between sequentiality in comics and continuity editing in film. While it is tempting to parallel the gutter to the straight continuity cut in cinema, readers experience gutter space differently from the imaginary diegetic space we infer between film cuts, in that, in comics, we can actually see the gutter. It belongs to comics discourse in a conscious way for both cartoonist and reader. Continuity editing constructs cinematic space by making certain parts of diegetic space absent during transitions. During a shot/reverse-shot sequence, rather than seeing a pan or track traveling from one point on the axis of action to another, the viewer suddenly sees one point on that line, then the other, and back again. Such cuts, though entirely discursive in nature, work to efface themselves in most commercial films, to hide their abridgment of space behind the temporal continuity that the sequence attempts to establish by keeping dialogue or movement or background mise-en-scène continuous across each cut. But the gutter is not diegetic space removed from the comics page. The gutter is not a tarp that blots out something lying between the panels. It is emphatically nondiegetic space. Groensteen distinguishes the comics frame from the cinematic frame by reminding us that, while the film frame excludes the physical space that lies beyond its edges, "the frame of a comics panel does not remove anything; it is contented to circumscribe."[39] The comics frame mimics the film frame's exclusion of offscreen space but in reality excludes nothing because there is no referential space to exclude in the first place. Instead, it creates spaces and arranges them rhetorically among the other such spaces on a page. Another way of putting this is that during comics production, the gutter belongs to the artist as a mode of dividing individual moments of space and time from one another, while during the act of reading, it belongs to the reader as a space that offers up for our inference temporality (how much time has passed between panel A and panel B?) and action (what action is not represented here, between the drawings?) without requiring us to project an *image* there, any more than we conjure up images of the spaces between cuts while watching a classically edited film.

The gutter frees Miller from the responsibility of keeping "screen" direction consistent from frame to frame in order to focus the reader's attention. As Hans-Christian Christiansen puts it, "the eyeline match and related figures are not essential factors in comics, as we are not situated at the centre of the diegesis and these techniques do not have the same [suture function] as in cinema (tying the spectator to the diegetic illusion). . . . Spatial continuity is not essential in comics, as the travel over time [from panel to panel] deconstructs continuity. . . . This discontinuity is not disruptive as it would have been in cinema."[40] Miller's *Daredevil* supports Christensen's claim in that Miller rarely attempts to create the kind of directional realism enforced by the 180-degree rule in film. The space of *Daredevil* is a 360-degree space that only gives the impression of 180-degree cinematic space, in that the eye still bounces back and forth from left to right as it passes from horizontal panel to horizontal panel, particularly during fight scenes, either to follow a character like Daredevil or to follow the lines of force. He also uses atmospheric and cognitive means of drawing the eye along the narrative through-line of a given page, such as coloring faraway figures and props monochromatically and closer figures more realistically and using bright colors or large blocks of saturated color to attract our immediate attention. Strategies like these allow him to compose an entire page for visual interest and emphasis at the expense of the law of directional consistency that rules continuity editing. Characters regularly flip sides of Miller's CinemaScope frames, so that as our eyes are drawn down, they follow an arabesque, a lazy S-shaped squiggle from left to right and back left again. He sometimes employs rigid patterns of panel size and arrangement in order to turn continuity itself into an aesthetic challenge, a problem to solve:

> Sometimes I'll enforce an arbitrary rule on myself just to make myself work within certain confines. Every once in a while, I'll decide that a job will be done in the classic six-grid, and then explore those shapes. I tend to go for images that are rather distinctly horizontal or vertical. To be confined by that square pushes me compositionally. And then there's always playing with time, the different ways the page can be laid out can really affect, I believe, the reader's sense of time, and . . . achieve a less metronome-like pace.[41]

For me, the Hand's attempt to kill Murdock by bombing his apartment in #174 is the most breathtaking example of Miller turning a preordained panel arrangement into a tour de force of temporal and spatial organization. It begins with Miller employing three straight pages of nothing but five horizontally oriented panels that run from edge to edge, then a page in which the same panel heights are used but two of the rows—2 and 5—are broken up into multiple panels to express the duration of a couple of events and Matt's reaction to them (one member of the Hand begins to dissolve; Matt ponders this while they all dissolve in unison). The next page begins with a clear visual transition to an adjacent locale: a vertically oriented, high-angle panel of Elektra standing over Matt's apartment building, with the mist of dissolving ninja bodies the only thing clarifying Elektra's proximity to Matt (figure 38). The change of orientation nicely characterizes the switch from fight (horizontal, with punches being thrown every which way) to still, standing figure (Elektra) while also calling attention to the revelation that Elektra is back in town and that her power over Matt, here expressed by both the point of view and the moment of surveillance it captures, remains undiminished. This panel also prepares us for a more substantial transition through story space. A second panel, also vertical but thinner than the panel of Elektra, displays the Kingpin's skyscraper from a low angle, dwarfing its only visible competitor. The Kingpin's phallic power—he is the all-seeing crime lord, more omniscient even than Don Corleone—thus forms a parallel with Elektra's man-killing power, but his is a power that places him above even Elektra in his control over the city.

Miller follows this transition by switching the locale to the Nelson and Murdock office, then using a fixed, repeated panel organization for three pages to switch points of view between Matt and Elektra: one horizontal panel that stops short of extending from edge to edge of the page, five vertical panels that resemble the earlier pages' layout turned ninety degrees, and a bottom panel mirroring the top one. Miller matches the visual symmetry with thematic symmetry. While Elektra stalks and then attacks the Hand assassins (who are stalking Murdock in turn) in panels 1 and 7, Matt tries to pull Foggy out of his funk in panels 2 through

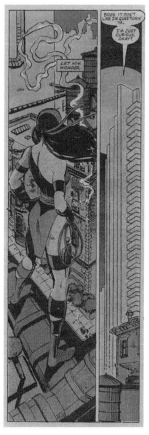

FIGURE 38. Frank Miller and Klaus Janson, "The Assassination of Matt Murdock," *Daredevil* #174 (Marvel, September 1981).

6. Then, on the final page of this fixed pattern, the two spaces become one as the story actions intersect: Elektra fails to stop one assassin from throwing a bomb into Nelson and Murdock's law office, the center panels show the impact, and a final panel focuses on Elektra's reaction—the wide-eyed honesty of her irrepressible urge to protect Matt (figures 39 and 40). And there are still eight pages left in issue #174, including a hospital scene, a car crash, and two climactic fight scenes, before it concludes with Elektra being targeted as the Hand's next victim.

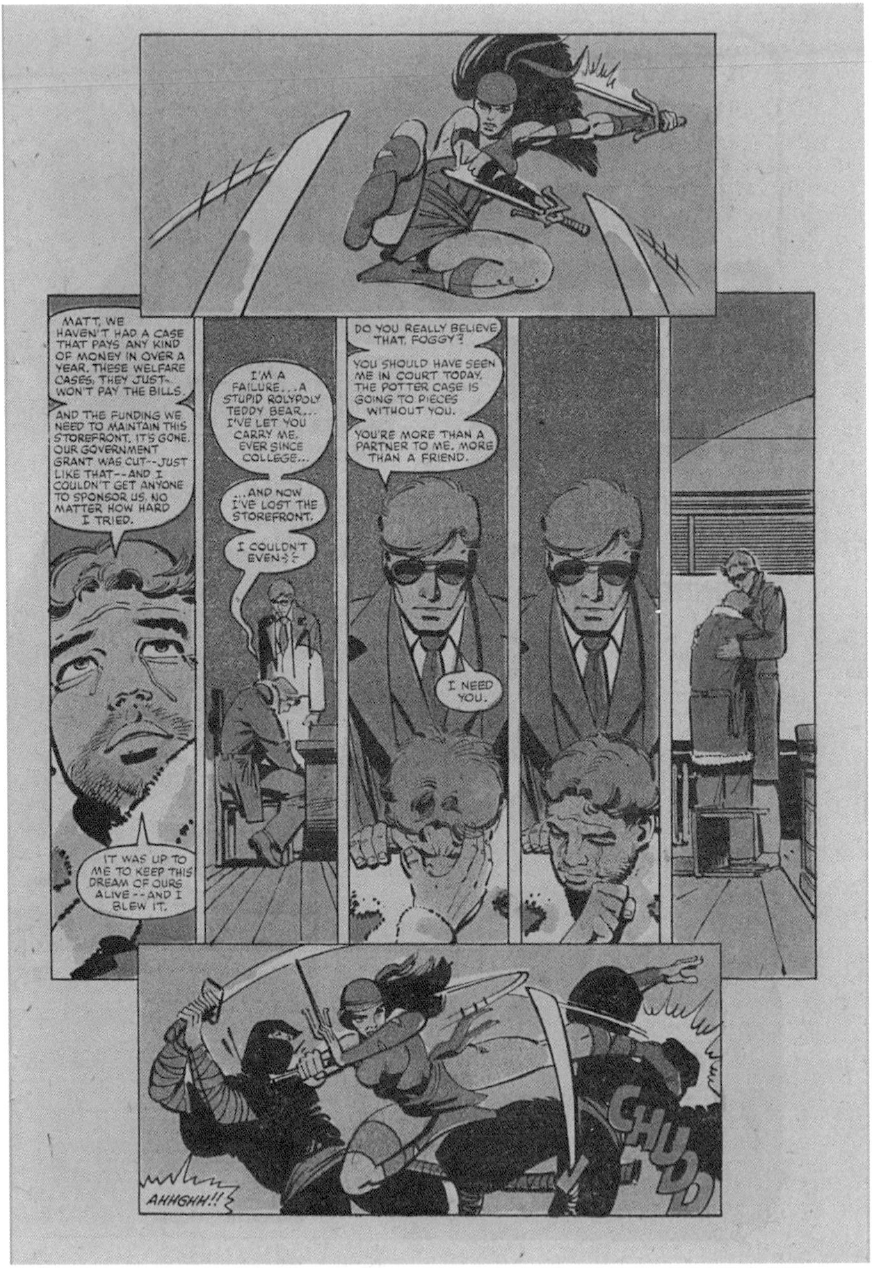
MATT, WE HAVEN'T HAD A CASE THAT PAYS ANY KIND OF MONEY IN OVER A YEAR. THESE WELFARE CASES, THEY JUST WON'T PAY THE BILLS.
AND THE FUNDING WE NEED TO MAINTAIN THIS STOREFRONT, IT'S GONE. OUR GOVERNMENT GRANT WAS CUT--JUST LIKE THAT--AND I COULDN'T GET ANYONE TO SPONSOR US, NO MATTER HOW HARD I TRIED.
IT WAS UP TO ME TO KEEP THIS DREAM OF OURS ALIVE--AND I BLEW IT.
I'M A FAILURE...A STUPID ROLYPOLY TEDDY BEAR... I'VE LET YOU CARRY ME, EVER SINCE COLLEGE...
...AND NOW I'VE LOST THE STOREFRONT.
I COULDN'T EVEN--
DO YOU REALLY BELIEVE THAT, FOGGY?
YOU SHOULD HAVE SEEN ME IN COURT TODAY. THE POTTER CASE IS GOING TO PIECES WITHOUT YOU.
YOU'RE MORE THAN A PARTNER TO ME. MORE THAN A FRIEND.
I NEED YOU.
AHHGHH!!
CHUDD

FIGURES 39 AND 40. Frank Miller and Klaus Janson, "The Assassination of Matt Murdock," *Daredevil* #174 (Marvel, September 1981).

Miller's choice of the identical panel shapes, sizes, and positions for these three consecutive pages sets productive limits on the layout while orienting readers just clearly enough to keep them focused on the events. The only hint that Miller gives us regarding the relative positioning of characters is the positions of the panels in which they appear, and as it turns out, these panel positions offer a sufficient representation of their locations, with the Hand assassins battling Elektra in the top and bottom panels, which overlap the page's center row as Matt and Foggy discuss legal business in the claustrophobic central panels. Over the course of these three pages, these central panels come to stand for the apartment building itself, where the two friends unwittingly stand in the eye of the storm. The drama of these pages is both virtuosic and breathlessly economical. Miller used repetition of panel layouts to generate humor, too. In issue #176, Wall-Eyed Pike, a semiprofessional pool hustler and professional criminal stooge, suffers three break-ins in a row perpetrated by Elektra, Turk, and Daredevil, all seeking information about the whereabouts of Stick. If repetition is the soul of comedy, Miller makes this scene funnier than it would have been otherwise by repeating the same panel arrangement for each event; it's the page layout equivalent to rolling one's eyes and moaning, "Here we go again." And if there's any doubt that this scene is supposed to be funny, Miller throws in a "plop-plop-fizz-fizz" sound effect when Pike drops Alka-Seltzer tablets into a glass of water. Where else but a comic book, where words only "make" the sounds we attach to them in our minds, could onomatopoeia from a TV jingle conjure up the sound of the product without changing the mood of the entire story from grim to goofy?

THE RECESSION OF THE IMAGE

The irony of Miller's experiments in fixed layout is that his *Daredevil* run also looks like it's deteriorating before our eyes. By this I do not mean that New York is physically crumbling (which, thanks to the Kingpin and Bullseye, it may as well be) or that Matt Murdock's life is falling to pieces (which it clearly is) but that the panel borders framing these diegetic matters figuratively and literally disappear over the course of the run. In the beginning, Miller frequently concretizes panel frames, as though they were physical features of Daredevil's world. In #158, Daredevil throws a punch from front to back while crouching with his knees nearly on the ground (an impossible feat worthy of a Kirby *Thor* panel). In the absence of any mise-en-scène beyond the figures of DD and Death-Stalker—only a sky-blue background setting off the all-black figures, the yellow of Death-Stalker's energy bolts and the symbolic flash of the punch's impact, and the red "THOK" sound effect—Daredevil is actually standing on the bottom of the frame, his feet making contact with the inked line. Of course, Carmine Infantino made his characters stand on the bottom frame line so consistently in his Batman stories from *Detective Comics* in the sixties that it looks as though we are witnessing the Dynamic Duo's exploits while lying on the floor. For Miller, however, this choice is more than a stylistic tic; it's a test, as if Miller were trying to steady himself for his first big professional challenge. By standing on the line, Daredevil claims his comic-book world as stable ground, perhaps the one solid thing he can count on in a world haunted by ghosts both supernatural (Death-Stalker, the resurrected Hand assassin Kirigi) and all too human (Elektra). By issue #173, seven issues after taking over as writer, Miller renders borderless panels on no fewer than eight pages per issue. The borders that remain seem increasingly permeable. Feet and elbows frequently cross them as though the characters—and Miller himself—have become frustrated by the limitations of the medium but are wary of leaving them behind.

Frameless panels don't necessarily signal formal self-consciousness so much as a cartoonist's attempt to vary his or her delivery of images. To name only a couple out of hundreds of potential examples, Wally Wood's much-reprinted memo to himself, "24 Panels That Always Work,"[42] contains a couple of open frames depicting entire cars and people, and Eisner eventually developed the frequent frameless panels of his *Spirit* stories into the completely borderless experiments of his later endeavors as a graphic novelist. But reflexivity in comics is as old as the medium itself. Tom Gunning cites a Winsor McCay *Little Sammy Sneeze* strip from 1905, in which Sammy's infamous sneeze shatters the very panel borders that contain him, to illustrate McCay's exploitation of a reflexivity that dates back at least to the nineteenth-century comic albums of Rodolphe Töpffer.[43] The oxymoronic quality of Miller's open-frame panels intrinsically troubles the diegetic focus of superhero comics. Opening the gutter, removing frame lines as Miller does as early as #158 alongside panels that insist on their impermeability, is a somewhat risky proposition for a cartoonist if we accept McCloud's point about gutters catalyzing closure for the reader. Depending on their size and frequency, frameless panels siphon away some of the reader's control over the temporality of sequences, because the panel then becomes, for lack of a better word, potentially timeless. A page full of closed panels functions a bit like one of Joseph Cornell's boxes in that they allow readers to peer into interconnected areas of interest that, taken together, constitute a world apart. But open panels offer readers involvement in a different order of space. While bordered panels provide access to discrete, successive moments, frameless panels give the impression that the figures "in" them stand above or outside the diegetic space. They now exist explicitly in the space of comics, the space where the experience of reading takes place. This space is not seen on the page or through it. It is the page itself.

Over the run, Miller's open frames become a barometer for the series's growing recognition of itself as a nothing more than a superhero comic, one doomed, like all superhero comics, to repeat itself infinitely. As early as #158, Miller hinders our eyes' forward momentum by plopping a single open panel in the center of a page made up of border-to-border horizontal views, coaxing our attention back the center of the page even after we have read past it. It's tempting to see such a choice as a rookie mistake, but soon enough it becomes a conventional feature of Miller's fight scenes. When Janson took over the penciling duties with issue #184, using Miller's thumbnail page layouts as his guide (figures 41 and 42), the frameless panels become more infrequent, but Miller continued a version of his experiment by laying out fewer frames per page and turning the blank gutters from narrow breaks between dense panels to the dominant space of the page. No longer ground to the panels' figures, the whitish space of the newsprint dominates the two-page spread depicting Matt and Heather's breakup in #189; emotional emptiness, as it turns out, has its icons too. But the ultimate disappearing act takes place in #191, Miller's final issue, for which he provided full pencils that were inked not by Janson but by Terry Austin, a gifted, slightly cartoony inker and a fan favorite for his earlier work over Marshall Rogers's Batman in *Detective Comics* and John Byrne's empire-founding pencils in *X-Men*. In this story, titled "Roulette," Miller makes both open frames and stark white figure backgrounds crucial to his compositions, to the point where they

FIGURE 41 (LEFT). Frank Miller, sketch design for splash page, *Daredevil* #188 (Marvel, November 1982). FIGURE 42 (RIGHT). Frank Miller (design) and Klaus Janson (pencils and inks), finished splash page for "The Widow's Bite," *Daredevil* #188 (Marvel, November 1982).

begin to make the framed panels and more fully rendered settings surrounding them—the standard icons of lushly composed comic-book worlds—look unnervingly artificial.

Daredevil, holding a gun for the second time in Miller's run, plays Russian roulette with Bullseye as the latter lies paralyzed in a hospital bed. The hospital room barely counts as a room at all. It lacks any indication of floor or ceiling save an occasional cast shadow, and it features only the bed, an IV bag, a chair, and rectangles of light shining on the figures and floor through nonexistent venetian blinds. Either the walls of the hospital room are missing, or they are papered with blank, gray-white newsprint, because that's all we see (figure 43).

The story is as stark as its surroundings. As I have discussed, Miller puts a .38 revolver in Daredevil's hand to externalize his burning desire to eliminate Bullseye for good but reveals at the climax that DD packs an unloaded gun. Over the course of the issue, he relates

FIGURE 44. Frank Miller and Terry Austin, "Roulette," *Daredevil* #191 (Marvel, February 1983).

some recent history to Bullseye (though he may be talking only to himself, as his tale is confined entirely to first-person narration boxes rather than word balloons). It's the story of Chuckie, a young boy whose father Murdock agrees to represent in an embezzlement case. Chuckie idolizes Daredevil to the point of telling his father at the dinner table that he *is* Daredevil, to Murdock's obvious chagrin. Murdock soon learns that the father is guilty, leading to a terrifying scene in which Chuckie witnesses his father pulling a gun on a coworker who has discovered the father's crime, then watches as Daredevil, his hero, punches his father out. Having done the right thing by the law (setting aside the physical assault), Daredevil finds that that his actions have driven Chuckie to identify with Bullseye instead. Chuckie then shoots a schoolmate with a pistol just like his father's. "Am I fighting violence—or teaching it?" Daredevil asks Bullseye, but the question is clearly posed to the reader, whom Miller then supplies with yet another knot to untie. When Murdock was a child, Battlin' Jack ordered him not to fight in school, then smacked his son across the face when he disobeyed. This was the moment when young Matt swore to himself to become a lawyer and uphold the rules that protect the innocent. What he didn't know at the time was that his future as a masked crusader would allow him to indulge in his father's violence just enough to grease the wheels of justice, but no more. Powerful as he is, undaunted by his weaknesses and fearless in his defense of the law, Daredevil has finally realized that he, too, is paralyzed. For years, he has expressed through violence his desire to retaliate against those who see ordinary people as prey, but his Catholic faith and his choice to supplement, not replace, the legal system have stopped him short of killing his enemies.

As Daredevil tortures Bullseye with the revolver and himself with his memories, his anger and restraint yank against each other so furiously that the result can only be a paralysis of will as overpowering as the physical paralysis of his bedridden enemy (figures 44 and 45). Anything he does as Daredevil now will only send Murdock straight back to this crisis of conscience, revealing anew the impossible binary that lies at the center of his crime-fighting career: the only thing worse than sin by commission, breaking both the law and God's commandment by killing those who relentlessly endanger the innocent, is sin by omission—the thought of leaving his fellow citizens vulnerable to Bullseye's violence and corruption by failing to end his enemy's life.

FIGURE 45. Frank Miller and Terry Austin, "Roulette," *Daredevil* #191 (Marvel, February 1983).

He is left with nothing to hope for. By stripping bare the stage for this revelation, Miller the expressionist has figured out how to make even emptiness expressive. And the emptiness spreads. While most depictions in #191 of settings beyond this room contain verisimilar props and bear at least a single color, the dining room in the home of Chuckie, the boy who idolizes Daredevil and fears his father, contains nothing but a table and chairs floating in space. It's a fitting arena for the father's humiliation of Chuckie in front of Murdock, a humiliation so quotidian that it drives Chuckie to withdraw into his dreams of violent heroism and watch a tape of DD's historic slugfest with Bullseye at the TV station over and over again. The weightless ambiguity of the physical world has ceased to matter compared to the vividness and moral clarity of the world within.

But the visual emptiness has another function as well, one in keeping with Miller's exploration of the superhero genre in all its conventionality. By showcasing the material conditions of the medium in this story of heroic paralysis, Miller acknowledges the bleak consequences of Marvel's "illusion of change" philosophy for the comic book as an

art form. While it's true that most of the panels in this story have clearly lined borders, at this point, the borders function merely to guide
the eye rather than to provide any illusionist sense that we are peering
into a window at the action; they simply separate drawings from other
drawings. The characters regress to lines on the page, an effect made
all the more potent by the assignment of Austin rather than Janson to
the task of inking Miller's full pencils. Janson's inks render Miller's layouts scratchy, caricatural, and urgent. He preserves the gestural quality that Miller has always brought to the page, as if his lines were too
busy to keep still because every image is tasked with both showing us
an event and anticipating the next threat and the next victory. Austin,
on the other hand, inks with such control that he seems to strip everything down to the sharpest single line possible. Daredevil and Bullseye
are minimalized both as figures against a nonexistent background and
as ciphers who take on meaning, ultimately, not as individual subjects
but only in relation to each other—the superheroic equivalent of Itchy
and Scratchy from *The Simpsons*, in which the only point of the central conflict is to kill, be killed, and anticipate the next setup to begin
the cycle all over again. "Guess we're stuck with each other, Bullseye,"
Daredevil thinks as the hospital room suddenly becomes an expanse
of black ink.

At the end of this story of marking time, published by the company
responsible for the convention that good can never quite win and evil
can never quite lose, Daredevil's final line pulls the back off the time-
piece that is the Marvel universe and reveals that there's nothing inside
but a single gear that never stops spinning. There is no room here for
the furtive sketches of the eager young cartoonist, only the finality of
the one essential line. Whatever happens in it, the story has already
been written, because everything is reversible except Daredevil's
refusal to kill his enemies and put an end to their reign of terror. Elektra is dead, but there was no Elektra until Miller invented her, and now
that Miller is gone, the series can plough forward as though she never
existed. Bullseye is paralyzed, but Bullseye was just another costumed
crook until Miller made him DD's worst nightmare—and supervillains
are a dime a dozen anyway. And really, what difference could a couple
of dozen stories make to readers of a series that was less than a year
short of its two hundredth issue? In mainstream superhero comics,
displacement is always, ultimately, zero. But upon Miller's departure

from *Daredevil*, he managed to cheat the seemingly inevitable return to square one. With #191, he lay Marvel's "illusion of change" philosophy bare. He turned the act of leaving Daredevil and his world the way he found them into an admission that superhero comics, stymied as much by commercial expediency as by the Comics Code, exist in a perpetual state of self-erasure. All we really have on the pages before us are a good guy, a bad guy, and a gun with no bullets.

DAREDEVIL VERSUS THE CATECHISM

NB: The following exchange is not intended to be blasphemous. Martin Luther, who liked to think that everybody had a valid opinion (except, presumably, when it came to his own anti-Semitism), would probably not mind it. It represents the convergence of my life as a nerd, a pastor's kid (or "PK"), and a comic-book fan whose mind wandered dramatically during Wednesday-evening Confirmation classes in the winter. Students in a Lutheran Confirmation class, as communicants and future full-fledged members of the Lutheran church, learn to respect, revere, and follow the beliefs appropriate to a devout church member primarily by memorizing a seemingly insurmountable quantity of doctrinal information. Among the memorized texts are Bible books and the order in which they appear, the Ten Commandments, a few prayers, and most of all, Luther's voluminous explanations of all of them. We wrote out much of what we memorized in a workbook supplied by one of the Lutheran supply stores; it contained short readings, memorization aids, and Mad Libs–style exercises that allowed for none of the random verbs, nouns, and adjectives that made Mad Libs actually enjoyable (imagine the sacrilegious consequences: "The LORD is my *backpack*, I shall not *punt*"). The margins of my workbook were filled in with hundreds of drawings of Spider-Man's head.

This mock workbook entry, presented as if filled in by a thirteen-year-old kid with a wild imagination and a tendency to let his mind wander on purpose whenever he could get away with it, is intended as a collapsed compendium of the author's early adolescence under the influence of Marvel Comics, Frank Miller, and *Daredevil*. As such, it is factually accurate save for its distortions of time, space, experience, memory, and events that occurred in objective reality. The author takes no responsibility for any such distortions. To summarize, this is a pubescent screen memory, so watch out.

NBB: This interlude is best read accompanied by a page-by-page reading of the scripture at hand: *Daredevil* #181 (April 1982). Granted, it's a thirty-year-old back issue, and we now live in an era when the merest whisper that a given hero will appear in a movie or TV show sends asking prices for the hero's key issues through the roof. However, as of early 2016, it's cheap by comparison to the poorly drawn first appearance of Deadpool in *New Mutants* #98, and the art and writing are much better. Don't cheat with a reprint. Buy the real deal from your local comics shop or a shifty online retailer, and then flip through it while reading this chapter. It's best to take it in ads and all, because they contribute to the pace and timing of the story.

CONFIRMATION WORKBOOK
The Lutheran Small Catechism, Distracted Teenager Edition
Section 8: *Daredevil* #181, "Last Hand," by Frank Miller (story/art), Klaus Janson (finished art and colors), Joe Rosen (letterer). Edited by Denny O'Neil. Jim Shooter, editor in chief (listed in credits as "Supervisor").

The First Commandment
You shall have no other gods.

What does this mean?
We should fear, love, and trust in God above all things.

What do you think about that?
I don't think you want to know.

Try me. God forgives tons of crazy sins.
Well, what I'm thinking about right now would probably count as a graven image that turns my head from the one true God. It's the splash page of "Last Hand," and I don't think God would be too keen on it. Daredevil is getting his head blown off. It looks like we're the ones pulling the trigger because there's a diagonal set of crosshairs between him and us. The "blood" spraying out of his head in all directions is

black, but the abstract color surrounding him is red and splattery like somebody spray-painted the page and left a white cloud around the superhero. Once you read the narration text, though, you realize that you're seeing someone's fantasy of killing Daredevil, through his eyes. This guy has got to be Bullseye, because he's on the cover, and he wants Daredevil dead more than anybody. But the cover also says, "Bullseye vs. Elektra: One Wins. One Dies." Looks like everybody's in the cross-hairs this time around.

This is a double-sized issue, although I think it's just advertising hype to call it double. I've never counted the pages of a "double-sized" issue to make sure. Maybe there will be fewer ads than usual. Most comic books don't print ads until at least three pages into the story, though, so we always get a nice two-page spread after the splash. The first spread starts with a stack of long panels that look like skinny windshields. The top panel shows nothing but Bullseye's eyes, looking straight at us, and that gets my attention right away. They're creepy, like the eyes Steve Ditko draws. They are too big and too close together, the pupils are giant, and they stare at me as if to scold me for getting excited about that first page. What grabbed me so thoroughly about it? Was it the blood? Was it because it looked like Daredevil died?

Why are you reading this? Your parents probably wouldn't approve. My brother Tim and I get a monthly newsletter from our mail-order comic subscription service. Other customers write in telling how amazing Frank Miller's *Daredevil* is, and people say the same thing in the comics fanzines they sell at the Pinball Place. I bike there on Saturdays to play Asteroids and Star Castle and look through the comics, and they're usually playing KRNA, which means that AC/DC's "You Shook Me All Night Long" is going to be on the radio while I'm there. It's a good soundtrack for firing photon torpedoes at hurtling space rocks. We bought a couple of issues of *Daredevil* a couple years ago and didn't stick with it. It was a bimonthly series, and it was hard to find back when we had to buy comics from the spinner rack at the 7-11. And besides, it looked weird and violent. Since then, I've changed my mind about violent or strange-looking comics and particularly about Miller's art. To succeed at drawing superheroes you've got to do something different from anyone else. Unlike most other artists these days, Miller isn't trying to make Daredevil and his supporting cast look like the characters in John Romita's *Spider-Man*. His New York looks scrubby, and so does everyone in it—Miller and Janson's line work isn't even trying to be clean like Romita's, and there's something liberating about that. Anyway, the rest of the panels on page 2 alternate between Bullseye's memories of Daredevil smacking him around and different angles on Bullseye sitting in a cage, empty except for him, grimacing like he's trying to grind his teeth into his gums. Nothing but bars everywhere. He hates being imprisoned, but he hates Daredevil even more because he once saved Bullseye's life. I didn't know about that because we don't have the issue it happened in, but all I need to know to get into this story is that Bullseye is *pissed*. He's thinking, "You had to pull me off the tracks so I could hear every snicker, every jibe." I guess he wanted Daredevil to leave him there to die, because he'd rather be dead than have everybody know that DD first defeated him, then spared him. He's thinking about how badly he wants to be known as "the man who killed Daredevil! Just wait . . ."

Then Bullseye is in the prison gym working out. He's holding onto the rings while hanging upright, so he's pretty strong. He kinda looks like he's floating in space because the panel he's in is tall and thin but still shorter than the comic page. I wonder why Miller lets so many of the narration text float on the blank part of the page like that with no frames around the words? A couple of people are talking to him now, but they're just silhouettes, looking through a window into the gym. They call him "Benjamin," probably to make him sound like a regular person instead of a code-named assassin. Miller doesn't allow us to see anything regular about him. But Bullseye plays along, acting calm so they'll think he wants to reform. To help him along that path, his doctors want him to be a guest on the Tom Snyde show. (Miller must not like that talk-show host Tom Snyder very much. Frankly, neither do I.)

Then Bullseye throws his head back and yells "ARRGHH." On the next page, the guard makes him put his arms into stationary cuffs, like the stocks in *The Scarlet Letter*, so he can give Bullseye his pills. The guard, Harry, mentions that Bullseye had a brain tumor that got removed. But he still gets headaches, and this headache you can see—there's this big red flash, like the black blood spurt on the splash page but even bigger, like now Bullseye is the one getting his head blown off. The red flash disappears as soon as Bullseye gets the pills, but because the guard acted like a dick and opened the pill bottle

really, really slowly—it took him five narrow vertical panels to do it—
Bullseye says, "You're a dead man, Harry." While he says that, there's
another series of similarly thin horizontal panels, each one framed a
little closer to Bullseye's eyes. At the bottom, his face turns from skin
color to this aquamarine tint, and suddenly there's a tiny Daredevil in
front of his eyes as he squints, angrily. He's thinking about how DD
is probably working out in his own gym just then, without "snotty
guards or bleeding heart parole officers" bothering him. There are
four or five Daredevils in every panel because Miller draws several
images of him in each one to show . . . I don't know, how complicated his moves are, with the flips and jujitsu punches and everything?
Miller doesn't use motion lines here like most artists would, but then
if he did, he couldn't display the big arcs of Matt's movements. These
multiple Daredevils take up the whole panel, which itself takes up the
whole row, and they all show him moving left to right, like he's going
forward. I just noticed that Bullseye is facing the other direction, to
the left, on the page before it. Ooo, symbolism! Like they're facing in
two different directions! I am being sarcastic because the metaphor
seems a little forced to me. But maybe it isn't. After all, I've never even
noticed a comic-book artist even trying something like that before.

The Second Commandment
You shall not take the name of the Lord, your God, in vain.

What does this mean?
It means I had better stay away from Jake, who is teaching me to swear
and teases me for being such a preacher's kid that I can't do it without
feeling guilty. But I met Paul Moellers through him, and Paul sold me
his old copy of *Daredevil* #168, which I had missed when I stopped
buying the book for a while. So at least I knew who Elektra was before
#181 came in the mail.

The Third Commandment
You shall keep thc day of rest holy.

What does this mean?
For one thing, I should not read comics in the middle of getting
dressed for church. I tend to forget what I was doing and just sit there

on the bed, reading away in my dress shirt, underwear, and socks until somebody yells at me to get with the program.

The Fourth Commandment
Honor your father and your mother, that it may be well with you, and that you may live long on the earth.

What does this mean?
Hm. Something in that one says to me, "Thou shalt stop buying comics." At tax time, when my dad gets mad about anybody spending money on anything that can't be eaten or worn, I decide not to buy them anymore, for about twenty seconds. Like that's going to happen. Someday Dad won't care that we bought all these comics. He might even be happy, if the comics gain some value. *Daredevil* #181 could be worth a hundred dollars someday because something important happened in it, and that raises demand. We bought something like four copies of it, and we ordered a couple of copies autographed by Miller, too.

Daredevil #181 is never going to be Giant-Size X-Men #1. But you will still keep your copies pristine because this issue will haunt you for the rest of your life. It even caused me to write this monograph . . . I mean, this catechism.
You make no sense. Are you going to kill my livestock and give me a skin rash like you did with Job?

I'm not God.
Luther, then. Whatever. Moses.

I'm you, in thirty, thirty-five years. I'm writing a book about Miller and Daredevil in which I try to figure out, maybe to justify, what compelled me so much about reading it when I was in junior high. This catechetical format is just a conceit.
Conceit? You're conceited?

Sorry, I forget that you're—I mean, I'm still thirteen where you are. No, I'm not conceited, I don't think, though my therapist says I have a narcissistic bent that causes me to hold my writing to such impossible standards that I paralyze myself and can't work. I think she's just unfamiliar with my condition, which is fairly common. It's called "being an academic from the Midwest."

I have no idea what you are talking about. You're writing a book about comics? About *Daredevil* #181? A book that's getting printed? And sold?

I don't know about sold, but it will get published, I think.

Wow. You can do that? I wish I could write about Miller and comics for a living. Fat chance of that. Liking comics or doing well in school makes you a nerd, and being a nerd means the only kind of attention you get for reading comics or doing well in school is the kind you'd rather not have.

I'm pretty sure the comics aren't the trouble here. If you let yourself like comics more, you might come out of junior high better than I did.

But I'm you, right? What do you mean by liking comics more?

You love them, but you're embarrassed by them. And they cost money, so you hide them from your parents because you don't want them to think you're wasting your allowance. You feel almost as guilty about spending that money as you do about putting quarters into pinball machines and video games. You don't talk about comics with anyone but your brother, and you like to draw but you don't throw yourself into it completely. It's as though you're worried about giving in to your love of comics and making up stories and forgetting about school and drama and band—the things you are pretty sure you're good at and that have the advantage of making adults proud of you.

You make it sound like my life with comic books is like a secret identity, but there's nothing cool about it like Cyclops's secret identity or Daredevil's. For one thing, those guys suffer in silence, and the beautiful women around them can't contain their desire to take these poor men in their arms and console them. I would love to have that power, the power to attract people's curiosity by brooding, but in my experience, brooding just means you're snooty and antisocial and gives other kids *more* reason to treat you like a nerd. When Elektra dies in *Daredevil* #181, Murdock suffers, but he does it nobly, in silence. He doesn't display how he feels because that might give away the fact that he's

Daredevil. He can't even tell anybody he's a human radar dish, because what would the supervillains do if they found out who he really is or that he is blind? He has all these powers and abilities, and he can't tell anybody. But he never gives his feelings away. He just stands there and pretends that nothing affects him. And Karen Page and the Black Widow and Heather Glenn and even his secretary, Becky, fall for him because he's so sad and tortured and won't express it. I only pretend to be sad and tortured because maybe it will make some girl think I'm fascinating, but I spoil the mystery by *explaining why I am sad and tortured.* The social stuff is way too complicated for me. You must remember what junior high was like: eating a shit sandwich, all day, every day.

I guess there's something to the idea of kids identifying with comic-book characters, after all. These days, identification is kind of a dead theory, at least when it comes to theorizing how people engage with movies. Maybe comics are different?
When I read *Daredevil,* I feel like I get to be Daredevil for a little while: righteously sad and tortured, admired and desired, and above all powerful beyond anybody's wildest dreams. He has discipline. And on top of all that, I get to be Frank Miller, too. I get to see a story the way he sees it. Sometimes I don't have the slightest idea why he visualizes things certain ways, but he thinks pretty carefully about how to arrange what we see and how we see it. He spends a lot more time making those decisions than hacks like Sal Buscema or Don Perlin do. How can my brother even *look* at Perlin's pencils in *The Defenders* without dry heaving, let alone try to convince me it read it, too?

Even the narration of *Daredevil* #181 is different. I like that Miller has Bullseye tell the story. You don't expect him to be the narrator because comics publish stories about heroes. But Bullseye telling the story makes Matt all the more the hero because Bullseye keeps guessing wrong about what Matt is thinking, and I get to enjoy how wrong he is, how much more in control of the situation Matt is because he knows how to keep his secrets. The best moment in #181 is when Bullseye almost figures out Daredevil's secret identity. Posing as a janitor, Bullseye sees Matt at the morgue identifying Elektra's body. (Why does he have to identify her when she died in his arms? Maybe Miller stages the morgue visit just to put Bullseye and Matt, out of costume, in the same scene to set up Bullseye's realization.) When Bullseye talks—he has killed the real janitor but tells a morgue employee that he "got . . . uh . . . McCaffrey's old job"—and Bullseye notices that Matt just freezes, like he recognizes Bullseye's voice—like maybe he's secretly Daredevil. This idea doesn't come to Bullseye out of the blue. He was thinking about it earlier when he was drunk, lying on the floor of a "fleabag" hotel room with a research file on Nelson and Murdock (see, Bullseye is gunning for Elektra, the assassin who took his job with the Kingpin when he went to prison) and laughing. "Wouldn't that be a kick—Daredevil, the blind superhero! Like I said, crazy idea." So when Bullseye sees how Matt reacts to his voice, he decides his "crazy idea" could've been right and decides to test it. He slings what is supposed to be a surgical knife (I *think*, but it looks like a piece of broken glass) at Matt, and instead of getting his throat cut, Matt nonchalantly whips out his cane and blocks it with a "THUNK." "Got news for you, Mattie boy. It's blown," Bullseye thinks, and Miller shows him running, in a bird's-eye view, from the top of the panel to the bottom—he's all motion, there's no background to get in the way of this panel or any other panel in the scene, except some people and like a grid of cold-looking tiles on the walls of the autopsy room. And there's so much white space on both pages of the scene that it looks like how you would stage a morgue scene in *Our Town*: no detail, hardly any props, everything is implied, stark. Even the color is missing. Elektra's skin is white, and there's still blood—black, Comics Code–approved blood— on her face from where Bullseye hit her and slashed her throat. It's horrible to think about, more haunting than if it was realistic, because Elektra looks like a China doll—something completely removed from the land of the living but not a B-movie zombie either. Her unearthly paleness gets across how it feels to be in a room with a dead body. At a funeral-home visitation, we pretend it makes sense that the body is wearing a nice suit or a dress, but everyone knows that this inanimate object is as far removed from wearing underwear or a tie as you can get. Still, I get the impression that Miller uses this starkness to tell us something about Bullseye's reaction to the space and the event, not Matt's. Remember, this is Bullseye's story. The empty setting doesn't express sadness. It just implies that all Bullseye cares about is whether the people in the autopsy room are alive or dead, because all he is thinking about, all he *ever* thinks about, is whom to kill next and how.

And now he thinks he's got Daredevil where he wants him. He's gonna take his revenge for Daredevil making him look weak and making the other inmates laugh at him, and we kind of think he's got DD where he wants him, too. But we also know that's not true. It doesn't cost Miller anything to let Bullseye tell the story. It's not like the Comics Code is gonna come down on Miller for glorifying violence. We know Bullseye won't win. The comic book isn't called *Bullseye*. But learning the hero's secret identity *and* preparing to kill him—that's the double whammy that gives this story a grim and consequential tone. It's like when the Joker was about to unmask the Dynamic Duo in front of TV cameras on the Adam West *Batman* show, and that's the cliffhanger, except that show is just dumb compared to this because nobody ever really seems to be in danger. The heroes will never die or lose or get their identities revealed. Well, I guess that's never going to happen to Daredevil either. Maybe the Batman show isn't so different from "serious" comics after all. But when all-out crime changes life into something as cheap as Bullseye makes it, it feels like there's really something at stake.

So anyway, Bullseye finally goes to see the Kingpin to tell him that Matt Murdock is Daredevil. Kingpin thinks this is a "pathetic ploy": Bullseye is just trying "to convince me to reinstate you as my chief assassin. Bring me Daredevil's body . . . and we will do business." The Kingpin has his doubts, and who can blame him? Bullseye is claiming that Matt went blind, yes, but he faked his "recovery" from the initial symptoms of the nuclear accident, which included the heightening of his remaining senses . . . that's what really happened in the comic book, but who would believe it in *Miller's* version of Daredevil's world, where nothing more metaphysical happens than a gun going off? Well, that's not quite true . . . the Hand's assassin Kirigi resurrected himself two or three times after Elektra killed him . . . but never mind that now. It doesn't matter to the Kingpin who Daredevil really is. The Kingpin just wants his head.

To get a-head, ha-ha, Bullseye breaks into Matt Murdock's bachelor pad and hears Matt talking, like he's dictating a legal document or something, something about the Fourth Amendment. That's pretty funny, because here's Bullseye creeping around Matt's apartment uninvited, and in Civics last term we learned about the Bill of Rights and how the Fourth Amendment bans illegal search and seizure.

You mean "unreasonable search and seizure," not "illegal." Search and seizure are not illegal if sanctioned and performed by the right authorities. If there's no warrant, however, and the plaintiff's counsel invokes the Fourth, courts are more likely to rule that the search and seizure was illegal. Then whatever evidence came up in the search is inadmissible in court. Theoretically, anyway.

Right, but Bullseye isn't an authority on anything but killing people, and he sure doesn't have a warrant to sneak around in Matt's apartment holding a luger.

Okay, so you're right, it's ironic and funny. But in fact the Fourth Amendment is only one factor in play in the text Matt is reading aloud as Bullseye sneaks into his apartment. Did you do a search for any specific phrases on the Internet? Didn't Miller write what Matt is reading? What's an Intern-Net?

Oops. Anachronism strikes. What Matt says goes like this: ". . . the Fourth Amendment contemplates a prior judicial judgment, not the risk that executive indiscretion may be reasonably exercised. . . . This judicial role accords with our basic constitutional doctrine . . . that individual freedoms will best be preserved

FIGURE 46. Frank Miller and Klaus Janson, "Last Hand," *Daredevil* #181 (Marvel, April 1982).

through a separation of powers and division of functions among the different branches and levels of government . . . prior review by a neutral and detached magistrate . . . ," and then DD's red-gloved hand falls onto Bullseye's shoulder from off-panel left. "No," Bullseye thinks. Turns out what we were "hearing" was a recording all along, and "like a dummy," Bullseye says, "I fell for it!" (figure 46).

Then Miller reveals that a dummy with a red wig and big sunglasses has been sitting at Matt's desk the whole time, holding a microphone and appearing to read from a book propped open in front of it. Big win for Daredevil; the text is just Matt's voice playing through the same tape recorder he's supposedly using to record dictation.

"Like a *dummy*." It's such a groaner, it's almost painful to read.

But it's efficient, how Miller gets across Matt's ruse—which took me nearly a paragraph to describe verbally—with a single image of a dummy and a tape recorder. We infer all the rest from the fact that we thought we "heard" Matt's voice on the preceding page, and Bullseye saying "dummy" is just the spark we need to make all the other connections. We never hear a peep from Matt himself about this plan to catch Bullseye, because Bullseye is telling the story! Neither the images nor the words could get all of this information across on their own; each needs the other to supply the necessary context.

In any event, here's where I was going with the Fourth Amendment, which is less important here in itself than it is for what it implies about legal overreaching and the excuses occasionally made for it in the name of justice. What Matt says on the tape is the text of a 1972 Supreme Court decision, 407 U.S. 297, in which the Nixon administration was told it couldn't bring surveillance tapes as evidence against the White Panthers, a leftist group affiliated with the Black Panthers, in a conspiracy case because the wiretap had not been properly authorized. John Mitchell, Nixon's attorney general at the time, claimed he had authorized it legally, but courts right up to the Supreme Court itself disagreed and ordered the recordings disclosed. The ruling meant that the executive branch of the US government had overstepped its bounds; it had to answer to the law of the land like everybody else.

So? Is this some kind of joke about Bullseye overhearing what turns out to be a tape used to fool him, a tape that doesn't tell the truth even though that's what tape recording seems to be for? It's a little late for

Tricky Dick jokes, isn't it? My mom hasn't baked a Watergate Cake in years.

Don't forget that it isn't just the Fourth Amendment Miller is citing. It's a specific invocation of it from the same year that Nixon campaign funds paid for a break-in at the Democratic National Committee office in the Watergate Hotel, before anyone was putting pistachios in their cakes and laughing about how "bugs" could be anywhere, recording everything we say.

So Miller is making Bullseye's break-in into a comment on the separation of powers? That's pretty obscure, isn't it? Checks and balances?

Is it really so obscure, Mr. I Like Social Studies?

Wait, the brief on Matt's tape is about the president breaking federal laws, right? Nobody is above the law to Daredevil, and if the courts won't get Bullseye, then he will. So Miller wants to remind us about that, quietly. We would have to know the case to know that, though.

I'm not sure that's so. The tape specifically mentions that the executive branch didn't honor the separation of powers. The White House didn't go through the proper authorities to get a warrant for those wiretaps. In other words, if the president isn't above the law, then no one is. Certainly not Bullseye. But not Daredevil, either. Yet Daredevil is taking the law into his own hands every time he puts on his red pants. He's a vigilante, a benign and compassionate one, sure, but a vigilante nonetheless. And some of the things he does in this very issue . . .

Oh. I think I see where this is going.

That brings us to the climax of the story. You said a few responses ago that we know before Daredevil #181 is over that Daredevil is still going to beat Bullseye and save his secret identity. We know there won't be long-term consequences.

Yeah, and we know that because we're used to never seeing permanent consequences in superhero comics, but like I said, there's something different about *Daredevil* on that front. When Miller is the one writing and drawing the story, you feel like there *could* be consequences. There could be consequences because people die all the time in this series.

Let's move on. The timing is pretty good for this next one.

The Fifth Commandment
You shall not kill. Especially if you're a superhero.

What does this mean?
"We should fear and love God, so that we do no bodily harm to our neighbor, but help and befriend him in every need."

Boy, is Bullseye ever in trouble.
Daredevil is a lot better at keeping this commandment than anybody else in this series, that's for sure. If Bullseye were Catholic like Daredevil, his penance would look like something out of Dante's *Inferno*.

Do you think Miller likes to portray people dying? He certainly does it often enough. Wait until you get all the back issues from Miller's run.
I keep going back to the pages in #181 right after the big panel of Bullseye laughing with that giant bottle of whiskey at the top of the page. (Why is the bottle so huge? Maybe some bottles of liquor really are that big, but I don't drink alcohol—I have the kind of guilty face that would get me caught immediately, and anyway, I think it's wrong to drink at my age—so maybe I will never know.) On that next couple of pages, Miller gives us one of those panels he uses so often to begin a scene, a tall, thin panel with nothing but a building in it to show us where we are, at the courthouse, and then he just plops all of Matt Murdock, head to toe, right on top of that panel like he was a paper doll pasted to the right side of it, standing in midair. He's pointing back to a woman in a wheelchair in the background as she hangs her head in sorrow. She's a fourth of the size of Matt, but they're both floating in the air: there's no courtroom walls or furniture or anything else behind them and no panel borders even. All the emphasis is on the act of compassion that Bullseye sees Matt undertaking. Matt wants this disabled woman, another person like himself who can do things no one expects that she can do, to get custody of her children. He's big in the picture, and he's a big presence to the woman symbolically, because he is helping her to help herself when nobody else would. But here again, the point of view belongs to Bullseye, so what we're really looking at when we see these ungrounded figures is a couple of

potential targets, the visually larger of the two being the man Bullseye thinks is his key adversary. This all leads Bullseye, himself sitting
incognito in the courtroom, to think, "He's like you in one way, Daredevil—he's a sap." So the opposite page shows Bullseye, who plants a
bug on Foggy in the courtroom when the hearing is over, hailing a
cab to follow Foggy, pulling out an ace of spades, and just flicking it
at the cab driver with no preamble whatsoever—and it cuts his throat,
so there's another big, black flash of blood coming out of it, and all he
gets for a last word is ". . . d-uuuurrggg!" while the card goes "SHTKK"
without any punctuation. Compared to the "WHAM!" and "CRACK!"
effects floating around a lot of fistfights in *Amazing Spider-Man*, leaving out the exclamation point makes the moment of violence seem a
lot more serious. And it reminds me again that Bullseye kills people as
nonchalantly as he would deal a card at a poker table (figure 47).

It's quiet, it's final. It's death without the supervillainous cackling
and posturing, comic-book death turned into something truly random and disturbing, with all the melodrama Stan Lee would squeeze
out of it just siphoned off. It's a lot scarier this way.

*And then Bullseye kills Elektra. If you'll excuse the Lutheran formula-
tion, "What does* this *mean?"*
Here comes the part of the issue I can't stop looking at. I hate that
I can't stop, because it's awful. Bullseye pursues Elektra because
he wants his old assassin job back. He wants to roll around in the

FIGURE 47. Frank Miller and Klaus Janson, "Last Hand," *Daredevil* #181 (Marvel,
April 1982).

Kingpin's paychecks like Scrooge McDuck swimming in his vault. At the moment he catches up to her, she has just let Foggy Nelson go. She was about to kill him on behalf of the Kingpin as a warning to Murdock not to screw with him in the future. Kingpin is pissed that Daredevil has ruined his chances to put his mouthpiece, Cherryh, in the mayor's office, and he feels he has to save face by sending a signal that he's still not to be messed with—and Foggy's life doesn't matter to anyone anyway (or so he thinks). But of course, it does matter in *Daredevil*, because it's a *life*. It's *his*, not Kingpin's and not Elektra's. And Elektra spares him—but not because his life belongs to him. Miller has made it pretty clear by her actions that she is long past valuing life for life's sake. Foggy's life only matters to her because it reminds her of Matt, his best friend, and she still can't get over her college romance. Lucky for Foggy she's got a sentimental streak, no matter how wire thin it is.

What does Bullseye do?
You're trying to sound like the catechism again, and that's good—God knows I love a good parody. To answer your question we have to go back to earlier in the issue. Bullseye has just sprung himself from the penitentiary. He has recently run into the Punisher, of all people, at the pen after he agrees to go on the Snyde show. The Punisher tells him that Kingpin doesn't need him anymore, because Elektra is Kingpin's head assassin now. So what does Bullseye do? Exactly what Punisher hopes he'll do with the news, and he even tells Bullseye this to his face: something stupid that might get him killed. Bullseye goes on the Snyde show, shackled hand and foot, and pretends to have another migraine. At this point, I understood why Bullseye's earlier headache had "caused" that huge flash of red to appear around his head: it's so we will understand that this time around, in the absence of the big red explosion, he's faking the symptoms. We're in Bullseye's head continuously in this issue, so if we saw the red flash of *his headache* earlier, another real headache would cause us see it again now, right? Then Harry pretends to have trouble opening the childproof bottle again, but this time, when Harry puts the red-and-white capsule in Bullseye's mouth, Bullseye holds it between his lips without swallowing it. . . . The first couple of times I read the issue, I thought that was the tip of his tongue sticking out of his lower lip—Miller draws stuff in pretty

bizarre ways a lot of the time; I can't always tell if he's just bad at drawing certain things or if he meant to make the capsule both a capsule
and Bullseye's tongue at the same time, a symbol of how he's razzing
Harry in his mind. He says, "Thanks . . ." and then—after making us
wait for the outcome by way of a page turn—completes his sentence:
". . . sucker!" and spits the capsule in Harry's eye. Then Miller takes us
into science-fiction territory, by exploiting Bullseye's status as a one-
man forensics team who knows exactly what projectile will hit what
surface with what kind of force. Harry the prison guard tries to shoot
him, which is just what he wanted Harry to do, because he can angle
his shackle belt just right to catch the bullet and break the chain holding his arms together. In just a few panels—all wide and thin, each one
filling up a whole row from left to right—Bullseye takes command of
the situation. He catches Snyde like a fish with the microphone cord.
And then we see that he's standing in a cage that looks just like Bullseye imagined his prison cell to look: bars, bars, and more bars, only
this time it's Harry who is sitting on the floor, helpless, and Bullseye
shoots him point blank. At least he keeps his promises.

And then?
And then he takes on Elektra, just when she's vulnerable because Foggy, a reminder of her past with Matt, caught her off-guard. First he
escapes from the Snyde show via helicopter, courtesy of more freshly
dead cops. Daredevil hears the news of his escape and gets ready for
action, just as Bullseye's narration speculates he's doing. Bullseye gets
to Mr. Slaughter, another assassin boss, and confirms that Kingpin has
hired Elektra to replace him. Then he laughs about Daredevil being
Matt Murdock—crazy idea—beside the Big Gulp–size bottle of whiskey. Then he goes to court to plant the bug on Foggy because he knows
Foggy is Elektra's next hit. And he kills the cabbie. And then he takes
her on. The whole fight lasts five pages. There haven't been any ads
since page 9 of the story, and the fight comes roughly in the middle of
a *twenty-two-page streak with no ads whatsoever.* I love double-sized
issues—nothing to break the mood for long stretches where it counts,
no Day-Glo Bubble Yum ads ruining the tension. But this battle is not
something you want to see. It is sadistic, and Miller takes full advantage of all the sympathy we've banked for Elektra (even though he has
given us plenty of reasons why she doesn't deserve it). Bullseye is all

offense, Elektra all defense. Bullseye pulls her head down by the hair so he can crack her jaw on his knee. She gets in one slice with her *sai*, which barely grazes Bullseye's cheek but turns him into an even crueler fighter. Lots of horizontal panels follow, the central one showing Bullseye's foot going all the way to the left edge of the page while Elektra's head, his foot's point of impact, swings all the way to the right. There's blood on her lips. By the bottom of the page, it looks like she's caught him by the neck with her headscarf. And then things gets really ugly. He pushes her back against the ground with a "KLUDD"; the panels turn vertical again for the top half of the page as the adversaries

stand still, recovering, and Bullseye grabs his second ace of spades in the issue. He's nearly rendered in 3D for a second, in a panel with no borders, the hand holding the card overlapping with the panel to the left, like Miller is preparing us for one of those SCTV Monster Chiller Horror Theater moments like "3D House of Pancakes," except what comes at us in the next panel isn't a syrup bottle but that fatal ace of spades. And it goes straight into Elektra's throat. I have never seen anything like that before, not in a movie and certainly not in a comic. I feel like pulling my head down into my T-shirt and gluing my chin to my

FIGURE 48. Frank Miller and Klaus Janson, "Last Hand," *Daredevil* #181 (Marvel, April 1982).

chest. Suddenly it's not my throat anymore. It's an opening for somebody who might want to end my life.

After that, there are horizontal panels again, three stacked up at the bottom of the page. Elektra lies there, legs sprawled so that her toes are practically pointing at each other. She has lost control of her body, might be unconscious, might even be dead. Bullseye is close. Next panel, he moves closer. He holds her in one arm like he's Clark Gable about to kiss her, but his left hand holds the *sai*. Last panel: their faces are close, as if he's going in for the clinch, but she's bleeding, and he is smiling like he's about to pull the wings off a dragonfly. "And, for my *next* trick," he says . . . (figures 48 and 49).

FIGURE 49. Frank Miller and Klaus Janson, "Last Hand," *Daredevil* #181 (Marvel, April 1982).

Turn the page. The background is a thin rectangle of spotty pinkish red, just like the bloody airbrush splash behind Daredevil in Bullseye's murderous daydream on page 1, but this time totally controlled, about an inch wide and running down the page from top to bottom. In front of the rectangle, there are no background props, no panel border, nothing but Bullseye, full figure, stabbing Elektra with her own sword, with the sword coming out of her back. He just killed her. I just witnessed a murder. It feels just like that.

There's something even uglier about it than you recognize. It's a rape.
What?

*It's a rape. A murder-rape. Miller says in that interview in one of the
DVD extras for the Ben Affleck Daredevil movie that he was* dumb-
founded *that the Comics Code, let alone his own editors at Marvel, let
him get away with showing a murder-rape in a Code-approved comic
book. In 1982.*
What? What the hell is a DVD? And there's nothing sexy about killing
someone. I don't care if they're members of the opposite sex. Do you
think that *sai* is supposed to be his penis or something?

*Well, I see one there, though not a biological one. And let's get some-
thing straight, kid: there is nothing "sexy" about rape either. Rape isn't
about sex. It's about power. And Bullseye's got all the power here. He gets
it from stealing all of hers. Figuratively—though it looks awfully literal,
doesn't it?—he's taking back the phallus from her, taking back his "right-
ful" position as The Man in this relationship, running her through with
her own weapon, mastering her in the ugliest way possible so she's left
with nothing. He has reduced her to what he was certain she already
was anyway: a marionette he can use to act out his sadistic fantasy of
mastering Daredevil, too. That's not to say he doesn't get pleasure out of
killing her. He's even laughing in open-mouthed ecstasy when he does it.*
I'm not even going to ask you what a phallus is, though I think I can
guess. But you're right, he's laughing, and that makes it even more horrible. Wait, are you suggesting that Frank Miller got off on drawing
this? Do you think he hates women? Is that the only mental place an
image like that can come from? If so, it's an even sicker panel than I
thought. Miller sure loved drawing her in quote-unquote athletic positions that were frankly pretty sexy, and that barely there ninja suit . . .

*I wish I could tell you what Miller's feelings were about women when
he drew that panel or what message about gender and power he is sending or thinks he's sending. When critics accuse a film director of sexism
or misogyny, I always wonder if that's misplaced ire. No matter how
deserved it is, even if the film exploits women and their bodies purely
for prurient pleasures or dehumanizes them in the name of mastery, so
many people are involved in making a film that the director can't shoul-*

der all the blame. When a sexist or misogynist comic book is written and drawn by the same person, though, it's obviously hard not to reach for the personal interpretation. What I feel I can say is, yes, this is a sensationalist, exploitative image, but Bullseye is as inhuman as any character I've seen in comics (except maybe Daken, Son of Wolverine, who not too long ago graphically decapitated the Punisher and chopped the rest of him into tiny pieces, but be glad you won't have to suffer through that or Wolverine mania for a few decades). Bullseye is not the hero. He's exactly the opposite of Daredevil because he has no empathy, no compassion, and we are supposed to hate him even more for the pleasure he takes in killing Elektra. None of this changes the fact that Elektra is less a character at this point than one of Gail Simone's "women in refrigerators"—injured or dead women in superhero comics who exist only to get men to punch each other out of revenge, protection, jealousy, or what have you. Seeing her hang there on the sai like a ragdoll aptly illustrates her function as Miller's narrative marionette.[1]

 This question makes me think of what Tania Modleski says about Alfred Hitchcock's tortured female characters, which is basically this: yes, Hitchcock probably got a rise out of having Janet Leigh's Psycho character stabbed to death while she was naked in the shower, but in that film and most of his others, the sharper focus is given not to the inscrutability or fickleness of the woman but to the inexplicable, out-of-control nature of the man whose sadism she suffers. Those films are "about" what women have to suffer through in a patriarchy, a society where men overtly and tacitly take control of women's bodies all the time.[2]

I'm not sure I get all that because I haven't seen any Hitchcock movies, but I think I see what you mean. You and I don't identify with Bullseye, especially at that moment. Elektra has done some horrible things in the past, like nearly chopping off Daredevil's foot with a bear trap, so maybe Miller is punishing her for that through Bullseye's act? But it's an unfair punishment considering Miller made her do those things, being the writer-artist. If either of them is a sympathetic character right now, just after Elektra lets Foggy go, it's obviously Elektra. But some unpleasant reader could conceivably enjoy watching Elektra suffer for being such a man-eater, especially while she's wearing that skimpy red ninja thing. You can't make people interpret a comic or a movie or a book the way you want them to. You can only steer them the best you can. It's chancy to use an image like this to make the point that what it depicts is awful. Some creep is going to like it just for what it literally shows, and to hell with the context.

I sincerely and enthusiastically doubt that I would have said any-thing like what you just said when I was thirteen. But hey, it's my screen memory, and I get to make myself a smarty-pants if I want.
So. Is Miller trying to turn us on or turn us off?

There's this scene in Daredevil #169 . . .
I don't have that one.

*You will. In thirty years, you will find it impossible to resist collect-ing all the Miller issues you missed. Anyway, I'll spoil it for you. Two nebbishy guys are in a movie theater watching The Maltese Falcon, the classic detective movie with Humphrey Bogart. Bullseye is hiding in the theater. Daredevil comes in after him, and they start to fight. The two guys in the theater love dark crime movies and start talking about how it's a classic of the genre. Then, while Bullseye kicks Daredevil in one direction, then the other, behind them, over two panels shown from the same point of view, one of the guys says, "The frightening, yet attractive nature of violence is the quintessential element of the detective genre . . ."
Now, I read a* Comics Journal *review from the early eighties that sug-gests that Miller is using the fight scene to undercut the movie fans' belief that violence is attractive as well as repellent. But seriously, Miller has drawn some beautiful fight scenes, and this is one of his prettier ones. The bodies of the adversaries are slim and sleek, they pose gorgeously for the "camera" when they're prepping their defenses, and when Bullseye throws a knife and apparently wounds Daredevil, he falls like he's doing a death scene in Swan Lake.*
If Miller is "saying" anything here, he can't possibly be saying that represented violence is unattractive. He's forcing us to look at the fact that it is *attractive, or at least that it can be attractive, square in the face. He wants his readers to think about the fact that they're enjoying this cartoon violence and make them squirm about their own enjoyment. I don't think that gets Miller off the hook for exploiting the female body in Elektra's murder scene. But at the very least, he's implicating readers who might enjoy it for that reason, and he's implicating himself for drawing it in the first place.*

If that's true, then he doesn't stop the implicating with that panel. He makes Elektra suffer even more. At the right side of the page, right after Bullseye stabs her, Miller gives us eight horizontal panels showing every awful moment of Elektra's last steps, as she tries and fails and tries again to stand up. There's this narrow triangle of black blood streaming out of her middle like she's still carrying the *sai* in her belly, and it just won't leave her alone. She half walks, half crawls to Matt Murdock's apartment, where he appears on the steps and holds her for the last seconds of her life. Miller shows their final embrace from three different angles, as if he's making a statue out of it, the panels getting darker one by one, drained of all color except a

FIGURE 50. Frank Miller and Klaus Janson, "Last Hand," *Daredevil* #181 (Marvel, April 1982).

steel-gray-blue. And at the bottom, among shocked, bluish onlookers standing against a background of solid bluish-purple color, stands Bullseye wearing the half-assed disguise of a flat cap and a jacket. He's lit up in an amber glow once again, this time because he's lighting a cigarette as he enjoys the show (figure 50). We can't help but see him. Janson's color scheme stacks the deck so we couldn't look away if we tried.

And there's something else going on visually here, too, but only if we remember a certain choice Miller made earlier. Remember when Bullseye gets that first headache, the real one, and everything at the bottom half of the page directs our eyes left, while the facing page—the one with Daredevil working out—pushes our *eyes again and again to the right?*

He's got the same directions assigned to each character here, once again with Bullseye on the left stabbing left and Matt turning, panel by panel, to face right. What does this mean?

That's pretty cool. It could be simple: it could just be a pun, where Matt is "right" and Bullseye goes in the opposite direction, and there's no compromising on either side. There's nothing these men can do with each other but destroy each other. The world can't hold both of them, a force for order and mercy versus a force for anarchy. I guess the repetition of those vectors at this more intense point in the story just emphasizes the fact that somebody has got to go down.

I guess so, but does that mean somebody has to win? Bullseye loses the battle, but what did Daredevil gain by defeating him? We were talking earlier about consequences for Daredevil, about the possibility of real peril to the hero that you say Miller manages to develop. He doesn't die, but does he win?

Maybe there won't be life-threatening consequences for Matt after this story is over, but there are long-lasting consequences for the world he lives in and the position where he places himself within it. And it takes its toll on him, heart and head. He has to go on living with all of Bullseye's old murders on his conscience and now the new ones, too, including and especially the murder of the first woman he loved, the one he long dreamed would return and then dreamed he could reform but couldn't. Those kinds of consequences don't stick around for long in Marvel comics, if death even comes. Aunt May dies, but then she doesn't; we find out that Mysterio faked her death to get her house or something. Gwen Stacy dies, but then she comes back as a clone. And Marvel is already sending out advance notice of their attempt to resurrect Jean Grey for a big DC crossover one-shot, with the Teen Titans. *X-Men* #137, where Jean dies because her Phoenix power gets out of control, isn't even two years old. In *Daredevil*, though, death feels real. People die just for standing in Bullseye's or Elektra's way. Life is cheap. But not to Daredevil. He has to put Bullseye away because if he doesn't, life gets even cheaper. So he drops him.

Right. Daredevil nearly murders Bullseye by dropping him from the electrical wires where they're fighting. Does that screw up your sense of Daredevil as a guy with a duty to fairness and the law and all of that? Is he not such a good Christian after all?

I'm a Christian, and that means that sinning is not the worst thing you can do. The worst thing you can do is stop trying to stop yourself from sinning. It's to have no conscience and answer to nobody, because then you don't even know what's sin and what isn't. You just do whatever you want to anybody because it makes you happy. If we had time to get to the Seventh Commandment, I'd tell you about the Greedo action figure I stole at church. I mean, I didn't exactly steal it, but I knew who it belonged to, and he left it behind at church on Sunday, and I found it and kept it. At home, I had Han Solo kill him the way he does in the first *Star Wars* movie for trying to sell him to Jabba the Hutt, even though I only have the Hoth Han Solo in a parka from *The Empire Strikes Back*, so it wasn't exactly a faithful restaging of the scene. Am I going to give Greedo back? Probably not. The kid doesn't care. He's probably too young even to remember he had it. Now, I fully realize that this whole line of thinking is terrible. It justifies stealing by pretending that certain circumstances make it okay. But it's not okay. Never in a million years would Daredevil rationalize a bad deed this way. But he wouldn't come after me with his billy club a-swingin' either. If he nabbed me for Grand Theft Action Figure, he would sit me down and talk me through my bullshit logic, not try to make me feel guilty or ashamed. He would try to show me how it hurts the other person to do something like that and how it hurts me, too, by making me care less about the rights of others.

But none of that sort of thinking stops Daredevil from dropping Bullseye. After a slew of pages that feature mostly horizontal panels that run from gutter to gutter, panels shaped to frame these guys beating the snot out of each other, chasing each other, having it out to the death, suddenly the orientation goes vertical—now they're at the mercy of great heights. They're falling off an elevated train—another train, like the one we know Daredevil rescued Bullseye from before, loving his neighbor even when his neighbor is a murdering scumbag—and they catch some telephone wires. Miller draws out the narrative tension by using three tall, narrow panels to show them pulling themselves up into tightrope walker positions, and then it happens: in six very small panels that run from top to bottom, each one framing just a face or a foot or a hand, Daredevil stands on the wire, jumps, returns to the wire without losing his balance, and catches Bullseye as he falls. It's so compact, so elegant. All it takes for us to know that Bullseye is falling is a panel of Daredevil's stable feet, a panel of Bullseye's feet going helter-skelter, an extreme close-up of Bullseye's upside-down face bathed in an amber-yellow tint like the caution light of a traffic signal, and a panel of a red hand grabbing a silver-gloved one. Daredevil is loving his loathsome neighbor yet again. And then, in five more tall, skinny panels on the page directly across, with all roads pointing straight down, Bullseye shouts "NO! You won't save me—not like before! Kill you! I'll kill—" and he swings his right hand—the one holding a sai he stole from Elektra just to twist the knife into Daredevil, so to speak—up to stab his savior and thus kill them both.

But Daredevil is no Jesus, loving even his worst neighbor to the bitter end. Instead of sacrificing himself, he drops Bullseye in a reprise of the grabbing panel, only stretched out from the top of the page to the bottom, as the red hand at the top drops the silver hand now grasping up from below. And at the bottom of the next and last panel on the page, Bullseye hits the pavement. So much for Christianity. Daredevil even says exactly the words he says to the Fixer's trigger man, Slade, when he pummels him in the origin recap in issue #164: "You'll kill no one—ever again!" You remember Slade, right? You bought that issue at the 7-11 you mentioned, and the Doc Ock issue after that too before you stopped getting Daredevil for a while. Slade killed Matt Murdock's father, and Daredevil beat the daylights out of Slade and effectively killed the man who gave the order. This is like that. This is revenge (figure 51).

Well . . . are you sure? Anybody would let go if the person he was holding onto suddenly came charging at him with a sword. It's probably automatic. As long as we're pretending this is a catechetical discussion, we might as well use a theological distinction: it doesn't have anything to do with free will.

You've been reading this catechism stuff pretty carefully, haven't you? Well, I would never do anything to disappoint my parents, especially when it has to do with church. Besides, if God is real, I don't want to get caught napping.

Good for you. I can't even remember the Nicene Creed half the time anymore, and I used to chant it without even looking at the hymnal. Well, don't tell that to Dad.

No. But you're wrong about the automatic reaction. Even as Daredevil makes the drop, he has the presence of mind to tell Bullseye that his

FIGURE 51. Frank Miller and Klaus Janson, "Last Hand," *Daredevil* #181 (Marvel, April 1982).

killing days are over as of now. He knows exactly what he's doing. He's terminating Bullseye's career as an assassin.

So who's guiltier here: the mass murderer or the guy who mangles him for life on purpose? It's not like Daredevil planned this ahead of time. He dropped Bullseye spontaneously, when they were in a totally unexpected situation and Bullseye was attacking him. What does it even mean to be Christian when you're in a situation like that? Does it mean saving this guy, the same guy you saved before who then went on to kill what seems like hundreds of innocent people and probably even more who weren't so innocent? Or does it mean saving all the people he would kill if he had another chance? I don't know if either one counts as a Christian decision. Maybe it's different for Catholics like Daredevil than for Lutherans, because Catholics have to pay penance every time they sin and Lutherans believe they're saved by the generosity of God's grace, not by their own confessions. And maybe Matt thinks of all the deaths Bullseye would cause as individual sins that he, Matt, would have to pay for in his heart. But if Bullseye were the only one to die, there would just be the one sin. Whereas for us Lutherans, sin is all about knowing you're always forgiven even before you sin but wanting to live up to expectations of good behavior as a way of saying, "Thanks for forgiving me." But who knows what Bullseye would have done with the rest of his life if Daredevil saved him again? Maybe he would turn into a hippie and smoke pot and smile on his brother, man, just because he hadn't tried that yet. Suuure he would.

Bullseye's got no opportunity to turn into anything, anymore. Daredevil, a.k.a. Matt Murdock, public defender of innocent and guilty alike, has condemned him to a hospital bed for the rest of his life. "My spine is shattered," Bullseye thinks in the narration boxes. "I can't feel my arms or legs. I can't even talk." The huge horizontal close-ups on his eyes, which mimic that very first panel on page 2 except they're all identical copies of each other this time, head up the last three pages of #181 and help obscure the fact that he's completely incapacitated until the final page, when the "camera" finally tracks back to show him in bed, bandaged like a mummy in a Hammer horror movie, plasma bag hanging next to his head. The picture plane moves because Bullseye can't; it's as if Miller were taunting him for his immobility, and once again, as at Rikers Island at the beginning, the only features we see in the room are bars—not steel bars this time but bars of shadow chopping him to ribbons as light seeps in between the venetian blinds. All he has left is his hate, he tells us, his hate for Daredevil: "and that'll be enough. No matter how many months and years it takes, I'm gonna put myself back together. And then I'll come for you again. Just wait. . . ." So even Daredevil's choice in favor of the many rather than the few didn't help anybody. Potentially.

I didn't notice before that Bullseye says "Just wait" again at the end, just as he did at the end of page 2 when he was stewing about Daredevil saving him in #169. I don't know why Miller has him repeat that line, exactly. Maybe the final repetition is a coy message from creators to readers: like Bullseye, we have to wait, we *always* have to wait, and we're always expected to think that there's something real, like the hero's life and death, at stake in some future issue of the series. There never really is, but we still wait, I and everybody else who reads comics and waits for their favorite villains to return. Why do we have "favorite" villains, anyway? Do we enjoy watching bad guys hurt innocents? Do we like to see people we care about, even just characters in a comic, in danger?

Come on. You never would have asked those questions when you were thirteen. You like Mad *magazine and* Cracked *and* Not Brand Echh! *and* Airplane!*, but I know for a fact that you don't think about reflexivity that deeply yet or wonder much about the attraction of violence.*

You're wrong about the second one. All I know is that I didn't just *read* this comic. It *happened* to me. I've already read it six times, and I'm gonna read it every time I come across it in our collection. And I'll turn straight to Elektra's murder even though I fully believe I don't want to see that page ever again. Elektra is not a likable character. She's a killer. But something happened to her when Foggy recognized her as "Matt's girl" and she spared him. She showed that even if nobody, not even Matt, could bring her back from what she has become, she was still more human than Bullseye. And human or inhuman, nobody deserves to die at the hands of someone else, especially someone who enjoys doing it as much as Bullseye did.

And by the way, I'll never wear a turtleneck again.

That's what you think.

So if you're not God, what will you do if I keep your commandments?

I'll let you write this book someday. Good luck with that. Meeting your past self in a thirty-four-year-old comic book that smells like a basement is a more chilling experience than you might think.

Oh, no you don't. You conjured me here, so I get the last word. I am the reason this book is so difficult to write, isn't it? You want to apologize for how much I loved what Miller was doing, and at the same time you want to continue loving it just the way I did. You can't have it both ways. Sell your *Daredevil* run and put away your fierce, guilty affection for Miller's run, or else own it—face whatever consequences it brings, reconcile yourself with it, and make your peace with him. Which is it going to be?

CONCLUSION

EXPOSÉ

Miller's *Daredevil* was the staging ground for his better-known block-busters *Batman: The Dark Knight Returns, Batman: Year One, Sin City,* and *300,* but it also proved a bellwether of dramatic changes in the comics industry's relationship to creators as well as its basic notion of the superhero. Without the convergence of multiple factors, from the rise of underground comix in the late 1960s and the emergence of a fan-creator generation at Marvel and DC in the 1970s to the dominance of blockbuster science-fiction films in Hollywood and the exhaustion of Marvel's Silver Age characterization formula—brood, bicker, save the world, get lambasted for demolishing New York in the process, repeat—Miller couldn't have kick-started this velvet revolution. Undergirding it all was the burgeoning direct sales system, in which distributors for the publishing companies shipped comics straight to dedicated comics shops rather than to newsstands, grocery stores, and the like and did not accept returned product as they did from those other venues. Direct sales, which proved its mettle when Marvel's *Dazzler* #1 (1981) broke sales records despite its exclusive distribution to specialty comics shops, left the shops' owners holding the unsold copies of a given book but also offered the possibility that those copies could be sold for higher prices as "back issues" in the future. Though problems with the no-returns policy loomed, at the time, direct sales seemed a clear move in favor of the publishers, for it made predicting circulation numbers much easier and also made it feasible for such small, independent publishers as Eclipse Comics, Pacific Comics, and Comico to get their monthly comics into circulation.

But it's still difficult to imagine either the feverish energy of the creators' rights movement or the looser, cartoonier drawing styles and non-Code-approved violence that characterize many of today's super-hero comics without Miller's original stint on *Daredevil*. Dick Giordano of DC Comics negotiated a stunningly lucrative contract with Miller for *Ronin* primarily because Miller had made *Daredevil* such a tremendous seller on the basis of the strength of his art and his writing rather than the popularity of the character. *Ronin* sold healthily for DC while Miller retained ownership of the characters and artwork, thus proving both Miller's value to the industry and the existence of a market for creator-driven material if handled correctly.

Mainstream success also offers the artist chances for greater independence; think of the filmmaker Steven Soderbergh, making lucrative, star-bloated *Ocean's Eleven* sequels and investing his royalties in purposely inexpensive, experimental projects such as *Bubble* or *The Girlfriend Experience*. Though the Batman character belongs to DC, Miller made loads of money in incentives off *Batman: The Dark Knight Returns*, thereby gaining the financial independence to take his work to smaller companies such as Dark Horse Comics, where the editor Diana Schutz was only too happy to let him retain character and story rights to *Sin City* and *300*. The more powerful he became, the more the industry listened, and Miller used that bully pulpit to support his fellow creators. He sat regularly and actively on creators' rights panels at comics conventions throughout the eighties and spoke fervently on behalf of Jack Kirby in his campaign to get back thousands of pages of original artwork from Marvel. Like many other creators who have labored under work-made-for-hire contracts at Marvel and DC, Miller has never claimed legal rights of ownership or control over characters that he designed under those terms: "I remember drawing Elektra for the first time and saying, 'I'm giving this to them [Marvel Comics].' And that was before royalties."[1] But when it came to a giant of the industry like Kirby or Steve Ditko being refused the right to his own artwork, a right enjoyed by Miller and his contemporaries but diluted by Marvel in the case of its biggest stars of the sixties, Miller was fearless in his support. Eventually Marvel returned to Kirby some of the pages he wanted, and not just because Miller advocated for him, of course—though the possibility that Miller would refuse to work for the company ever again if it stood firm surely dented Marvel's armor at least a bit.

Miller's work here and on the four-issue Wolverine miniseries also indicated a potential adult market for superhero comics. However enormous the circulation numbers were on Chris Claremont's *X-Men* series, no matter who drew it, the X-Men were characters for kids. Claremont played up the student-as-awkward-misfit angle in ways that few teenage fanboys could resist.[2] Miller knew that *Daredevil* was a comic marketed primarily to kids and claims he held back on the violence because he was producing "morality plays for children," but even though *Sin City* plays it much less coy with the gore and sadism, we have to remember that Code-approved comics couldn't even print the word "werewolf" until the mid-1970s, let alone portray an assassin flicking a razor-sharp ace of spades into a cab driver's throat. Discreet though that panel from *Daredevil* #181 seems now, with its small flash of black blood and its oblique angle on the playing card's contact with the victim's flesh, by comparison to the rest of the product on the market it was as though Miller had splattered the page with real blood. To me at age thirteen, it was horrible and sad and most of all thrillingly forbidden, a vision of the irreversibility of violence that I didn't expect to see until I was old enough to go to R-rated movies unaccompanied.

When *Batman: The Dark Knight Returns* was first released as a miniseries in four installments in 1986, everyone knew from *Ronin* what to expect from a Frank Miller comic published in a prestige format and distributed only to specialty shops: superheroic violence with the Code gloves off. Intriguingly, the intensity of graphic violence and gore in *The Dark Knight Returns* was scarcely higher or its instances more frequent than they had been in *Daredevil*, save for the penetration of the Joker's eyeball with a tiny blade, a clear poke in the you-know-what to the psychiatrist Dr. Fredric Wertham for the distaste for such images he expressed in his censorship-baiting screed *The Seduction of the Innocent* (1954). The expensive square-bound format and subtle color reproduction of the new miniseries screamed "for adults," and adults simply hadn't paid attention to Miller's *Daredevil* unless they were grown-up fans. So far as most adult readers knew, *The Dark Knight Returns* represented the first time anyone had ever bled in a superhero story. If there was a difference between *Daredevil* and *Dark Knight* in purely structural terms, it was in which character perpetrated the violence. The blade protruding from the Joker's eyeball wasn't a juvenile delinquent's shiv but a tiny Batarang. Portraying the hero as the most ruthless figure in the series gestured back to Daredevil kicking in Turk's windshield just to pump him for underworld information, but this time it was consistent and tied directly to the nature of Batman the character as Miller understood him. That was different, and its effects are visible everywhere in comics today, no less on the newsstand or the comics shop "New Arrivals" display than in graphic novels.

Along with the British writer Alan Moore's *Swamp Thing* and *Watchmen*, Miller's *Daredevil* popularized another "adult" trend in the mideighties: reflexivity, a postmodernist irreverence regarding the ontological boundary between fiction and physical reality. Underground comix opened that gate more than a decade earlier, expanding a healthy tradition of playing games with the fourth wall begun by newspaper comic strips at the turn of the twentieth century, but thus far, mainstream superhero creators had largely limited that self-awareness to allegories about Marvel or DC office politics or flat-out parodies in *Mad* or *Not Brand Echh!*. Moore and the penciler-inker-letterer Dave Gibbons's hit miniseries *Watchmen* (DC, 1986) quickly became the most lauded of these explorations of superhero comics' conventions and limits, but *Watchmen*'s monolithic shadow should not be allowed to obscure *Daredevil*'s subtle yet definite moves in the direction of self-aware comics. Sure, before Miller, characters got injured, broken, even killed in mainstream superhero comic books, but it never happened as suddenly or without warning as the multiple murders that sometimes took place in a single Elektra-versus-ninjas battle; and that level of violence brought the artificiality of superhero comics into sharp relief. Miller achieved this level of metatextual "realism" with *Daredevil*—the acknowledgment of the conventions of a genre as conventions, highly coded constructs—by transforming the traditionally bloodless punches and gunshots of superhero comics into acts with permanent consequences.

While long-standing comics readers may have welcomed Miller's forthright approach to violence, public reaction was mixed at best. Law-enforcement officials and public-safety pundits, certain that comics were intrinsically a children's medium, freaked out upon discovering violence and sex in *any* comics sold by the growing number of specialty stores. Shop owners wrote letters to industry magazines begging for a ratings system after the manager of Friendly Frank's Comics in Lansing, Illinois, was arrested and the shop closed down for selling such "adults only" titles as *Omaha the Cat Dancer* and *Bizarre Sex*.[3] Miller was as outspoken about the industry's response to such threats as he was about giving Jack Kirby his due.

After the Friendly Frank's bust, publishers and many creators saw ratings as protection against federal or state censorship. On this point, Miller's position was more extreme. He campaigned not only against censorship but also against a cover-labeling system for which even Gary Groth, a crusader for comics as art who has also published hardcore sex comics under the Eros banner, expressed support. Miller accused publishers of being as craven in the eighties as they were in the fifties, when EC's horror and crime comics drew Congress's ire while the rest of the industry cowered behind a promise to self-censor.[4] "As far as I know, the comics industry has never done a fucking thing for the First Amendment," he told Groth in 1987.[5] He objected most vehemently to DC's and Marvel's apparent plans to institute ratings without consulting their creators first. His stand against censorship was as uncompromising as his ideal hero: anyone advocating censorship was "evil," trying to "take my freedoms away from me." But when Groth pressed him on this point, Miller recognized the gray area that his argument denied. Miller had earlier professed that he wouldn't want his own child, "were [he] to have one," to be exposed by comics to graphic violence, superwomen wearing bondage gear, or even super-heroes who become powerful by getting angry (Hulk, anyone?).[6] This time out, he agreed again that kids shouldn't have access to some comics, and Groth told him, "when you make these absolutist comments about how all censorship is wrong, and then you back away . . . and say, 'Oh, well, this censorship is right. And that censorship is right,' it damages your position." Miller responded, "If you're getting into an absolute discussion of censorship, or suppression, which really seems to be more what we're talking about, you can't come down on every act that you call censorship, because very soon you'll find yourself defending murder, arguing for the creative freedom of the makers of snuff films, I don't believe I ever put the position that broadly." "Well . . . ," Groth replied, with Miller then adding, "I might have. I was pretty excited."[7] There have always been two Millers, to my mind, both of whom make an appearance in this exchange: the absolutist who gets "excited" and fiercely defends his blanket definitions of a concept or problem and the listener who tries hard to identify with the opposing position.

Until recently, Miller the listener was the one who wrote and drew most of the comics published under his name. His complex engagement with violence in the *Daredevil* comics themselves is a case in point. There Miller focused on a structuring assumption of the superhero genre—the intrinsic goodness of vigilante justice—that was long overdue for scrutiny. Miller portrayed Daredevil's choice to fight crime outside the justice system not simply as a problem of character psychology but as a hypothetical point where individual rights and collective rights collide. Daredevil smashes alleged bad guys' noses without answering to assault laws and does so in the name of justice. He bypasses the legal system even more blatantly by taking retribution into his own hands when pursuing his father's murderer. At such moments, he becomes a vehicle not just for testing the limits of media violence but also for examining it and provoking more debate about its consequences. It's this version of Daredevil—this "most Christian of heroes," as Miller once called him—that tends to get lost when Miller's early work is adapted for film or television.[8] Mark Steven Johnson's 2003 film *Daredevil*, with its much-reviled performance of the titular hero by Ben Affleck, takes its cues from Miller's first run when it comes to noir tone and specific story elements—Miller's Elektra is one of DD's major nemeses, and she dies at Bullseye's hand essentially as she did in *Daredevil* #181—but it also opens with a scene in which Daredevil kills a petty crook. If Johnson intended such scenes to pay tribute to Miller's version of the character, he didn't read the run carefully enough. The first season of Netflix's *Daredevil* series (2015) also borrows liberally from Miller, putting young Matt Murdock in the same black pants, shirt, and turban-like mask he wears in Miller and John Romita Jr.'s *Daredevil: The Man without Fear* miniseries (1993–94) and standing by as he ping-pongs between sides of the law while attempting to maintain a consistent ethical center. But Charlie Cox's Murdock is much angrier than Miller's and has a lot less to say, which translates on screen into a bringer of vengeance pure and simple. Miller's Murdock wants revenge for his father's death, too, but the essential twist there is that Miller's Murdock refuses to acknowledge that fact, preferring to believe he has risen above such sinful thoughts. It is difficult for me to avoid judging the entire Netflix series on the basis of its misreading of Miller, though as I hope I've made clear by now,

Miller finished his run by making Daredevil realize that his allegiance to the legal system cannot be reconciled with his impulse to vigilantism—and freezing him at the moment of that realization. If to Miller's mind that incarnation of Daredevil had no future, perhaps it's unfair of me to judge all later incarnations against that example; I relish the atmosphere of the Netflix series and admire its determination to re-create the clarity of mood and action that *Daredevil* might never have acquired without Miller's intervention, even if it doesn't entirely succeed. Nothing will stop writers, cartoonists, and media creators of all stripes from trying to reinvent Miller's wheel, at least superficially; without his decisive vision of Hell's Kitchen as seen through an angel's devilish eyes, it's debatable whether Daredevil would be such a hot property today.

In issue #191's "Roulette," Miller brings Daredevil back to Bullseye, the character that personifies the paradox of Matt's lawyer-vigilante status. That conundrum had been on Miller's mind at least since the introduction of Elektra in #168. Bullseye has been hospitalized, conscious but completely immobile, since his fall from the electrical wires in #181. This issue is what it's all been leading up to, for here Daredevil faces, for the last time on Miller's watch, the adversary whose murder of Elektra tested Daredevil's ability to set personal feelings aside and let the law do its work. Now, as before, Bullseye demonstrates that the contradiction inherent in the lawyer-vigilante is inescapable, that it cannot be resolved by action or any other means. For even when Bullseye is completely immobilized, his mere existence—and in terms of volition, his physical state reduces him to little more than inert matter—motivates Daredevil to simulate a revenge fantasy that he cannot fulfill. Someone whose superego aligns so tightly to the Law could hardly bring his relationship with his lover's killer to the conclusion that his personal desires demand. The game of Russian roulette reduces Daredevil's physical duel with Bullseye in #181 to its simplest elements; it's like a duel to the death from a psychologically complex video game such as The Last of Us has taken the external form of a Pong match. This chilling final scene is drawn based on a suspense principle that Miller learned from Hitchcock, Griffith, and countless other film directors and editors, cutting back and forth between increasingly close, photocopied images of Bullseye's face as Daredevil's pistol centers on his forehead and extreme close-ups of the hammer of the pistol as Daredevil inches back the trigger. The outcome, however, is never in doubt: Daredevil has never killed anyone before, and he's not about to start now.

This scene flouts the expectation of closure on which criminal justice is based. Despite punishment, the legal system provides no satisfactory closure for crime victims or their families, and as the current state of the US prison system exemplifies, we can incarcerate millions of convicts without even coming close to eliminating the fact of crime; after a certain point, the sheer population of penitentiaries begins to look like an obscene totem supplicating the gods to protect us from criminal behavior rather than a socially engineered disincentive. It also comments on the circular nature of superhero serials. No series ever ends (unless sales are poor); there's always a new bad guy to defeat or a past baddie back from prison or the dead who needs to be put away. And there's the unraveling of the superhero as agent of decency as well. If heroes defeat bad guys and make society safer for the upstanding citizens among us, what do those heroes have to be like? How do they—and we—reconcile their status as role models who save kittens and make children feel better about themselves with the naked fact of their love of thrills and their reliance on punching and hitting and kicking in the final instance to make their point? For Miller, all of Daredevil's legalistic soul-searching, from his refusal to let Bullseye die even if he escapes conviction to his indecision regarding capturing Elektra and turning her in, leads up to the last page of "Roulette," in which Daredevil's sixth and final pull of the trigger reveals what can only be read as an admission of what Miller perceives as the impotence of his otherwise phallic career: "My gun has no bullets." Daredevil, the quintessential masked vigilante who never hurts anybody and makes sure justice is always done, cannot eliminate Bullseye or crime in general because he can't—won't—kill. It's no wonder that the backgrounds have simply disappeared in this issue, replaced by a clinical white backdrop, or rather the color of no color at all—the color of newsprint, which is in this case also an avatar of comic-book reflexivity, a canvas that never lets us forget that it's flat.

I return to *Daredevil* #191 fairly frequently when thinking about the history of the character and how Miller reinterpreted it. But what still surprises me when I actually open the issue is Miller's thoughtful examination of media violence, both its effects and the discourse surrounding it. Miller once said that his "job" as an artist is not to be liked but to provoke, and his unapologetic violence was high on the list of provocations. He puts his money where his mouth is in #191 by scrutinizing the effects of media violence, including the kind he'd been generating for the past four years. Chuckie sees Daredevil on TV (replaying a scene from *Daredevil* #146, June 1977, written by Jim Shooter with pencils by Gil Kane) in a fight that was already pretty reflexive about media violence in that it took place in a TV studio that Bullseye had commandeered. In #146, Bullseye was undone by his delight in his own showmanship: he meant to shoot a bound hostage but, unable to resist the challenge, shot the cord that suspended him instead, giving Daredevil opportunities both to save the hostages and to apprehend Bullseye. In #159, when Bullseye put a contract on Daredevil's head, he provided Mr. Slaughter with a videotape of that fight. This time around, these same video images of Daredevil doing his thing amount to a Miller *Daredevil* comic minus the more complicated plot threads and the debate that Miller sponsors regarding the rightness of Daredevil's vigilantism. It's a taped television broadcast in the book, but what we're actually looking at are drawings of a fight, and not just any fight—it's Daredevil fighting Bullseye, the same "show" Miller broadcast intermittently from issue #168 until Bullseye's near-fatal accident in #181. It's a cartoon show with blood and guts. The boy's parents don't stop him from watching it. And it turns out that the father is actually corrupt. Miller then investigates not only the potential influence of violence on kids—seemingly toeing the censorship line—but also the psychology of childhood development.

When Chuckie sees Daredevil subduing his gun-toting father, his identification shifts from Daredevil to his father, whom he now perceives as flawed. If he has to pick a superpowered surrogate for his father, the boy feels obligated by the father's corruption to identify not with Daredevil but with Bullseye, and so he takes a revolver just like his father's to school and wounds another kid on the playground. The last image of Chuckie in the story is an extreme-long-shot panel, unbound by a frame line, of his tiny silhouette against a flat, white (that is, uncolored) newsprint background. "We won't really know how Chuckie is until he starts talking again . . .". Daredevil finishes that story with an anguished examination of his chosen "profession" that is, ultimately, Miller's self-examination too. I've quoted a bit of it already, but the censorship discussion here begs fuller context: "So I keep asking myself again and again . . . what made Chuckie like he was? What am I giving people, by running around in tights and punching crooks? What am I showing them? Am I showing them that *good wins out*, that *crime does not pay*, that *the cavalry is always on its way*—or am I showing them that any idiot with fists for brains can get his way if he's fast enough and strong enough and mean enough? Am I fighting violence—or teaching it?" Miller offers no up-or-down verdict here. He does not advocate censorship, but neither does he rule it out. Rather, he displaces the question of censorship onto the more powerful influence that parents have on their children's behavior and on the processes by which children piece together the meanings of media violence on the basis of familial and other influences.

Chuckie's father is largely responsible for his son's breakdown, it seems, but that doesn't let Daredevil off the hook. The plot of #191 by its nature acknowledges the danger of exposing children to violent entertainment, but its outcome complicates the notion that represented violence is responsible for violent childhood impulses in some straightforward or predictable way. Chuckie would never have identified with Bullseye, the story implies, had not his father turned out to be not only a tyrant but also a corrupt businessman whom Daredevil must subdue—not just a mean father but a Bad Guy according to the Law, Daredevil's avowed standard. It's the tendency to draw a black-and-white distinction between good and evil—a tendency that even Silver Age Marvel comics proliferated—that does Chuckie in. Despite Murdock's determination not to be fooled by appearances of guilt or innocence, he, too, plays a zero-sum game in which Bad Guys are Bad Guys and Good Guys can do no wrong. For Miller's Daredevil, no gray area exists between the legal and the illegal; it's just that he determines to do the detective work necessary to make the distinction in terms not of what can be seen but of history, a willfully hidden but discoverable past of illicit acts.

This issue puts a fitting conclusion on a run so action packed that it has, until now, cleverly hidden its own muddying of the conventional good-evil dichotomy that comics held to fervently from DC's first Superman stories through Marvel's Silver Age. Miller, unlike his verbose predecessors of the socially conscious seventies,[9] uses story action rather than exposition to do the deconstructing. Daredevil reveals his own motivation for superadventuring to Chuckie not as a maxim but as a flashback to his own past, in the form of the preorigin story that Miller had written for himself long before its publication in #191, in which Matt comes home bloodied and bragging about his prowess in a street fight, and his father, drunk and furious that Matt has disobeyed, slaps his son. The image of Matt perched atop the Brooklyn Bridge, looking as small and alone as Chuckie sitting before his television, cements the contrast between him and Chuckie. Young Matt faces in the opposite direction from Chuckie and has no mass medium to cloud his reason: people need rules, Matt realizes, no matter who they are to you or how they justify their actions. But the parallel also compares the two kids as kids who make big decisions about their adult futures on the basis of a child's emotional and psychological reactions to childhood experience. Perhaps no one can slip the noose of childhood Oedipal trauma entirely, but Chuckie and young Matt are poster children for the cause of being vigilant about the uncompromising control that formative experiences can exert over one's moral sense thereafter.

As we readers sit alone, perhaps in silhouette ourselves (if anyone's looking) while we read this issue, we at least have the benefit of a media experience that deconstructs the same moral dichotomization that its key players face in *Daredevil* #191. But there doesn't seem to be much point in opening a comic book ever again to look for answers to the questions raised by #191; Daredevil certainly doesn't have any, though at least the creator pulling the strings cares that we understand that fact. Besides, this has all been for us, as the book readily admits. Daredevil's narration, ostensibly a dialogue with Bullseye, is not truly dialogue but rather narration, communicated to us in rectangular boxes rather than roundish balloons. This trope implies that, to an ear within the diegesis, Daredevil is *saying* nothing at all but only thinking it. And as the nondiegetic narrator who lies behind the diegetic one, Miller is saying what he says directly to the readers with only a thin veil of character standing between him and us.

Miller's censorship dustups of the eighties similarly recognized the complexity of morality and ethics in the real world as opposed to the narrow good-guys-versus-bad-guys spectrum of comics. Miller said in his very first interview with the *Comics Journal* that the Comics Code Authority didn't bother him; it was, if anything, a set of rules that, like genre conventions, actually assisted the artist as well as ensuring that the industry, not the law, controlled content: "If I wanted to do something that didn't fit with the Code . . . I simply wouldn't do it in *Daredevil*. . . . I don't mewl and puke about the Comics Code or about how I'm not allowed to do naked women or whatever. You need walls to push against. I've seen very little good work that's been created without supervision of some sort or another, without fairly strict rules. Even when I've gotten a great degree of freedom, I've set myself rigid rules to follow."[10] Miller also expressed concern that many writers and artists "who want to do comics for adults . . . slip inappropriate material into the kid stuff," such as heroes who "become more powerful and more effective and more successful every time they lose their temper," "women . . . dressed in B&D costumes," and "coy little sex references" that come in a constant stream. "We need to have comics done for adults," Miller said in 1985, while recognizing the difficulty of doing so in a culture that dismissed comics as junk from within a publishing industry that considered branching out an untenable risk.[11]

Miller could have held his own feet to the fire on several counts for his representations of women. He dressed Elektra in a high-cut minileotard and gave her gloves and footwear that resembled bondage gear wrapped around her by someone in a big hurry; he once even let his picture plane drift coyly away from Matt and Heather in Central Park as they apparently begin fooling around behind the bushes (issue #171). But at least once he addressed the issue of appropriate subject matter in *Daredevil* by telling a story *about* S&M that resonated with his criticism of dropping innuendo into comics bearing a Code seal. With "Mikey," the strapping, gimp-masked villain of "Lady Killer" (*Daredevil* #173, August 1981), Miller takes a poke at the White Queen's bodice-and-garter business suits in Byrne and Claremont's *X-Men* the previous year. In full leather regalia like a Nazi biker boy straight out of Kenneth Anger's *Scorpio Rising*, Mikey is revealed as the rapist who put Becky, Matt and Foggy's legal secretary, in a wheelchair and forces Daredevil into a helpless and humiliating position in a bar fight. "Can't move," Daredevil thinks as Mikey and his pals hold him down and pour their beers on him, then move in to administer a beating. "Helpless . . . I'm helpless . . . at his mercy . . ." Finally, as Daredevil gets socked over the course of three increasingly tight panels, his words leave his thought balloon and become block letters like those that usually signify sound effects, neon words that turn from orange to red as the panels progress: "JUST" "LIKE" "BECKY" (Figure 52). The simile here, suggestive as it is of is of a man's epiphanic empathy for a woman's experience of rape, is more than a little dubious. A rich and powerful white guy even when he isn't playing superhero, Matt/Daredevil is not exactly subject to the rape culture that makes Becky feel so responsible for her own assault that she refuses to turn Mikey in. And by putting the bad guy in leather, Miller fills out a stereotype about the evils of "deviant" sexuality. While these are hardly moot points, there's also a valid critique on display here of halfhearted self-censorship in the comics industry as it stood then, before *Maus*, *The Dark Knight Returns*, and *Watchmen* proved that adults would buy and read picture books with word balloons: bringing adult themes into children's entertainment risks destroying the superhero comic in that it shows how much the offending creators think about their own pleasure and how little they care about that of their audience.

But Miller clearly found the Code more and more constraining and stretched its limits thinner as he moved on to other projects. Wolverine from the X-Men apparently never interested Miller very much until he and Claremont got stuck in a taxi together and wound up plotting a four-issue miniseries featuring the character.[12] *Wolverine* (1982) was to be Miller's last penciling work for Marvel outside the occasional pinup or inventory story and the hardcover graphic novel *Elektra Lives Again* (1990), which he and Lynn Varley produced sans Code restrictions for Marvel's Epic Comics line. But in Wolverine, Miller latched onto a character uncompromised by Daredevil's sympathy for the rights of alleged lawbreakers. When ninjas attack Daredevil, he tries to subdue them and pump them for information as he does with petty thugs, but he stops far short of deadly force. When ninjas attack Wolverine upon his arrival in Japan, it is kill or be killed, and unlike the Lawyer without Fear, Wolverine enjoys the blood sport for its own sake. In *Wolverine* #4 (December 1982), when Wolverine confronts the adversary behind the attacks, he extends his claws and kills the crime lord out of frame, only his eyes and the "snikt" sound effect visible in the frame as he does so, but Glynis Wein, presumably at Miller's direction or at least with his blessing, colors his eyes blood red just for that moment.

Slowly and steadily, Miller was maneuvering out of Code territory into the world of frankly adult themes and pressing harder and

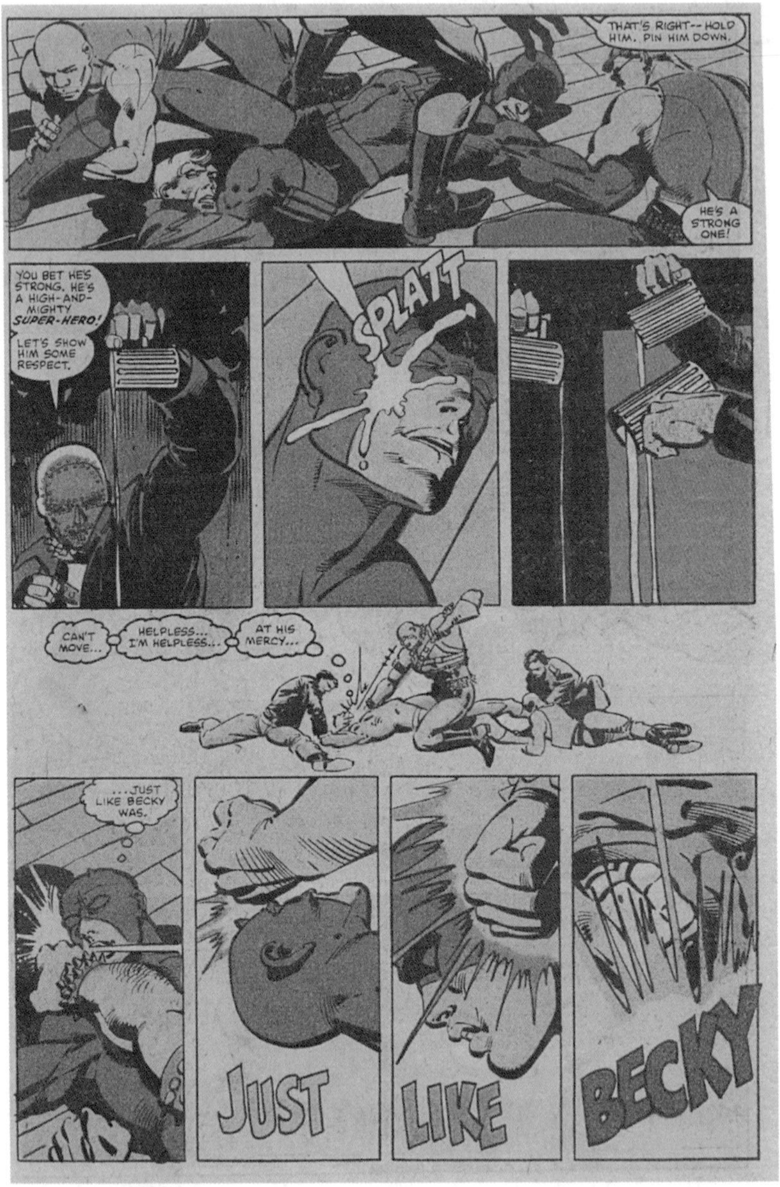
THAT'S RIGHT-- HOLD HIM. PIN HIM DOWN.
HE'S A STRONG ONE!
YOU BET HE'S STRONG. HE'S A HIGH-AND-MIGHTY SUPER-HERO!
LET'S SHOW HIM SOME RESPECT.
SPLATT
CAN'T MOVE...
HELPLESS... I'M HELPLESS...
AT HIS MERCY...
...JUST LIKE BECKY WAS.
JUST
LIKE
BECKY

FIGURE 52. Frank Miller and Klaus Janson, "Lady Killer," *Daredevil* #173 (Marvel, August 1981).

harder on the contradictions on which a traditional concept of heroism depends. Miller's *The Dark Knight Returns* steps even further into that world even as it sets up new "walls" to push against, namely, the postsixties culture of liberal humanism and so-called moral relativism. Miller's Batman has all of Daredevil's desire for justice but lacks any of DD's concern for the civil rights of the alleged perpetrators; indeed, if Daredevil's primary concern is with the victims, as Jim Shooter taught Miller, then Batman's primary concern is with crushing the perps. And he gets called on it throughout *The Dark Knight Returns* by loads of liberal-sounding talking heads who claim that Two-Face and the Joker were actually turned into supervillains by Batman's example, that even convicted homicidal maniacs deserve a second chance, and so forth. What Miller has done is to take Daredevil's line of legal thinking regarding the rights of criminal defendants, the same line that made him save Bullseye from being mashed on the subway tracks, and put it in the mouths of comic-relief characters such as the brain surgeons and psychologists who try to make Two-Face a productive member of society again. Miller's Batman, by contrast, is an epic hero who refuses to mistake good for evil or vice versa, and he gets to define on his own what each term means. Miller's Matt Murdock refuses such a metaphysical view of good and evil as all-or-nothing opposites on idealist grounds of a different sort. Matt believes that obscured innocence and hidden guilt have to be brought to light intellectually by finding proof and testing it, while Batman, who was at one time represented as a detective at heart, relies entirely on instinct when Miller has the reins.

To be fair, Miller presents the crudeness of Batman's worldview as a serious problem and has even done so in the midst of a conflict that seemed to many Americans to draw the brightest possible line between the national Us and a foreign Them. DC had already published the first issue of Miller and the colorist Lynn Varley's *Dark Knight* sequel, *Batman: The Dark Knight Strikes Again!*, when al-Qaeda operatives commandeered the planes that destroyed the World Trade Center on September 11, 2001, an event that, Miller told Groth, made it impossible to leave Batman's catchphrase about "striking terror into the hearts" of evildoers unannotated. As I've mentioned, Batman's dialogue in *The Dark Knight Strikes Again!*—even the dialogue written before 9/11—makes the ugliness of his philosophy unmistakable: "Striking terror. Best part of the job." Groth even points out to Miller that one Batman speech, in which he refers to American capitalists and the federal government as "tyrants" and promises that he and his team will "strike like lightning and . . . melt into the night like ghosts," sounds uncannily like "the point of view of radical Islamists" toward the United States.[13] Miller doesn't take such a crack at the obvious bad guys, however. Rather, he immediately pounces on the political reaction to the bad guys and how the George Bushes, Dick Cheneys, and John Ashcrofts of the world use crises like 9/11 for their own purposes. They stand in for the heroes we think we need in tumultuous times but slip the bounds of law at every turn—and Miller attempts to reduce our sympathy for them. This Miller, chastened by the 9/11 attacks but ever the shrewd critic of the media that deliver such disasters to us, digs into the fascistic politics of superhero comics, the news media's role in sensationalizing global politics and inciting fanatical nationalism, and the real-world politics of vigilante justice all at once. He claims comics as a space to explore what "heroism" means—and not necessarily to him but rather to contemporary US culture. If the one who "saves" us from tyranny, even the tyranny of our own leaders, claims he has to act like a terrorist to do it, do we even want to be saved?

At the same time, both Miller's comics and his interviews have long scrutinized the insolubility of the paradox—heroism is necessary to restore order, but it's also authoritarian in its purest form, even fascistic—as a necessary evil. Batman seems the purer Miller "hero" in that Batman's sense of justice is unencumbered by any complicating factors. He metes it out as he sees fit, on the basis of an Old Testament version of righteousness: you take my eye, I'll take yours, score settled. This hero is no model for quotidian life, but as in such classical Hollywood Westerns as John Ford's *The Searchers* (1956), the frontier will remain forever a chaotic wilderness without him. Only Ford's half-wild hero Ethan Edwards (John Wayne) can save his niece from hostile Comanche in post–Civil War Texas, but his intense race hatred makes him a relic, unfit to cross the threshold into the orderly world of law, family, and home that his very wildness has helped bring to the western frontier. The civic-minded Daredevil would be welcome in any such home, but for the later Miller especially, that taste for civilization and its rules reads as an "impurity," a liberal-humanist streak within traditional superheroism that Miller once talked about strictly in terms of character type (it's the difference between Batman and his "purer" doppelgänger, the Punisher) but that lately he describes as a moral fault, without any of the irony he mustered up a decade ago. There are signs dating back to 1986's *Batman: The Dark Knight Returns* that this irony was ambivalent anyway, considering the extent to which Batman adopts the Western hero's ruthless stance when taming the "frontier" of racialized criminals, right down to trading in the Batmobile for a horse.[14]

The progressive reverence with which Miller's comics after *Daredevil* treat that definition of heroism has everything to do with 9/11 and the scale of twenty-first-century global terrorism as Miller has processed it since *The Dark Knight Strikes Again!*. Back in 2003, he told Groth, "For at least the foreseeable future, [9/11 is] the whole point of my work. I'm going to play around with doing some propagandizing,"[15] but this sentiment did not prevent him from making the US government's reaction to the disaster a target for satire in his second *Dark Knight* story or lambasting the Bush administration for branding disagreement with its policies as providing solace to terrorists. By contrast, the Fixer, the costumed hero of Miller's frankly propagandistic graphic novel *Holy Terror* (Legendary Comics, 2011), doesn't care whether he gets thrown out of the house or not; his lot is to make the world safe for civilization, American style, not to inhabit it, and he likes it that way. The Fixer, a behemoth who shares a name with a character that Miller created for his high school newspaper's comics page, kills terrorists like a sledgehammer breaks pavement. There's no second-guessing motives or anything else; as far as the Fixer is concerned, if you're Muslim, you've got a bomb strapped to your midsection, so there's no danger that he will smash the wrong face.

Unsurprisingly, the character originally at the center of *Holy Terror* was Batman. Finally, Miller had freed the character of its impurities. To do that, he also had to burn off the "impurities" of the fundamentalist foe by painting al-Qaeda as representatives of all Islam and all Muslims and playing on every Arab stereotype he could scratch onto his Bristol board, from big noses to using Evil English to express delight in the torture and murder of "infidels." He has matched such images with political commentaries on National Public Radio, his personal blog, and elsewhere that show none of the critical distance that once made his work as jarring and energizing intellectually as the best Dashiell Hammett novel you've ever read. Our terrorist enemy, Miller has said, is "pernicious, deceptive and merciless and wants nothing less than [our] total destruction." Never mind that the majority of victims of al-Qaida and now ISIS are, in fact, Muslims.[16]

The hardline right position that Miller takes in *Holy Terror* differs so dramatically from that expressed in interviews dating back to the early 1980s that one has to wonder if he's been replaced by a Life Model Decoy from Nick Fury's supply closet. But *Holy Terror* was a critical disaster, prompting fans and critics alike to swear off any future Miller work and even to claim that his comics have rallied around a "sexist, fascist" flagpole since as far back as *The Dark Knight Returns* and possibly even before. Spencer Ackerman echoes the most scathing reviews when he writes in *Wired*, "Frank Miller doesn't do things halfway. One of the true comic-book greats, he's created several of the most extraordinary stories ever to grace the art form. So perhaps it's fitting that now he's produced one of the most appalling, offensive and vindictive comics of all time."[17] An opinion piece by "Kevin" on *Unleash the Fanboy* is equally representative of blogdom's take on the book:

> Miller's artistic downturn also coincides with what many see as a shift in his personality. The once astute social observer has been replaced by a *racist, sexist, homophobic, xenophobic, paranoid* nutcase. But there's a problem here and the problem is this: Miller's work was always kinda shitty. In fact, Miller's work has always been uneven and sometimes laughable, and there have been more than a few hints at the fascist, misogynist, bigot he eventually became publicly. . . . For all the praise it's gotten for being *the* Batman story, *DKR* [*Dark Knight Returns*] manages to paint an extremely out of character Batman. If people thought Miller's depiction of Batman as an abusive and *thuggish prick* in [Miller and Jim Lee's recent miniseries] *All-Star Batman* is off base, they should look back into *DKR* because he's essentially the same creature. Miller's Batman does not think; he punches. He's not a detective; he's a brawler. His solution to every problem, from gang violence to political corruption, is violence.[18]

I can't subscribe to such uses of Miller's Batman to evaluate Miller's own character. Critics have been mistaking the positions Miller examines in his comics for his own convictions for decades. Indeed,

Miller would agree with every one of Kevin's criticisms of Batman and even offer an aesthetic justification for this portrayal that depends on a dramatic irony that is difficult to locate, precisely because superhero comics have always traded in absolutes; criticism of those absolutes would understandably be less obvious to a dedicated reader of superhero comics, not to mention a nonreader convinced of superheroes' intrinsic lack of sophistication, than to someone interested in exploring or exploding the limits of the Batman mythos. Now, however, it not only looks like Miller has given away his critical distance; he also wants everyone to know it and to decide for themselves whether what he's done is worthless as a result, as comics or as political activism.

Back in 1998, discussing *300* with Christopher Brayshaw in the *Comics Journal*, Miller acknowledges the historical irony of Greece, the epitome of civil organization and intellectualism in the ancient West, needing a nation-state of cold-blooded warriors to fight its battles. In another context, he tells Brayshaw, he might have invited readers to ponder that irony and consider its paradoxical relationship to the development of democratic ideals.[19] He does not do so in this context, however. For Miller, *300* is all about the necessity of saving civilization—*Western* civilization—from barbarism. The three hundred Spartans did what was necessary; they lost the battle, badly, but without their sacrifice, discipline, and utterly unambiguous worldview, we would apparently still be living in mud huts today.

Even with *300*, though, Miller argues that he's playing around just a tiny bit with our tendency to collapse *heroes* with *role models*. Miller makes Leonidas admirable but not likable and renders most of the other 299 Spartans as less admirable and even less likable. But maybe, Miller has said not only about the Spartans but about the Punisher, Batman, and Superman, cultures need guys like that, and I do mean guys—the reckless male narcissists who can't or won't make subtle distinctions between good and evil—to do the dirty work of "preserving civilization as we know it." Usually, as in *The Dark Knight Returns* and *The Dark Knight Strikes Again!* and to a certain extent the noir riff on Dante's *Inferno* that is *Sin City*, Miller lets us sit with that ugly possibility, lets us squirm at our own enjoyment and/or disgust. He forces us to wonder if peace and forward movement are *ever* possible without the bright lines between good and evil and at the same time makes us ponder whether by drawing those lines, we put our humanity at risk. The generous way to interpret what Miller says here is that, like Hitchcock, he's casting doubt on the very notion of heroism that rules superhero comics, that is, the fantasy that superheroes could do what they do and yet remain "ordinary" people. Miller turned Batman into a living symbol of the fear that criminals should feel when threatened by "good," at least in a Platonist universe, but don't. However, when it's no longer comics, the First Amendment, or aesthetic complexity at stake but national security, take-no-prisoners tactics—in art as well as war—look to Miller like the only way to go. Even the Occupy Wall Street movement, which has its own ax to grind with tyranny in the form of the "1 percent's" economic mastery and the license it grants, is to Miller "nothing but a pack of louts, thieves, and rapists, an unruly mob, fed by Woodstock-era nostalgia and putrid false righteousness":

> These clowns can do nothing but harm America. This is no popular uprising. This is garbage. And goodness knows they're spewing their garbage—both politically and physically—every which way they can find.
>
> Wake up, pond scum. America is at war against a ruthless enemy.
>
> Maybe, between bouts of self-pity and all the other tasty tidbits of narcissism you've been served up in your sheltered, comfy little worlds, you've heard terms like al-Qaeda and Islamicism.
>
> And this enemy of mine—not of yours, apparently—must be getting a dark chuckle, if not an outright horselaugh—out of your vain, childish, self-destructive spectacle.

The commentary space below this post, his last to date on frank-millerink.com (a site no longer accessible as of November 2014), drew leftist humanists and right-wing hawks into a verbal battle that runs for pages and still got the occasional post right up to the time of the site's removal. The Right urges Miller on by characterizing the "Occutards" as lazy welfare royalty who love the terrorists as much as Miller says they do and are in any event too cowardly and stupid to enlist in the armed forces and kill off the *real* cancer on global society once and for all. The Left curses Miller for drawing us-or-them lines around everything and characterizing even a critique of capitalism as dangerously un-American—tactics that he once publicly abhorred. Rick

Moody, the author of *The Ice Storm* and other fictions of suburban angst, responded with an opinion piece for the *Guardian* (UK):

> Miller tries to repel the OWS [Occupy Wall Street] message ("Maybe, between bouts of self-pity and all the other tasty tit-bits [*sic*] of narcissism you've been served up in your sheltered, comfy little worlds, you've heard terms like al-Qaeda and Islami-cism") by reminding us that we are at war. This despite the fact that OWS is focused primarily on income inequality, and thus mainly taken up with domestic politics, such that OWS doesn't really take a position on the "ruthless enemy" and doesn't need to. Miller's particular approach, the warmongering approach, is self-evidently reminiscent of the Bush/Cheney years, in which any domestic reversal was followed by an elevated level on the colour-coded risk-assessment wheel.[20]

Moody is about as ham-fisted as Miller in his summary judgments. To Miller's accusation that Occupy Wall Street "schmucks" spend too much time playing World of Warcraft to take the terrorist threat seriously, Moody responds, "no one is more likely to play *World of Warcraft* than the kind of adolescent boy who also thinks [the film adaptation of] *300* is quality cinematic product."[21] Tiresome as it is to watch Moody plop gamers into the cryptofascist-escapist category, however, he manages to produce a fitting description of how obsessed Miller is with the 9/11 attacks, how it has become for him a funhouse mirror masquerading as a telescope through which he sees nothing on the horizon but barbaric leeches, consumers of American and European technological and cultural acumen who (according to Miller) have never produced anything worth consuming in return, preparing to destroy "us."

In what I want to believe is a triumph of Miller the listener over the absolutist Miller who sneers at the same First Amendment he once sacrificed his industry goodwill to defend, Miller now refuses to comment further on his anti-Occupy rant. Perhaps he thinks it all speaks for itself, or perhaps he has accepted certain tenets of his critics just as he graciously (and legitimately, it seems) accepted the differing opinions of Groth and other interviewers as recently as a decade ago. Either way, he has stopped talking much about politics of any stripe.

His blog is now abandoned due to "computer problems," Miller says, glowering during an interview for a *Wired* profile when Sean Howe suggests he find "a better technician" to fix it. "I will," Miller says, after a long silence.[22]

Look back on Daredevil's nemeses from the '79–'82 run with Miller's current anti-Islamicism in mind, though, and watch the ambiguities and nuances of his first major achievement get harder to pinpoint. Bullseye is a psychopath, complete with brain damage caused by cancer to guarantee it. Elektra is irredeemable despite her ostensibly clean bill of mental health: "The feeling I've been trying to get across is that she's betrayed something. She was meant to be something better than she is."[23] But once you've fallen from grace, that's it. Some people are evil, through and through—think of the "reformed" Harvey Dent/Two-Face in *The Dark Knight Returns*, whose ruined mind no amount of reconstructive surgery can repair—and they must be punished, locked away for good, dismissed, disposed of. There's no other way to get the cancer out of society. Miller dates the rising scale of violent crime in *Daredevil* back to his getting mugged and robbed in New York: "The experience filled me with anger, and that translated right into my comics."[24] As he got angrier, however, the struggle over right and wrong that plagued Daredevil seemed to get a lot less interesting to him than staking an unwavering claim to right.

Howe shrewdly characterizes Miller's use of secondary characters as a kind of misdirection: "*Daredevil*'s dastardly supporting cast allowed Miller to have it both ways by making Daredevil's barrage of kicks and punches look reasonable in comparison."[25] The bleak view on Miller's career would paint it as a slow but momentous roll past such apologies for superheroic vigilantism and into the stark light of the Fixer's gleeful, openly sadistic rampages, a development that Howe connects to Miller's personal victimization by crime prior to plotting *Batman: The Dark Knight Returns*:

> As Miller's career was taking off, the everyday violence in Manhattan at the time was taking its toll. "New York is no longer fit for human habitation," Miller told one friend. After enduring three robberies in the course of a month, he and [the colorist and his then-girlfriend Lynn] Varley decided to escape to LA. While she went out west to search for a home, he stayed behind

to set up more work to get them out of debt. He had a check in his pocket when, once again, someone tried to rob him. "Frank just went berserk on the guy," Varley says. "He didn't hit him or anything, he just went so berserk the guy backed off and ran away. We were on edge."[26]

Such anger floats to the surface of his work with a bang in 1986, the year I graduated from high school, with not one but two smash-hit stories about characters that didn't belong to him: *Batman: The Dark Knight Returns* and Miller's most lauded Daredevil story, *Daredevil: Born Again*, his 1986 return to the *Daredevil* series, penciled by David Mazzucchelli.

Born Again appeared in seven consecutive issues of *Daredevil* beginning with #227 and ending with #233. It begins with the Kingpin learning Daredevil's secret identity through channels leading back to Matt's former love interest Karen Page, whose failed Hollywood career has left her scraping the bottom of the media barrel, starring in cheap pornos and providing sex and information in exchange for her next heroin fix. (We're already in *Sin City* territory, where the bad things that happen to good people are both hyperbolic and creepily eroticized.) Like any good CEO, Kingpin uses this insider information to destroy the competition via economic channels, closing down Matt's bank accounts, shutting off his heat and water, and decimating his credit rating. But it's only when the Kingpin, at heart an old-fashioned gangster who can't resist a good hit, blows up Matt's condominium that Matt reaches the bottom he has to hit in order to be reborn: "It was the perfect crime, Kingpin. You shouldn't have signed it." He now has the evidence of a real antagonist—entropic destruction may be realistic, but it doesn't give you a sparring partner—but he soon loses his grip on sanity. The splash pages of the first three issues display bird's-eye views of Matt curled in various fetal poses, and after Kingpin has blown up his home real good, as SCTV's "Farm Film Celebrity Blow-up" hosts used to say around that time, that position visualizes Matt as a human caterpillar, cocooning himself both in body and mind as he staggers through streets and makes deranged phone calls to Foggy and to his girlfriend, Gloriana (in a move that allowed the feminist comics blogger and writer Gail Simone to put another Woman in Refrigerator notch in her belt, the writer Denny O'Neil had Heather Glenn commit suicide in *Daredevil* #220). Matt eventually confronts the Kingpin, gets the living shit kicked out of him, and winds up at a Catholic mission in Hell's Kitchen where his mother—pronounced dead way back in *Daredevil* #1 but retconned by Miller with all the audacity one would expect from the guy who concocted Elektra—is now an official Sister of Mercy, habit and all.

Miller sponsors a position here rather than taking it; he is not more religious than before ("I'm an atheist, Gary," he told Groth in 2003, and his first comic about 9/11 was a laconic but scathing critique of all religious faith),[27] but he is no less willing to let a god he doesn't believe in provide transformative illumination to his character. In the end, after a nut-ball subplot in which Nuke, a pill-popping, Looney Tunes cross between a Special Ops agent and the Punisher, is called in by the Kingpin to finish his failed assassination, the disbarred Matt turns losing everything he valued into an opportunity to become nothing more or less than the principal defender of his old neighborhood against the Forces of Evil. Daredevil still wears the same costume, but everything else about him has burned away, allowing him to focus solely on policing his territory. *Born Again* celebrates hatred as a crucible for the heroic soul, burning away needless subtleties of character and helping Matt regain the sanity to fulfill the revenge impulse he picked up while losing his mind. He has become Miller's Batman without all the technological toys, purged of his straight-arrow lawyer's love of the law by anger and madness—just the sort of Hulkish release Miller used to characterize as a lousy lesson to teach comics-reading kids.

It's a hell of a second coming for a character whose series stubbornly still bore a Comics Code seal. I won't fault Miller for the anger of that story today any more than I did when I read *Born Again* at seventeen; on the contrary, I still believe there's not much point in going through adolescence in the United States without some rebel-themed mass culture to embrace for the sole reason that your parents would hate it. Still, I marvel at how much Miller's perspective on his audience had changed between 1983's "Roulette" and the *Born Again* story line in 1985–86. According to Howe's account of Marvel in the eighties, Miller's inspiration for *Born Again* was losing everything himself. Ramped up on the success of *Ronin* and eager to get away from the city that fostered at least one person's transformation into a real-life vigilante ("one Bernard Goetz is enough"), Miller moved to Los Angeles, found himself dead broke, and decided to pitch a new Daredevil story that started with Matt Murdock in similar straits.[28] No doubt it was satisfying to create a world in which a bloated mob boss—somebody, anybody—could actually be held accountable for downturns of fortune, instead of such mundane external forces as random robberies or astronomically high rent. But *Born Again* also recommends interpretations of Miller's work as reflective of his worldview, making it more difficult to give him the benefit of the doubt when he says he is investigating the justification of defensive violence rather than sponsoring it.

Still, after Miller stripped bare the superhero myth so completely with his initial *Daredevil* run, it's difficult to see where one could go with the premise from there except backward. The conclusion of issue #191 genuinely reaches a dead end for superheroic fantasies that law enforcement could be practiced extralegally without causing ugly consequences. Chuckie's father is outed as an embezzler and a committer of domestic violence, and the implication is that he will be punished for it. But his infractions hurt no one more than Chuckie, whose worship of Daredevil turns to emulation of Bullseye when he sees DD subdue his father. Those Xeroxed panels of the pistol aimed at Bullseye's head, color draining out of each successive panel as we are edged closer and closer to the intended point of impact, exposes for good and all the circularity of DD's career and the cycle of accidental negative consequences that such vigilante activity might have for its younger readers in thought or deed. This is not a critique of funnybook idealism but the demolition of the superhero myth itself.

Less than five years after *Daredevil* #191, however, Miller tries to reconstruct what he so thoroughly demolished. *Batman: The Dark Knight Returns* begins, cautiously, Miller's long celebration of superhero fantasy as fantasy, for its own sake. Upon the publication of *The Dark Knight Returns* and *Watchmen* in 1986, Miller told Groth twelve years later, they were "falsely believed to [represent] a revival of the superhero," when to him, they "look[ed] more like the end of something than any kind of beginning." He recounted joking with Alan Moore that Moore's *Watchmen* was an autopsy of the already-dead superheroic dream, while *The Dark Knight Returns* was its "brass-band funeral."[29] If that's so, then *The Dark Knight Strikes Again!* is its full-blown resurrection. Everything silly about men and women in tights that creators from Englehart, Gerber, and Starlin to Moore, Miller, and

Grant Morrison had forced readers to confront has been boiled down to its essence once again. The figures have hands as big as their heads, women are all angles, and in general, Adams-style realism has finally, completely disintegrated in the name of returning to basic, fun, fantastical questions raised by more-than-human characters: what would it be like, exactly, to shrink oneself down to the size of a molecule? Miller's introduction of the Atom, which begins with a primitive-looking man (the Atom himself) fighting off monsters many times his size, seems to have bounded out of a *Twilight Zone*–ish Ditko story from *Amazing Adult Fantasy*, where the twist always involves concealing some irregularity in the story's world until the very end. He reduces all the characters to their most brutal political-epic elements: Green Arrow is a hippie/commie/anarchist court jester, Superman is even more a shill for the US government than he was in *The Dark Knight Returns*, Wonder Woman finally looks and sounds like the ancient god she was always suspected of being and has rough (though not explicit) sex with Superman in midair.

Miller's attraction to this sort of frankness differs considerably from his much-earlier irritation with the "fuck scene" (as Miller delicately put it in 1985) between Superman and Lois Lane in Richard Donner's *Superman II* (1980). Miller's complaint was that the scene was both tonally inappropriate and simply redundant: they "had already made love in the first one [*Superman*, Donner, 1978], flying over the city; that's how superheroes do it." The first film, in other words, had produced a metaphor for sex appropriate both to the character and to the character's target audience of kids simply by remaining within the bounds of the superhero genre and doing it artfully.[30] Today, to Miller, getting back to basics seems to mean revisiting not the original creators' treatment of the characters but rather following his own instinct regarding their essences, which are effectively feral versions of themselves.

Certainly one could interpret these caricatures as critical portraits drawn by taking the essence of each character and exposing its ugliness by exaggerating it, reducing the character to nothing but a machine for expressing that essence. From this perspective, Batman is a villain, not a hero. But how can one deny that Batman is the intended hero of *Batman: The Dark Knight Strikes Again!* or of any other book that bears his name? Structurally at least, we're rooting for him. Miller can make us question the rightness of "right" here, just as Hitchcock does, according to Robin Wood, by exposing that "bourgeois 'normality' is empty and unsatisfying, everything beyond it . . . terrifying."[31] When the law comes to put everything right at the end of a Hitchcock film, we're left with a lurking sense that the good guys didn't necessarily win, that Guy Haines of *Strangers on a Train* was a killer at heart rather than the innocent victim of Bruno Antony, and that Guy's own struggle with anger and violence remains unresolved. The characters haven't necessarily learned to respect one another's rights, only how to avoid punishment by keeping their contempt for each other a secret. All that has changed by the end is that the playing pieces have been returned to their proper squares—which is to say, nothing has changed at all, and the audience is made to feel this in the form of a lurking anomie or even disgust.

There are flashes of that sort of nuance here and there in Miller's twenty-first-century work, though you won't find them in *Sin City* or *300*, which both draw the differences between good and bad more starkly than even the Batman stories do. They provide little evidence of the kind of double reversal that Miller told Groth he was pulling in *The Dark Knight Strikes Again!*, in which we (might) suddenly realize that we've been tricked into identifying with a reprehensible idealism about crime and punishment.

But Miller's broadest strokes have deep roots, as well. *Give Me Liberty* (drawn by Dave Gibbons, 1990–91), in which a victim of political oppression in a dystopian future evolves from terrified child to disciplined revolutionary, reads to me now a bit like a manual from the National Rifle Association intended to show children how to beat back the evil federal government that the Tea Party has taught us so much about; the fact that this child is an African American named Martha Washington with a most legitimate bone to pick with "her" government can't quite mitigate my gut reaction that Miller chose a black girl for his protagonist in order to make the horse-sized pill of martial law easier to swallow.

Miller has also deflected the charge of oversimplifying political shades of gray through satire. The cartoonist Geof Darrow turned Miller's concept for *Hard Boiled* (1992) from a fairly conventional noir story into a gargantuan satire of Dirty Harry, a choice with which Miller gleefully complied when writing the dialogue. And—lest

I forget one of his most experimental forays into his Daredevil universe—there's the miniseries *Elektra: Assassin* (1986–87, drawn and painted by Bill Sienkiewicz), which pulls no satirical punches in making the presidential candidate Ken Wind a dead ringer for Dan Quayle and revealing him as the Beast, a force of pure evil that exists only to rain destruction on all humans. Elektra employs (more like possesses) a half-crazed, half-robotic S.H.I.E.L.D. agent named Garrett to help her fight the Beast, who hides his nefarious intentions for the world behind a bleeding-heart liberal stance. The conclusion brings us Garrett, now inhabiting Ken Wind's body and sitting pretty in the Oval Office, nonchalantly waving a semiautomatic rifle around and announcing that he possesses the mythical "button" that would nuke the Russkies into the Stone Age. Am I supposed to feel safer now than when the Beast had the world by the tail?

Back in the first decade of Miller's career, even when he cut broad categories regarding his convictions, he was still willing to entertain dissenting views. When Marvel and DC began drafting comics ratings policies in the mideighties without requesting input from creators, he preached to anyone who would listen the gospel of the First Amendment, portraying the moment you allow someone to slap ratings on works of free expression as the very moment you relinquish your right to free speech; you need only await the jackbooted thugs to march down your street to make it official. When Groth pressed him on his paradoxical logic—you don't want kids to read certain kinds of material, but you refuse to sanction *any* mode of signaling such material to potential readers?—he seemed to recognize that he hadn't considered all the consequences of his ideas.[32] How *do* you keep kids from reading inappropriate material if their parents don't care? And is clearing up all ambiguity about the "adult" nature of the material behind that letter rating on the cover of your comic book really equivalent to banishing the possibility of ever publishing any such material again, at least not as a comic?

Miller brought that thoughtfulness into his first creator-owned series. The brilliance of *Ronin*, it seems to me, is not in its unique transplantation of *Lone Wolf and Cub*'s masterless samurai conceit into a futuristic America or its critique of how multinational capital writes and enforces its own laws. The brilliance of *Ronin* is in its musing on the effects of media violence on children. Billy, a quadriplegic adult with the mind of a ten-year-old, has tremendous telekinetic powers that he uses to reincarnate a samurai for a powerful artificial intelligence called Virgo, the creation of the Aquarius corporation. In the end, through a haze of provocatively cloudy insinuation, we discover that this ronin that Billy created with biomechanical technology is (probably) not a historical figure after all but rather (more or less) an amalgam drawn from samurai movies he has watched on television under Virgo's supervision. The ronin is made by Virgo to believe he actually is a ronin and a hero, and Virgo manipulates him through that fantasy into killing everyone who stands in the way of her taking over Aquarius and turning the global thermonuclear age into her playground. It's the Age of Aquarius all right; Miller's suspicion of sixties counterculture has now become scathing parody, right down to the aging, peace-sign-wearing hippie who cruelly appropriates the ronin as his protector and meal ticket as they wander the deadly slums of a ruined New York. Hypocrisy permeates every social relationship, and violence in the media—exemplified by *Ronin* itself—is only good for turning children into soldiers for somebody else's cause, right?

Not quite. The violence that Billy witnesses on television might be suspect in itself, even to Miller, but *Ronin* displays what individuals actually *do* with their encounters with media violence in a more optimistic light. Miller went on record many times in the eighties saying that he wouldn't want any children of his to read the violent, adult-themed comics he was beginning to create, but *Ronin* explores the inevitability of children coming into contact with media violence and places its faith in children's ability to use such images to challenge their understandings of ethics, human rights, and what sorts of things are worth fighting for. Billy breaks free of Virgo's influence and, directed by a much more benevolent guide named Casey, who is also Aquarius's chief security officer, overthrows the AI and saves the world. Without *chanbara* films on late-night TV, Billy would have been helpless to prevent Virgo from burning everything down. Not that samurai movies saved the world all by themselves, but in the right mind with the right upbringing, Miller hints, even they could become a vehicle for renewal.

The days of such thematic subtlety are long behind Miller now. He seems to have become a full-time curmudgeon, from his one-dimensional stories of punching, shooting, and decapitating anything he doesn't like right down to his sallow appearance. Indeed, for whatever reason (I won't dignify rumor by repeating any of it here), he even looks like a curmudgeon. Promotional photos of Miller released before the premiere of *Sin City: A Dame to Kill For* in late 2014 present a bony, wrinkled, stooped figure who looks twenty years older than his actual age of fifty-seven. The Bleeding Cool website reported on December 3, 2014, that Miller and the current *Batman* scripter Scott Snyder are furiously cowriting a second sequel to *The Dark Knight Returns*, but "Miller is too unwell to draw the book" himself.[33] The DC Comics website now lists Brian Azzarello (the writer of Vertigo's *100 Bullets* and DC's "New 52" reboot of *Wonder Woman*) as Miller's collaborator on what the site calls "DK III: The Master Race"; "artists for the project," the press release concludes, "have yet to be announced," though as of late 2015, penciler Andy Kubert and Klaus Janson, the inker of Miller's *Daredevil* and the first *Dark Knight* series, have been added to the creative team.[34] It must tear Miller's heart out to leave the art of a new *Dark Knight* series to others, no matter how well they know his interests and preoccupations. I am worried about him. I want my Frank Miller back. That's selfish, of course, as well as delusional in a way fans are accustomed to being delusional after years of obsessing over stars of mass culture. Today's Frank Miller is not *my* Frank Miller—but of course, he wasn't mine in 1982 either. He never wanted to be anybody's artist but his own. If his goal as an artist is to piss people off, he's succeeded mightily; even a progressive critic who disagrees with Miller's current views on Islam and terrorism has professed admiration for *Holy Terror* on the grounds that Miller is still trying to force us to face the demons that reside in our fantasies of revenge.[35] Is it too much to hope for that the subtitle *The Master Race* might signal not a sneer at critics who have called Miller's Batman fascistic but rather some kind of return to Bernard Krigstein's "Master Race" for EC, a story characterized by chillingly stark graphics and a real will to examine the dark impulses that burst forth when circumstances back us against the wall?

So how do we locate politically Miller's first crack at *Daredevil*, with respect to works like *Holy Terror*? Here's a possibility, perhaps the most optimistic one I can imagine. Read the end of *Daredevil* #191 not as the final irony of superhero justice but as the desperation of a character who suddenly realizes that's what he is: a character, a Wile E. Coyote stuck in an endless loop of coyote-versus-road-runner violence in which all other plot points represent nothing more than a brief reprieve from the recurring conflict. Daredevil and Bullseye really are stuck with each other, and Miller both reports this and exposes the futility of its logic because it can never—for this is a genre product aimed largely at kids (at least so long as Marvel reported to the Comics Code Authority)—allow Daredevil to kill his enemy.

The stripped-back nature of this moment exposes a textual logic of superheroic angst in Marvel Comics beginning with the Silver Age, a logic in which no story ever concludes, displacement is always zero—in other words, nothing gets done. Even death is never final; the next time Phoenix dies in an *X-Men* book, you won't have to count the months for very long before somebody figures out a way to bring her back, whether it's by burying her "real" body in the ocean while the "Phoenix-Force" runs amok or going back in time to retrieve the original, pre-Phoenix Jean Grey from 1963. Miller has exposed a strictly commercial nerve here, outed the superheroic version of serial anxiety and added a twist of self-deprecation and self-loathing, a sense that the Lacanian *objet petit a* not only will continue to elude Daredevil but will never even reveal what it's *pretending* to be, let alone what it is. *Daredevil* #191 also reports on Miller's ultimate frustration at the limitations of superhero comics, which he's pushed against to good ends for nearly four years by now, and a volley in favor of a more stripped-bare heroism, in which his thrill at drawing expressionistically can open out into new modes of conflict. Looking back, this issue marks the beginning of the end of Miller's willingness to think further through the problem of illegal heroism or perhaps an admission that there's nowhere further to think at all. He reached the end of that line of inquiry so early in his career that he has had to reinvent and renew the old dichotomies of superhero comics in his work since just to have something to bash his head against. But his reaction to 9/11 made those dichotomies useful to him again in an unselfconscious way, and he's reverted to them as his medium pure and simple rather than his intellectual tango partner.

On the hunt for some kind of closure for this book or maybe for a reason to forgive Frank Miller for turning his back on the ambiguities of heroism, right, and wrong, I went to see *Frank Miller's Sin City: A Dame to Kill For* (codirected by Miller with Robert Rodriguez, 2014) in a theater a couple of months before I submitted this book. I had to dig through Fandango to find a nearby theater screening a 3D print of the film, which does Miller's graphic novels up in black-and-white with isolated color details and a near-religious replication of Miller's panel compositions. I drove forty-five minutes in a mild fog to get there. A few minutes in, Joseph Gordon-Levitt appears as Johnny, a gambler with lucky hands whose hard-boiled voice-over says that casinos are like women: somebody has to win.

Or something like that. I won't be going back to the film to check the dialogue, probably because the line so crassly subordinates gender to the noir male's drive for linguistic mastery of everything—especially women—that one wonders how Miller could ever have produced even as crude a study in cross-gender empathy as "Lady Killer" (*Daredevil* #173). For all that story's naivety about the ideology of gender power dynamics, it approaches a surprising level of empathy for victims of assault like Becky. The story is hardly the pinnacle of feminist analysis. There's nothing like delivering to a woman crippled by her attacker not one but two man-splanations of why she shouldn't feel ashamed of being attacked, especially when each reason is employed not to comfort her but rather to coax her into testifying. But it does attempt to understand from a masculinist perspective what causes the victim of rape such shame even if it completely misses the point that in rape culture, men (rapists and appointed protectors alike) hold women responsible simply for being women and therefore "causing" sexual assaults in the first place. At least Miller the young turk made the attempt to grasp a perspective that wasn't his own.

These days Miller uses the once-productive limits of genre as a barricade he erects around himself and his material to protect it from such complexities. In the film of *A Dame to Kill For*, Gordon-Levitt's Johnny picks up a young woman named Marcie (Julia Garner) at the casino, takes her to the back-room poker parlor for "luck," and winds up winning thousands of dollars at the poker table, enraging Senator Roark (Powers Boothe), a machine politician with glints of green postproduction "light" flashing in his evil eyes. Apparently having no place else to go and nothing to do besides being picked up by a hunky young man, Marcie gets aroused by Johnny's good fortune and generosity and, becoming quite tender toward him during the five minutes of screen time they've known each other, agrees to meet him at his hotel later. The next time we see her, she's just a head lying on the floor of the hotel room, the victim of Roarke's retribution against Johnny. This heinous act motivates Johnny to destroy Roarke—big surprise there. In the end, it's the renowned stripper Jessica Alba who shoots Roarke in the head, so I guess in Miller's mind, the women win after all. Tell that to Marcie, a totem stripped of any value except to motivate somebody else's righteous retribution. In itself, to paraphrase Budd Boetticher, her head has not the slightest importance.

There's still a tinge of the *Daredevil* Miller lurking in the second *Sin City* film, if you can stand watching it long enough to catch a glimpse of it. Characters like Dwight (Josh Brolin) find themselves doing exactly the opposite of what they know is good for them but are completely unable and unwilling to stop themselves; that would rob them of the pleasure of wallowing in self-hatred while puzzling over their self-destructive drives. Dwight shares with Daredevil a bewilderment at his own motives; his subconscious desires and immediate bodily needs—he wants his old lover Ava (Eva Green) back, a desire she feeds by lying around naked and begging him like a frightened child to follow her orders—override his instinct for self-protection. Dwight is perhaps further gone than Matt Murdock. At least Murdock had the ego to refuse to recognize his contradictory behavior toward Elektra, choosing instead to believe that he was going to do his sworn duty to justice by "bringing her in" eventually even as his emotions were generating new justifications for letting her go free. Dwight is fully conscious that he's destroying himself and can't do anything about it. More than this, though, what has changed is that only the fact of the contradiction itself seems to interest Miller any longer, because it motivates a lot of cathartic violence, not to mention a neat little double reference to *Double Indemnity* and *The Strange Love of Martha Ivers*, film noirs that end with Barbara Stanwyck at last declaring her love to her erstwhile male victim just as he shoots her to death (though to be fair, Martha Ivers shoots her guy right back).

Watching Dwight shoot Ava in *Sin City: A Dame to Kill For* got me thinking about Miller's interest in heroism again. Did Dwight's resistance to the femme fatale stem from the same idealized heroism of Matt Murdock filtered through Leonidas in *300*, where right actions are sometimes drawn from the gut rather than the legal code? Did Miller think Daredevil did the right thing on some objective plane when he dropped Bullseye from the power lines to the street in #181, or was that moment supposed to haunt us the way it haunted Matt for the last eleven issues of Miller's stint, to force our recognition of the irreconcilability of public justice with its private counterpart in the self-justifiable moral universe of the individual mind?

Richard Rosenbaum has recently made the compelling case that Miller's Batman, even the universally reviled "I'm the goddamn Batman" Batman of Miller and Jim Lee's unfinished *All-Star Batman and Robin* miniseries (2005–8), resonates deeply with the contemporary conservative moral mind-set to the point where it manages to analyze that position better than just about anyone else, certainly better than most conservative pundits and politicians. What Miller recognizes, Rosenbaum argues, is that Batman is afraid, that he understands that only fear will cause his fellow do-gooders to make the hard choices necessary to protect their constituencies from havoc.

> Batman is afraid because he knows exactly what is out there in the world, he anticipates every possibility in order to prevent or counter it. Batman's viewpoint is fundamentally a conservative one: Batman needs order and control; he wants to personally ensure that the only people who get hurt are the ones who deserve to. . . .
>
> Miller, a conservative, understands this probably more than any other modern Batman writer, but he needs to exaggerate Batman's neuroses more and more to make the point as we become more and more accustomed as a society to Batman, his motivations and his *modus operandi*: Batman's foes are not alien warlords or evil interdimensional clones—they are people who take advantage of other people, people who cause the innocent masses to live in fear. His perspective on crime is fundamentally conservative because he doesn't believe that going after "root causes" of crime is good enough; Bruce Wayne operates orphanages and donates beyond generously to charity, but in the final analysis Batman believes that what will stop criminals is only the fear of being caught and punished. He's no "bleeding heart" like Superman or Green Lantern. He's a "law and order" type. He knows that criminals are a cowardly, superstitious lot. He knows that criminals will respond to fear, because *he* responds to fear.
>
> Does that make you uncomfortable? Should it?[36]

Rosenbaum takes a generous leap of faith when he suggests that Miller is simply doing what Miller has always done, which is to give an intransigent point of view to a character and then follow it through to its logical conclusion, whether Miller agrees with that perspective or not. I'm just not sure whether I can attribute Rosenbaum's reading of *All-Star Batman and Robin* to Miller's brilliance as an artist so much as to a mounting intolerance that his stories express toward anyone who doesn't fit his definition of the true hero. The ideal Miller hero rejects the rule of law, follows his own moral code, and disregards the rights of all others, up to and including their right to exist. What Miller considers heroic thinking at present looks a lot like narcissistic personality disorder to me, and that kills my appreciation for his recent work. I would be the first to admit that my reactions to Miller's twenty-first-century comics say as much about my current political convictions as they do about his. Perhaps the reason I can't abide by a brilliance driven by fear and hatred is that fear and hatred make for lousy foreign policy, as so much of "antiterrorist" military activity since 9/11 has stemmed from following irrational fear directly into irrational action. I'm not coming out of this study smelling like a rose any more than Miller is. At least I've learned from him that gut reactions are not to be ignored but confronted.

So long, Frank. Whatever else you've done with your career, your first big hit helped me to mature first as a comic-book fan and later as a media critic who has learned to confront his own blind spots. Thanks for *Daredevil*, which forced me to think and rethink the consequences of my love for corporate superhero comics and to appreciate the complexity of the ethical dilemmas that haunt them. I doubt we'll meet again.

NOTES

INTRODUCTION: DEALING WITH THE DEVIL

1 Scott McCloud, *Understanding Comics: The Invisible Art* (1993; repr., New York: Kitchen Sink / Harper Perennial, 1994), 70.

2 Al Feldstein and Bernard Krigstein, "Master Race," *Impact* #1 (EC, April 1954). An even more incremental example of this tendency occurs in Krigstein's final page of the story "The Desert Rat," *Journey into Mystery* #46 (Atlas [Marvel], May 1957).

3 On the differences between Miller's use of graphic violence and the "grim 'n' gritty" violence of 1990s mainstream comics, see Julian Darius, "What Fall from Grace? Reappraising the Chichester Years," in *The Devil Is in the Details: Examining Matt Murdock and Daredevil*, ed. Ryan K. Lindsay (Edwardsville, IL: Sequart Research & Literacy Organization, 2013), 170–71.

4 For the definitive discussion of autobiographical comics by women from their undersung origins in underground comix to the lauded works of Bechdel and Marjane Satrapi, see Hillary L. Chute, *Graphic Women: Life Narrative and Contemporary Comics* (New York: Columbia University Press, 2010).

5 Hereafter all dates associated with single issues are cover dates unless otherwise noted. Until quite recently, comics, like most monthly magazines, carried a cover date later than the actual month of publication and release (between two and four months at the beginning of the Silver Age, for example); cover dates indicate to regular retail sellers when to return unsold copies to the distributor for a refund.

6 Lee's philosophy of projecting change without actually changing anything was driven by Marvel's interest in making its characters instantly appropriable by potential merchandising and television licensees. Inevitably, however, the generation of writers after Lee found the philosophy frustrating. For an excellent discussion of the "illusion of change" mandate and its longevity, see Sean

Howe, *Marvel Comics: The Untold Story* (New York: HarperCollins, 2012), 100–101, 136–37, 178.

7 Though I don't wish to downplay the historical and critical importance of Miller's *Batman: The Dark Knight Returns*, that miniseries attracted more mainstream press attention and larger sales than *Daredevil* did then and now at least in part because of Batman's greater recognizability compared to Daredevil, and arguably because Miller gave the historically protean Batman character more definition (as a ruthless, hard-boiled crime fighter) than it had enjoyed at any point since the early 1970s.

8 The one academic collection focused on Daredevil analyzes plots and characters exhaustively but offers little to no discussion of images. Its authors treat covers, panels, pages, and individual issues as more or less objective containers for story material and subordinate the differences among disparate creators' *Daredevil* runs to an interest in describing character traits and development as consistent and believable. See Lindsay, *Devil Is in the Details*.

CHAPTER ONE: OUR STORY SO FAR

1 As Peter Coogan argues, Clark Kent in his earliest appearances "only uses his Superman identity to enable him to get the story and write the exposé" for his newspaper the *Daily Planet*. Within two years of his introduction in 1938, however, Superman shifts from being a proponent of "public-spirited vigilantism"—a mission-driven social reformer, even a radical one—to being a reactive figure, only taking action when the community is unsettled by the fiendish plan of a supervillain. Peter Coogan, *Superhero: The Secret Origin of a Genre* (Austin, TX: Monkeybrain, 2006), 203, 114. Coogan is right to assert the dominance of the passive model in serial superhero stories ever since, because the alternative, the proactive superhero like Moore's Ozymandias (from *Watchmen*) and Miracleman, "risks becoming a ruler, savior, or destroyer, essentially a villain in the first and last roles" (ibid., 114). As I'll discuss in later chapters, Miller hangs Daredevil up on this paradox of the proactive superhero with respect to Bullseye, an unreformable villain whose reign of terror can apparently only be ended by his death or total incapacitation.

2 Dwight Decker, "Interview One" (1981), in *Frank Miller: The Interviews: 1981–2003*, ed. Milo George (Seattle: Fantagraphics, 2003), 20. For the record, the credits for Wood's run are more complicated than Miller suggests. Lee wrote issues #5–9 and #11; Wood wrote #10 himself; and Wood and Bob Powell shared the layout, rendering, and inking duties on issues #9–11, before Wood left Marvel to help establish a competing company, Tower Comics.

3 According to Will Murray, due to Everett's tight schedule at his personal studio, the backgrounds for *Daredevil* #1 were completed by Steve Ditko, George

Roussos, and Sol Brodsky. Will Murray, "A Different Daredevil," in *The Devil Is in the Details: Examining Matt Murdock and Daredevil* (Edwardsville, IL: Sequart, 2013), 7.

4 See *Marvel Two-in-One* #3 (May 1974) and *Daredevil* #110–112 (June, July, and August 1974).

5 Kuljit Mithra, "Interview with Marv Wolfman (November 1997)," ManWith-outFear.com, 1997, http://www.manwithoutfear.com/daredevil-interviews/Wolfman.

6 Richard Howell and Carol Kalish, "An Interview with Frank Miller," *Comics Feature* 14 (December 1981): 18.

7 Robbins may well have intended his single issue of *Daredevil* as satire or at least a loud rebuttal of a genre that didn't quite fit his aesthetic if he wasn't drawing "historical" titles like *The Invaders*, a Marvel team book set during the Second World War. Though Sean Howe writes that Robbins left the *Daredevil* assignment that issue because he retired to Mexico, I wonder whether Robbins, a forty-year veteran of the adventure comic strips *Scorchy Smith* and *Johnny Hazard* and an artist-writer for DC and Marvel through the 1970s, drew that issue the way he did to get himself fired from the series. At the time, superhero comics demanded consistent, mundane realism from issue to issue and artist to artist. As Miller notes, Robbins's work on that issue "looked about 20 years out of date": "It was culture shock. That was one of the most bizarre things I ever saw. I don't think it was successful." Peter Sanderson, "The Frank Miller/Klaus Janson Interview," in *The Daredevil Chronicles*, ed. Mitch Cohn (Albany, NY: FantaCo, 1982), 23. Yet Miller respects Robbins for precisely that uncompromising streak, his persistence in drawing exactly as he wants to draw, no matter what conventions he bucks. He calls Robbins's art "dangerous" in the most complimentary sense: it's bold, grotesque, and unique enough to repel all but the most dedicated *Daredevil* readers in an era when Neal Adams's realist approach ruled the industry. See Sean Howe, *Marvel Comics: The Untold Story* (New York: Harper Perennial, 2012), 223; Sanderson, "Frank Miller/Klaus Janson," 13.

8 Murray, "Different Daredevil," 8–9.

9 Thomas Pynchon, *The Crying of Lot 49* (1965; repr., New York: Perennial, 1999), 52.

10 "Frank Miller (Earth-1218)," Marvel Database, http://marvel.wikia.com/Frank_Miller_(Earth-1218) (accessed June 11, 2013).

11 "*Daredevil* #158! Rare 1979 Dave Cockrum Cover Sketch! Frank Miller! Marvel Comics!," *Big Glee! The Albert Bryan Bigley Archives!*, November 8, 2010, http://bigglee.blogspot.com/.

12 Decker, "Interview One," 21, 31.

13 Christopher Brayshaw, "Interview Four" (1998), in George, *Frank Miller: The Interviews*, 81.

14 Sanderson, "Frank Miller/Klaus Janson," 18.

15 Charles Hatfield, *Hand of Fire: The Comics Art of Jack Kirby* (Jackson: University Press of Mississippi, 2012), 92. See also Howe, *Marvel Comics*, 50.

16 Hatfield, *Hand of Fire*, 91.

17 Les Daniels, *Marvel: Five Fabulous Decades of the World's Greatest Comics* (New York: Harry N. Abrams, 1991), 99.

18 Decker, "Interview One," 22.

19 I was led to this hypothesis by Hatfield's intriguing speculation about the challenge Lee faced whenever he got drawn pages back from Kirby: "[Lee] did not have to worry about dialogue until confronting nearly-finished pages, a mercy that allowed him to attack the pages as found objects, with a certain improvisatory élan that helps account for the freshness and jouncing vivacity of his best scripting (as well as the blithe excesses of his worst)." Hatfield, *Hand of Fire*, 92.

20 Though I don't have the space to explore the point here, the generic limits of superhero psychology in mainstream comics might be a consequence of Marvel's division of labor. Lee's soap-operatic interior monologues may have given the impression of greater depth than DC's characters without providing much more than a melodramatic externalization of character. I do not wish to understate the advance that this technique represents or to slight the expressive power of such externalization, but Silver Age readers' appreciation of this form of roundedness may have hindered the pursuit of other kinds of psychological complexity.

21 Howell and Kalish, "Interview with Frank Miller," 20.

22 Sanderson, "Frank Miller/Klaus Janson," 21.

23 Sanderson, "Frank Miller/Klaus Janson," 18.

24 Sanderson, "Frank Miller/Klaus Janson," 17.

25 Decker, "Interview One," 20; Sanderson, "Frank Miller/Klaus Johnson," 20.

26 Sanderson, "Frank Miller/Klaus Janson," 18.

27 Howell and Kalish, "Interview with Frank Miller," 24.

28 Ed Via, "Miller's *Daredevil*: Morality amid Violence and Corruption," *Comics Journal* 70 (Winter 1981–82): 94–95.

29 Sanderson, "Frank Miller/Klaus Janson," 18.

30 Howell and Kalish, "Interview with Frank Miller," 24. Johnny Blaze in Marvel's *Ghost Rider* title (1973–83; first appearance in *Marvel Spotlight* #5, 1972) provides another precedent for a character who acknowledges and works actively at the performance of superheroics. Blaze regularly trades in his slangy local-color speech for prepare-to-meet-your-maker rhetoric right out of Tolkien whenever he turns into a blazing skeleton on a motorcycle, all the

while commenting via thought balloons on how out of character his elevated language sounds.

31 Sanderson, "Frank Miller/Klaus Janson," 20.

32 Sally Kempton, "Super-Anti Hero in Forest Hills," *Village Voice*, April 1, 1965. The *Esquire* article, a better-known feature including interviews with college-age Marvel fans, makes more implicit comparisons to DC (as "Brand Echh," Marvel's pet name for the Distinguished Competition). See "O.K., You Passed the 2-S Test—Now You're Smart Enough for Comic Books," *Esquire*, September 1966, 115–16, and "As Barry Jenkins, Ohio '69, Says: 'A Person Has to Have Intelligence to Read Them,'" *Esquire*, September 1966, 117–18.

33 Howell and Kalish, "Interview with Frank Miller," 24.

34 Sanderson, "Frank Miller/Klaus Janson," 20.

35 Howell and Kalish, "Interview with Frank Miller," 24.

36 Decker, "Interview One," 24.

37 Sanderson, "Frank Miller/Klaus Janson," 20.

38 R. C. Harvey, "The Reticulated Rainbow: McKenzie and Miller's *Daredevil*: A Skillful Use of the Medium," *Comics Journal* 58 (September 1980): 94.

39 Art Spiegelman, "Comix 101: Ballbuster: Bernard Krigstein's Life between the Panels," *New Yorker*, July 22, 2002, http://www.newyorker.com/magazine/2002/07/22/ballbuster.

40 John Benson, David Kasakove, and Art Spiegelman, "An Examination of *Master Race*" (1967), in *A Comics Studies Reader*, ed. Jeet Heer and Kent Worcester (Jackson: University of Mississippi Press, 2009), 291.

41 Ibid., 303–4.

42 Decker, "Interview One," 20.

43 José Alaniz, *Death, Disability, and the Superhero: The Silver Age and Beyond* (Jackson: University Press of Mississippi, 2014), 77, 76.

44 Theo Finigan, "'To the Stables, Robin!': Regenerating the Frontier in Frank Miller's *Batman: The Dark Knight Returns*," *ImageTexT* 5, no. 1 (2010), sections 3 and 10, http://www.english.ufl.edu/imagetext/archives/v5_1/finigan/.

45 Decker, "Interview One," 24.

46 Miller, quoted in Michael Catron, "Devil's Advocate: For the Man without Fear, It's Miller Time," *Amazing Heroes* 4 (September 1981): 51.

47 Sanderson, "Frank Miller/Klaus Janson," 20.

48 Ibid., 21.

49 Ibid.; see also Decker, "Interview One," 24.

CHAPTER TWO: INTO THE SNAKE PIT

1 Gary Groth, "Interview Five" (1998), in *Frank Miller: The Interviews: 1981–2003*, ed. Milo George (Seattle: Fantagraphics, 2003), 101.

2 Dwight Decker, "Interview One" (1981), in George, *Frank Miller: The Interviews*, 20.
3 Joey Cavalieri and Mitch Cohn, "The Denny O'Neil Interview," in *The Daredevil Chronicles*, ed. Mitch Cohn (Albany, NY: FantaCo, 1982), 40.
4 Decker, "Interview One," 25.
5 Ibid., 28, 30.
6 Richard Howell and Carol Kalish, "An Interview with Frank Miller," *Comics Feature* 14 (December 1981): 22, 23.
7 Howell and Kalish, "Interview with Frank Miller," 22.
8 Laura Mulvey, "Visual Pleasure and Narrative Cinema" (1975), in *Narrative, Apparatus, Ideology*, ed. Philip Rosen (New York: Columbia University Press, 1986), 202–3.
9 Howell and Kalish, "Interview with Frank Miller," 22.
10 Decker, "Interview One," 21.
11 Ibid., 29.
12 Ibid., 16.
13 Scott McCloud, *Understanding Comics: The Invisible Art* (1993; repr., New York: Kitchen Sink/Harper Perennial, 1994), 36–39.
14 Groth, "Interview Five," 101.
15 Christopher Brayshaw, "Interview Four" (1998), in George, *Frank Miller: The Interviews*, 81.
16 See Peter Sanderson, "The Frank Miller/Klaus Janson Interview," in Cohn, *Daredevil Chronicles*, 21–22.
17 Decker, "Interview One," 24.
18 Howell and Kalish, "Interview with Frank Miller," 20, 21.
19 Miller's statement about Daredevil's motivation to protect and defend, which I've already quoted from earlier, is worth presenting in full: "It's an essential part of the Daredevil character that he's a lawyer—a defense lawyer, particularly. It's something I had a hard time dealing with when I first worked on the character, because my first reaction was, 'He should be a prosecutor, he hunts down criminals,' but it became clear to me at one point—I think [Jim] Shooter pointed it out to me—that Murdock's concern—and Daredevil's concern—is with the *victim* of a crime, not with the criminal. And someone falsely charged with a crime is a victim of the crime, as well." Ibid., 20.
20 Ibid., 26.
21 Christopher Irving, "Frank Miller Part 1: Dames, Dark Knights, Devils, and Heroes," NYC Graphic, December 1, 2010, http://www.nycgraphicnovelists.com/2010/12/frank-miller-part-1-dames-dark-knights.html.
22 Timothy Callahan, "Being Mike Murdock," in *The Devil Is in the Details: Examining Matt Murdock and Daredevil*, ed. Ryan K. Lindsay (Edwardsville, IL: Sequart, 2013), 29.

23 Groth, "Interview Five," 110, 111.

24 Kim Thompson, "Interview Two" (1985), in George, *Frank Miller: The Interviews*, 35.

25 Charles Hatfield, *Hand of Fire: The Comics Art of Jack Kirby* (Jackson: University Press of Mississippi, 2012), 110.

26 Brayshaw, "Interview Four," 72.

27 Brian Michael Bendis, "Brian Michael Bendis's Farewell to Daredevil," in *Daredevil by Brian Michael Bendis and Alex Maleev Ultimate Collection*, book 3, ed. Jennifer Grünwald (New York: Marvel, 2010).

CHAPTER THREE: THE UNHOLY THREE

The epigraph to this chapter comes from Peter Sanderson, "The Frank Miller/Klaus Janson Interview," in *The Daredevil Chronicles*, ed. Mitch Cohn (Albany, NY: FantaCo, 1982), 17.

1 Frank Miller interview, in *The Men without Fear: Creating Daredevil* (2003), produced by John Mefford, Marc Ostrick, and Eric Young, cinematography by Marc Ostrick and Mac Kenny, editing by Marc Ostrick, on *Daredevil*, dir. Mark Steven Johnson, Twentieth Century-Fox Film Corp, 2003, DVD.

2 Sanderson, "Frank Miller/Klaus Janson," 16.

3 Miller interview, *Men without Fear*.

4 Alan Moore, "The Importance of Being Frank," *Daredevils* #1 (Marvel UK, 1981), 15.

5 Frank Miller, fan letter published in Marvel's *The Claws of the Cat* #3, cover date April 1973.

6 Larry Rodman, "New Blood: A Frank Miller Career Overview," in *Frank Miller: The Interviews: 1981–2003*, ed. Milo George (Seattle: Fantagraphics, 2003), 123.

7 Miller interview, *Men without Fear*.

8 Sanderson, "Frank Miller/Klaus Janson," 23.

9 See E. Ann Kaplan, ed., *Women in Film Noir*, rev. ed. (London: British Film Institute, 1998).

10 Dwight Decker, "Interview One" (1981), in George, *Frank Miller: The Interviews*, 29.

11 Ibid., 26.

12 Miller interview, *Men without Fear*.

13 Decker, "Interview One," 21.

14 See Laura Mulvey, "Visual Pleasure and Narrative Cinema" (1975), in *Narrative, Apparatus, Ideology*, ed. Philip Rosen (New York: Columbia University Press, 1986), 203.

15 Decker, "Interview One," 26.

16 Miller interview, *Men without Fear*.

17 Decker, "Interview One," 26.

18 Sanderson, "Frank Miller/Klaus Janson," 26.

19 See Robin Wood, *Hitchcock's Films Revisited* (New York: Columbia University Press, 1989), 93–94.

20 See D. G. Chichester, Gregory Wright, Scott McDaniel, et al., *Daredevil Epic Collection: Fall from Grace* (1993–94; repr., New York: Marvel, 2014). In a further act of spitting in Miller's eye in the name of paying tribute, McDaniel changed his drawing style completely with that story beginning in *Daredevil* #319 (August 1993), making it resemble nothing so much as a color version of Miller's *Sin City* with its stark contrasts, spidery inking, and open-panel page designs. It seems McDaniel wanted to give readers the sensation of seeing how Miller might have depicted Elektra's return, ten years on. It's hardly a perfect "homage," however. I, for one, can barely make out what most of McDaniel's squiggly drawings and imaginary anatomies are supposed to depict, and Chichester's story features so many guest stars—contemporary "hot" Marvel characters like Venom, Morbius, Silver Sable, Siege, and others—and so much needless exposition and overwriting that there's simply no time left to spend on Daredevil's reaction to her resurrection.

21 "A person counts as an *asshole* when, and only when, he systematically allows himself to enjoy special advantages in interpersonal relations out of an entrenched sense of entitlement that immunizes him against the complaints of other people." Aaron James, *Assholes: A Theory* (2012; repr., New York: Anchor, 2014), 4–5.

22 Richard Howell and Carol Kalish, "An Interview with Frank Miller," *Comics Feature* 14 (December 1981): 20.

23 Kuljit Mithra, "Interview with Marv Wolfman (November 1997)," ManWithoutFear.com, 1997, http://www.manwithoutfear.com/daredevil-interviews/Wolfman.

CHAPTER FOUR: COMICS FOR COMICS' SAKE

1 Peter Sanderson, "The Frank Miller/Klaus Janson Interview," in *The Daredevil Chronicles*, ed. Mitch Cohn (Albany, NY: FantaCo, 1982), 17.

2 Charles Hatfield, *Hand of Fire: The Comics Art of Jack Kirby* (Jackson: University Press of Mississippi, 2012), 36.

3 Kim Thompson, "Run of the Miller," *Comics Journal* #82 (July 1983), http://www.tcj.com/run-of-the-miller/.

4 Ibid. (italics in original).

5 On the waxing and waning of the "writer-editor" position at Marvel, see Sean Howe, *Marvel Comics: The Untold Story* (New York: HarperCollins, 2012), 152–202.

6 Ibid., 200–202.

7 APA-5 has been referred to as the precursor to the independent company Dark Horse Comics, which published Miller's *Sin City*, *300*, and other works in the 1990s and first decade of the twenty-first century. The first issue of *Dark Horse Presents* (1986) featured work by then-current APA-5 members such as Paul Chadwick and Randy Emberlin. See Shaun Manning, "[Mike] Richardson on the Return of 'Dark Horse Presents,'" *Comic Book Resources*, December 31, 2010, http://www.comicbookresources.com/?id=30108&page=article. Miller's path to the professional market resembles that of many third-generation Marvel (and DC) creators of the seventies. A group of fan writers and artists, among them Bob Layton, Roger Stern, and John Byrne, founded a fan collective called the CPL Gang (for Contemporary Pictorial Literature) to publish a few fanzines, the most famous being the *Charlton Bullseye*, a tribute to the superhero industry's last minor-league club. The *Bullseye*, with the blessing of the fading Charlton Comics company, printed unpublished Charlton Comics action stories by Steve Ditko, Alex Toth, and Jeff Jones along with fan art and written tributes to Charlton's action and horror comics. Many members of the CPL Gang worked their way up from the *Bullseye* and Charlton series (John Byrne drew a Charlton science-fiction series called *Doomsday + 1* and a children's cartoon tie-in, *Wheelie and the Chopper Bunch*) into tryouts with Marvel and DC. Reliable information on the CPL Gang is difficult to come by, but the fan page *Splitting Atoms: A Captain Atom Blog* by "FKAJason" carries the authority of a longtime fan historian who has read and reviewed the full run of the *Charlton Bullseye*. See "*Charlton Bullseye* #1," *Splitting Atoms*, October 30, 2013, https://splittingatomsblog.wordpress.com/2013/10/30/charlton-bullseye-1-1975/.

8 Sanderson, "Frank Miller/Klaus Janson," 14.

9 Joey Cavalieri and Mitch Cohn, "The Denny O'Neil Interview," in *The Daredevil Chronicles*, ed. Mitch Cohn (Albany, NY: FantaCo, 1982), 39.

10 Sanderson, "Frank Miller/Klaus Janson," 13.

11 Hatfield, *Hand of Fire*, 75.

12 Scott McCloud, *Understanding Comics: The Invisible Art* (1993; repr., New York: Kitchen Sink/Harper Perennial, 1994), 70.

13 Kim Thompson, "Interview Two" (1985), in *Frank Miller: The Interviews: 1981–2003*, ed. Milo George (Seattle: Fantagraphics, 2003), 45.

14 See John Benson, David Kasakove, and Art Spiegelman, "An Examination of 'Master Race'" (1975), in *A Comics Studies Reader*, ed. Jeet Heer and Kent Worcester (Jackson: University Press of Mississippi, 2009), 288–305.

15 Thierry Groensteen, *Comics and Narration* (2011), trans. Ann Miller (Jackson: University Press of Mississippi, 2013), 149–150.

16 Benoît Peeters, "Les aventures de la page," quoted in Thierry Groensteen, *The System of Comics*, trans. Bart Beaty and Nick Nguyen (Jackson: University Press of Mississippi, 2007), 93. For a full English translation of the Peeters argument, see "'Four Conceptions of the Page,' from *Case, planche, recit: lire la bande dessinee*," trans. Jesse Cohn, *ImageTexT* 3, no. 3 (2007), http://www.english.ufl.edu/imagetext/archives/v3_3/peeters/.

17 Sanderson, "Frank Miller/Klaus Janson," 18.

18 Larry Rodman, "The Gene Colan Interview," *Comics Journal* 231 (March 2001), http://www.tcj.com/the-gene-colan-interview/.

19 Sanderson, "Frank Miller/Klaus Janson," 15.

20 Dwight Decker, "Interview One" (1981), in George, *Frank Miller: The Interviews*, 22.

21 Ibid., 23.

22 Christopher Brayshaw, "Interview Four" (1998), in George, *Frank Miller: The Interviews*, 84.

23 Decker, "Interview One," 23.

24 Sanderson, "Frank Miller/Klaus Janson," 14.

25 Ibid., 23.

26 Ibid., 13.

27 Decker, "Interview One," 23. A decade later, Miller recasts this approach in more comics-centered terms: "Some admirers have called [Miller's] style 'expressionism,' but Miller finds that [term] 'a little lofty. The term I really like to use is 'cartoon.' It's a language in line; that's what my eye wants to see.'" Les Daniels, *Marvel: Five Fabulous Decades of the World's Greatest Comics* (New York: Harry N. Abrams, 1991), 188.

28 Sanderson, "Frank Miller/Klaus Janson," 9.

29 Ibid., 11.

30 Kurt Olsson, "Frank Miller Makes *Daredevil* Come Alive," *Comics Feature* 14 (December 1981): 28, 29.

31 Sanderson, "Frank Miller/Klaus Janson," 13.

32 Thompson, "Interview Two," 35. The reader who knows of Ditko's Objectivist worldview and is interested (or pained) by Miller's preoccupation with rugged individualism may notice that I have not addressed whether Miller, too, subscribes to the philosophy of Ayn Rand. I prefer to leave this question to the reader. He has mentioned Rand in interviews from time to time, and his concept of heroism without mercy or compassion resonates with Rand's; but after reading twenty years' worth of interviews, I find it difficult to believe that the sheer dogmatism of Objectivism could ever get past Miller's passionately libertarian stance. For a qualified statement of admiration for Rand, see Miller in Decker, "Interview One," 28.

33 Decker, "Interview One," 18.

34 Decker, "Interview One," 16.

35 Peeters, "Four Conceptions of the Page," section 22.

36 Thierry Groensteen, *Comics and Narration* (2011), trans. Ann Miller (Jackson: University of Mississippi Press, 2013), 46.

37 McCloud, *Understanding Comics*, 63.

38 Ibid., 67, 69.

39 Groensteen, *The System of Comics*, 40.

40 Hans-Christian Christiansen, "Comics and Film: A Narrative Perspective," in *Comics & Culture: Analytical and Theoretical Approaches to Comics*, ed. Anne Magnussen and Hans-Christian Christiansen (Aarhus, Denmark: University of Copenhagen/Museum Tusculanum, 2000), 116–117.

41 Brayshaw, "Interview Four," 86.

42 See the original twenty-four (not twenty-two) "Panels That Always Work," in *The Wallace Wood Sketchbook* (New York: B Crouch/Wallace Wood, 1980).

43 Tom Gunning, "The Art of Succession: Reading, Writing, and Watching Comics," *Critical Inquiry* 40, no. 3 (2014): 41–42.

INTERLUDE: DAREDEVIL VS. THE CATECHISM

1 See Gail Simone's Women in Refrigerators website, where (beginning in 1999) she began listing female comics characters who had been "depowered, raped, . . . cut up and stuck in the refrigerator" as plot devices to motivate male superheroes and asked fans and creators to begin a conversation about why this happened so disproportionately to women. Simone, Women in Refrigerators website, http://lby3.com/wir/r-gsimone.html (accessed July 29, 2015). Simone has since become a writer of superhero comics herself, including most notably *Birds of Prey* and *Batgirl* for DC and *Red Sonja* for Dynamite Entertainment.

2 See Tania Modleski, "Introduction: Hitchcock, Feminism, and the Patriarchal Unconscious," in *The Women Who Knew Too Much: Hitchcock and Feminist Theory*, 2nd ed. (New York: Routledge, 2005), 1–14.

CONCLUSION: EXPOSÉ

1 Gary Groth, "Interview Six" (2003), in *Frank Miller: The Interviews, 1981–2003*, ed. Milo George (Seattle: Fantagraphics, 2003), 113.

2 "Claremont and Cockrum's X-Men were [like] the members of a halfway house, where everyone tried to figure out how to live in close quarters without letting their emotional baggage get in the way." Sean Howe, *Marvel Comics: The Untold Story* (New York: Harper Perennial, 2012), 196.

3 "Scoop" [Joe] Sacco with Thom Powers, "Comic Shop Busted," *Comics Journal*

114 (February 1987): 13–15. See also Comic Book Legal Defense Fund, "CBLDF Case Files: Illinois v. Correa," http://cbldf.org/about-us/case-files/cbldf-case-files/correa/ (accessed August 19, 2014).

4 See David Hajdu, *The Ten-Cent Plague: The Great Comic-Book Scare and How It Changed America* (New York: Farrar, Straus, and Giroux, 2008).

5 Gary Groth, "Interview Three" (1987), in George, *Frank Miller: The Interviews*, 53.

6 Kim Thompson, "Interview Two" (1985), in George, *Frank Miller: The Interviews*, 38; see also Groth, "Interview Three," 61–62.

7 Groth, "Interview Three," 63.

8 Howe, *Marvel Comics*, 241.

9 Don McGregor's politically charged Black Panther stories in the ill-titled series *Jungle Action* (1972–76) led the pack in verbosity, but in general, Marvel's momentum in the midseventies was generated by writers more than artists, as it had been in the preceding decade. On McGregor's political commitment to writing a comic about black characters and the dialogue-crammed panels that announced that commitment (and eventually got McGregor fired from the follow-up series *The Black Panther*), see Howe, *Marvel Comics*, 130–33 and 179–81.

10 Dwight Decker, "Interview One" (1981), in George, *Frank Miller: The Interviews*, 27, 28.

11 Thompson, "Interview Two," 38.

12 Howe, *Marvel Comics*, 243.

13 Groth, "Interview Six," 110.

14 Theo Finigan, "'To the Stables, Robin!': Regenerating the Frontier in Frank Miller's *Batman: The Dark Knight Returns*," *ImageTexT* 5, no. 1 (2010), sections 1, 2, and 20, http://www.english.ufl.edu/imagetext/archives/v5_1/finigan/.

15 Groth, "Interview Six," 110.

16 Spencer Ackerman, "Frank Miller's *Holy Terror* Is Fodder for Anti-Islam Set," *Wired*, September 28, 2011, http://www.wired.com/2011/09/holy-terror-frank-miller/.

17 Ibid.

18 Kevin, "Contrarian Fanboy: Frank Miller Has Always Been a Sexist, Fascist, Racist Prick," *Unleash the Fanboy* (blog), March 7, 2013, http://www.unleashthefanboy.com/news/the-dark-knight-returns-fascist-power-fantasy/45802#!bLo4QL.

19 Christopher Brayshaw, "Interview Four" (1998), in George, *Frank Miller: The Interviews*, 73.

20 Rick Moody, "Frank Miller and the Rise of Cryptofascist Hollywood," *Guardian* (UK), November 24, 2011, http://www.theguardian.com/culture/2011/nov/24/frank-miller-hollywood-fascism.

21 Ibid.

22 Sean Howe, "After His Public Downfall, *Sin City*'s Frank Miller Is Back (and Not Sorry)," *Wired*, August 20, 2014, http://www.wired.com/2014/08/frank-miller-sin-city-a-dame-to-kill-for/. By March 2015, frankmillerink.com had content once again, but not much—only a sparse pencil sketch of Batman against a white field, with the words "Under Construction!" scribbled above it. As of this writing (July 28, 2015), the sketch remains unchanged, though Miller returned to Twitter earlier in the year.

23 Decker, "Interview One," 21.

24 Howe, *Marvel Comics*, 240.

25 Ibid.

26 Howe, "After His Public Downfall."

27 See Frank Miller's contribution in *9-11: Artists Respond*, vol. 1 (Milwaukie, OR: Dark Horse/Chaos!/Image, 2002), 64–65.

28 Howe, *Marvel Comics*, 285.

29 Gary Groth, "Interview Five" (1998), in George, *Frank Miller: The Interviews*, 104–5.

30 Thompson, "Interview Two," 38.

31 Robin Wood, "Retrospective" (1977), in *Hitchcock's Films Revisited* (New York: Columbia University Press, 1989), 220.

32 Groth, "Interview Three," 63.

33 Rich Johnston, "Frank Miller and Scott Snyder Planning to Write *Dark Knight 3* Together," Bleeding Cool, December 3, 2014, http://www.bleedingcool.com/2014/12/03/frank-miller-and-scott-snyder-to-write-dark-knight-3/.

34 DC Comics, "Superstar Writer/Artist Frank Miller Returns to Batman!," press release, April 24, 2015, http://www.dccomics.com/blog/2015/04/24/superstar-writerartist-frank-miller-returns-to-batman.

35 For a defense of *Holy Terror* on aesthetic grounds, see Tim Callahan, "Once upon a Batman: Frank Miller's *Holy Terror*," Tor.com, September 29, 2011, http://www.tor.com/2011/09/once-upon-a-batman-frank-millers-holy-terror.

36 Richard Rosenbaum, "The Dark Knight Confounds: Why Is Frank Miller's Batman So Alienating?," Overthinking It, May 20, 2014, http://www.over-thinkingit.com/2014/05/20/dark-knight-confounds-frank-miller-batman-alienating/.

INDEX

ABOUT THE AUTHOR

Paul Young is an associate professor of film and media studies at Dartmouth College. He is the author of *The Cinema Dreams Its Rivals: Media Fantasy Films from Radio to the Internet* (2006) and articles and chapters on early cinema, American literature, film sound, and video games. Currently he is at work on a book about reflexive visual storytelling in the early US feature film.

"An incisive and focused discussion of an understudied era in the *Daredevil* series that provides a rewarding exploration of how the superhero reflects and shapes broader areas of culture."

—José Alaniz, author of *Death, Disability, and the Superhero: The Silver Age and Beyond*

"Knowledgeable with regard to the commercial and aesthetic contexts of the superhero genre, but also willing to risk more personal reflection, Young helps us to read these pivotal, powerful works of popular culture afresh."

—Benjamin Saunders, director of Comics Studies, The University of Oregon

In the late 1970s and early 1980s, writer-artist Frank Miller turned *Daredevil* from a tepid-selling comic into an industry-wide success story, doubling its sales within three years. Lawyer by day and costumed vigilante by night, the character of *Daredevil* was the perfect vehicle for the explorations of heroic ideals and violence that would come to define Miller's work.

Frank Miller's Daredevil and the Ends of Heroism is both a rigorous study of Miller's artistic influences and innovations and a reflection on how his visionary work on *Daredevil* impacted generations of comics publishers, creators, and fans. Paul Young explores the accomplishments of Miller the writer, who reimagined Kingpin (a classic Spider-Man nemesis), overhauled the garden-variety villain Bullseye, and invented a new kind of

Daredevil adversary in Elektra. Young also offers a vivid appreciation of the indelible panels drawn by Miller the artist, taking a fresh look at his distinctive page layouts and lines.

A childhood fan of Miller's *Daredevil*, Young takes readers on a personal journey as he seeks to reconcile his love for the comic with his distaste for the fascistic overtones of Miller's controversial later work. What he finds will resonate not only with *Daredevil* fans, but with anyone who has contemplated what it means to be a hero in a heartless world.

PAUL YOUNG is an associate professor of film and media studies at Dartmouth College in Hanover, New Hampshire. He is the author of *The Cinema Dreams Its Rivals: Media Fantasy Films from Radio to the Internet*.

A volume in the Comics Culture series, edited by Corey Creekmur

ISBN 9780813563817

9 780813 563817

RUTGERS
UNIVERSITY PRESS

Cover design by Lindsay Starr

Visit our website at rutgerspress.rutgers.edu